Unlocking the Scriptures for You

GALATIANS
EPHESIANS
LeRoy Lawson

**STANDARD
BIBLE STUDIES**

STANDARD PUBLISHING
Cincinnati, Ohio   40109

Library of Congress Cataloging in Publication data:

Lawson, E. LeRoy, 1938-
  Galatians/Ephesians

  (Standard Bible studies)
  1. Bible. N.T. Galatians—Commentaries. 2. Bible.
N.T. Ephesians—Commentaries. I. Title. II. Series.
BS2685.3.L38 1987   227'.407   86-30154
ISBN 0-87403-169-9

CONTENTS

Part One

Galatians

INTRODUCTION TO GALATIANS

Paul to the defense!

The opening words of this letter are from a man who is in no mood to be trifled with. "Paul, an apostle—sent not from men nor by man, but by Jesus Christ and God the Father...." An apostle is a man on a mission. He is under orders. His words and his actions are not his own; he speaks and acts for another. In this case, that Other is God, and His word is law, and Paul is His spokesman.

This very personal letter bristles with indignation. The apostle is on the defensive, on his own behalf as well as on behalf of his readers. His apostleship is being attacked and the foundation of the churches he established is being undermined. What is at stake is the eternal destiny of his Galatian brothers and sisters. His anger flashes out against perverters of the gospel who are luring the young Christians away from the truth and into heresy.

Don't expect to find here the leisurely discussion and rather lofty tone that you are familiar with in Paul's epistle to the Romans. There the apostle treats a similar theme but in a more objective manner. Romans is a well-reasoned treatise; Galatians an empassioned appeal. You don't write a carefully reasoned treatise when you are burning with passion. Paul has Galatian lives to save and his own reputation to rescue. If he tosses aside the niceties of precise exposition for the more persuasive appeals to his personal testimony and his rich relationship with these friends, so be it. If he confuses twentieth-century readers with his rabbinical argument in chapters 3 and 4, you'll just have to remember that he wasn't writing with us in mind. He borrows the tools of his time in order to convince the people of his time that the truth of the gospel must not be made to conform to the time's prevailing religious customs.

That is not to say that there isn't any order in the epistle. There is. In the first place, Paul adopts the proper form for letters. He (1) begins with an opening greeting, (2) offers a prayer for the health of the recipients, (3) devotes the main body of the letter to the subject at hand, and (4) closes with final greetings. There is a slight departure from the norm here. Usually the writer includes (between points 2 and 3) a word of thanksgiving for the virtues of the recipients. In Paul's haste to address the issue, he rushes right past this formality.

In the second place, we can trace an orderly argument in the main body. In this simple outline, we can quickly discern the logical progression of his thought:

Introduction (1:1-5)

I. Paul defends his authority as an apostle (1:6—2:21)

II. Paul defends the gospel he has preached (3:1—4:31)
   A. Salvation is by faith in Christ (3:1-14)
   B. Law's effectiveness (3:15-22)
   C. Sonship in Christ is better than slavery to the law (3:23—4:1)

III. Paul celebrates and explains our freedom in Christ (5:1—6:18)
   A. Freedom from legalism (5:1-12)
   B. Freedom from self-indulgence (5:13-26)
   C. Freedom to love and serve (6:1-10)
   D. Freedom to be a new creation (6:11-18)

The main argument celebrates our freedom in Christ, freedom based on the grace that saves us, a liberty that the Galatians are dangerously close to throwing away. Paul takes his stand here because it is on this issue that his opponents have chosen to do battle against him. (How glad we can be, by the way, that even in the earliest days of the Christian church there were disturbers of the peace. Thanks to them, we have the New Testament epistles to guide our churches through today's very same problems. The names and faces have changed through the centuries, but the issues have remained very much the same.)

These first-century troublemakers are known to us today by the name Judaizers. They did not see themselves as enemies of the gospel, but as defenders of the true faith. They were Christians, disciples of Christ, all right; but as lifelong Jews, they could not bring themselves to believe that salvation was possible through Jesus alone. More was needed, and that more was obedience to the law of Moses. The proof of their allegiance to Moses was circumcision.

Behind their argument was the racial conviction that only the Jews were the true people of God. Yet most of the Galatian Christians were Gentiles, and not Jews. Was it really possible that God was accepting these non-Jews as equal with Jews? Such a thought was unthinkable. God would not open the gates of membership in the exclusive club of "His People" to non-Jews. So the only solution was to insist that in addition to baptism into Christ, these Galatian Christians must also undergo initiation into Moses. They must be circumcised. Without circumcision and obedience to other prescriptions of the law of Moses, they would be condemned.

As I have already said, Paul deals with this same subject in Romans, but in a more dispassionate way. A major difference in the two letters is in his treatment of the law. In Romans, Paul freely admits the law's holiness (7:12) and attributes its failures less to itself than to human sinfulness. He starts with the same assumption in Galatians, but the emphasis shifts. The law is "weak and miserable" (4:9), unable to save. Since Christ is the only Savior, anyone who trusts the law for salvation has turned his back on the grace of God and is thereby condemned (5:4).

In both Romans and Galatians, Paul points out that there can be salvation in spite of one's transgression of the law, but he also strongly affirms his conviction that the law itself can never save. Both letters raise the question, "How can one come into a right relationship with God?" That is, "How can one be justified before God?" Both give the same answer: "There is no justification in the law. Faith, not law, justifies." The Judaizers, in teaching that belief in Christ must be joined with conformity to Jewish law in order for a person to be saved, are wrong. Worse than that, they are dangerous, since they lead the innocent away from salvation. They would rob Christians of one of their most precious gifts from God, their freedom.

It is freedom that this letter fights to protect.

11

Who Were the Galatians?

Some nagging problems have frustrated Bible scholars for a long time. For example, we have no doubt that the apostle Paul wrote this letter, and that he sent it to the Galatians. What we don't know, however, is exactly who the Galatians were. There are two distinct possibilities, giving rise to the North Galatia and the South Galatia theories.

In the first century, *Galatia* was the term designating a large territory in what we now call north-central Asia Minor, the name being derived from the Celtic tribes that lived in the area. In 189 B.C., Rome brought these warlike people into submission and combined their territory with the territory to the south of them into a larger administrative district or subject kingdom of the Empire.

That introduces the problem. The term by the first century A.D. had taken on two different meanings. It could refer to the specific region inhabited by "the Galatians," or it could refer to the larger administrative district that included (and generally specifically referred to) the southern, more populated region. There in the south were the cities of Antioch, Iconium, Lystra, and Derbe.

When Paul writes "Galatians," then, if he is thinking of the Roman province, he has the area of these cities in mind (the South Galatia theory); if he is thinking of the geographical area settled by the Celtic tribes, then the North Galatia theory is correct.

Which should we choose? In the crossfire of debate, I take refuge in my conviction that if a scholarly issue like this one doesn't affect the truth of the passage in question, then we should concentrate on the truth that we do know instead of speculating on what we don't know. The message of Galatians remains the same, whether you choose South Galatia or North Galatia. I tend to favor the former, because of Paul's habit of going to major population centers to plant churches (and the major cities are found in the South), because there were more Jews in proportion to Gentiles in these urban areas (and the letter in places speaks directly to Jews and to Gentiles familiar with Jewish teaching), and because it seems more likely to me that Paul's enemies would have more readily pursued him into the southern than the northern region. In addition, Paul seems to have followed the practice of using the names of Roman provinces rather than geographical territories for the places he visited.

What impresses me in reading Galatians is the near irrelevance of the original recipients of the letter. They cannot be dismissed, of course, since one of the principles of Bible study is to take into consideration the importance of when a particular passage was written, to whom, and for what purpose. What is so remarkable about Galatians, however, is that even if we did not know the answers to these questions, we could still appreciate this letter for its relevance to today's church. We don't call them Judaizers

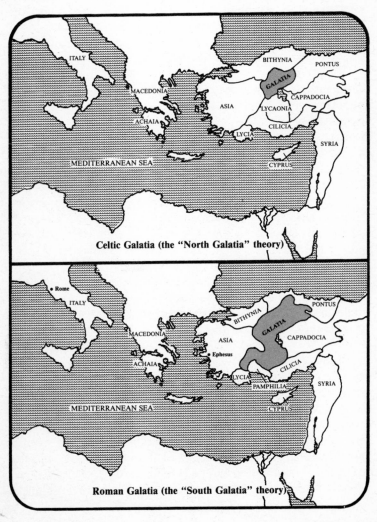

Celtic Galatia (the "North Galatia" theory)

Roman Galatia (the "South Galatia" theory)

anymore, but we still have false teachers of every description who would, if they could, persuade us to forsake our freedom in Christ, so graciously given, for bondage in this or that form of religious legalism. Freedom in Christ is constantly under fire. Paul's urgent appeal to believers to be diligent in its protection could not be more timely than it is today.

When, then, was this letter written? Assuming that it was written to the churches that Paul planted in his first missionary journey (the South Galatia theory), we can feel pretty comfortable in assigning a date just about mid-century, A.D. 50 or 51. This date makes Galatians one of the earliest letters in the New Testament.

Reading Galatians

With this brief introduction, we are ready to read the letter. May I suggest that you read all six chapters of Galatians before concentrating on any single passage. It helps our study if we remember that this is a real letter, initially intended to be read clear through at a single sitting. We do an injustice to Scripture sometimes when we insist on pulling out a verse, or a few verses, to find "what this means to me." To be more honest Bible students, we need to read an epistle in its entirety so that we can grasp the larger themes and the interrelatedness of the various passages. Only then should we concentrate on a particular verse.

Then, after reading it all, you are ready to begin your study. My book is not, as you will quickly discover, an authoritative commentary. It is one Bible lover's comments. I have tried to read with honesty. I have studied the historical context of the letter and I have analyzed the original language, paying attention to the way Paul constructs his sentences and organizes his ideas. I have tried to be faithful to its first-century setting, but I haven't stopped there. As a twentieth-century reader, I have brought along with me the questions and peculiar points of view of my era. My reading in other disciplines, as well as in the daily newspapers and news magazines, and my experiences as a pastor will be in evidence on these pages. For these intrusions into "pure" Bible study I don't apologize, being convinced as I am that the Bible came into being in living history and comes most alive today when it rubs shoulders with the minds of the marketplace.

I hope this little book will be helpful to you. I offer it to you with my love and to God with my heartfelt thanks for freedom in Christ.

CHAPTER ONE

The Good News of Freedom

Galatians 1:1-5

We need more synonyms. Even with the help of such near equivalents as *liberty* and *independence* and *emancipation* (no one of which quite captures the full impact of what it means to be set free in the Lord), I'm afraid we may still wear out the word *freedom* before we complete our study of Galatians. It has been called the "Magna Carta of Christian Liberty," and the title fits. The apostle Paul's theme is the incomparable freedom we have in Christ. In every chapter, he celebrates this gift, examining its many facets so that in the end we will cherish it as he does. There is no word quite like freedom, and no freedom equal to our freedom in Christ.

The good news of this freedom in Christ seems almost too good to be true, as a woman recently discovered. She accepted Christ as her Savior after eight years as a member of the Children of God cult. A friend of mine had patiently and lovingly led her to faith in Jesus Christ. At first tentatively, then more courageously, she embraced the Lord and was baptized into Him.

Then she told my ministerial friend, "I've committed my life to Christ just as you urged. So *now* are you going to tell me the rules?"

He didn't answer her directly. Instead, he handed her a copy of my little book *The Family of God* and asked her to read the brief chapter entitled, "What Are the Rules?" My first sentence answers the question: "There aren't any."[1]

When she finished reading, she asked him, "You really meant that, didn't you?"

---

[1] LeRoy Lawson, *The Family of God* (Cincinnati: Standard Publishing, 1980) p. 40.

He did, and so do I. We both preach the message of Galatians: "It is for freedom that Christ has set us free. Stand firm, then, and do not let yourselves be burdened again by a yoke of slavery" (Galatians 5:1). No more rules! Over and over again, Paul returns to this central affirmation of the gospel: God wants you free!

The Galatian letter explains how life without overbearing rules is possible.

The Messenger of the Gospel (1:1, 2)

There is even a hint of God's desire for our freedom in the opening words of greeting. "Paul, an apostle" (Galatians 1:1). An apostle is a "sent one," a messenger dispatched to deliver a specific message from the sender, an ambassador with no authority of his own but with delegated power from the one he represents. Paul will quickly adopt a very authoritative tone in this letter. His use of his title right at the beginning reminds his readers that he has a right to speak to them in that tone. He's an apostle, and his message is from Christ! Acts tells the story of Paul's call to apostolic office three different times (in chapters 9, 22, and 26). He has no doubt about who called him, Christ, or what He called Paul to do: "This man is my chosen instrument to carry my name before the Gentiles and their kings and before the people of Israel" (Acts 9:15). Paul never wavers in his conviction that he has been sent to the Gentiles as surely as Peter has been sent to the Jews (Galatians 2:7).

In the New Testament, *apostle* is used in two ways. It designates one of the twelve disciples whom Jesus called to be with Him during His earthly ministry and to be witnesses of His death and resurrection. They laid the foundations of the church on the day of Pentecost. Paul was not one of these.

In a broader sense, it also simply means *messenger* and is used of Jesus himself (Hebrews 3:1), Epaphroditus (Philippians 2:25), Matthias (Acts 1:26), Paul and Barnabas (Acts 14:4, 14), James the Lord's brother (Galatians 1:19), and Junias and Andronicus (Romans 16:7). Paul, who was called to his responsibilities after the resurrection of Christ, could not claim authority because of close association with Jesus, but he made no apology for his apostolic office because he was appointed somewhat later than the others. He nonetheless was "sent not from men nor by man, but by Jesus Christ and God the Father." His credentials are not in doubt.

16

The Christ of the Gospel (1:1-5)

Paul telescopes much information about Jesus into this first sentence (Galatians 1:1).

He is "Jesus" (a form of the Hebrew name *Joshua*) of Nazareth, born of Mary, reared in the home of Joseph the carpenter, circumcised on the eighth day, presented in the temple in His twelfth year, baptized by John the Baptist in the Jordan, partaker of human life as a true member of the nation of Israel and the tribe of Judah, fully human, fully man, fully one of us (Matthew 1—3, Luke 1, 2).

He is the "Christ," (*Messiah* in the Hebrew), the One anointed of God like kings and priests and prophets of old, the Promised One who would save Israel (1 Kings 19:16, Isaiah 61:1, Exodus 29:21, 1 Samuel 9:16, 16:3; Isaiah 53; John 1:1-14, Mark 14:61, 62).

And He is the Son of "God the Father, who raised Him from the dead." The resurrection is crucial to the good news of freedom. Had Jesus not been raised from the dead, all His promises would have come to nought, and all His followers would have believed in vain (1 Corinthians 15:1-8, 12-28). This fact separates Jesus from the world's great men (Socrates, for example, or Buddha, Mohammed, Moses, or Michelangelo). They can "give life" to ideas, perhaps, or create the illusion of vitality on canvas or in stone, but they cannot revivify decaying flesh.

History records that before the resurrection, when Jesus lay dead in the tomb of Joseph of Arimathea, His despondent disciples scattered. They had seen the crucifixion; they had to concede their Lord's—and their own—defeat. Only when the risen Lord appeared did their spirits revive. They experienced more than revival. They were transformed from timid, dependent disciples into bold, aggressive apostles. They began preaching the message that cannot be silenced. "He is not dead. He is risen, as He said. He died for you, so that you can live in the freedom that only He can give."

Therefore we call Him "the Lord Jesus Christ" (Galatians 1:3). His title connotes the majesty and authority of the only Person worthy of our allegiance. He "who gave himself for our sins to rescue us from the present evil age (Galatians 1:4) deserves our gratitude and loyalty. In Him, the great God of the universe paid the price to set us free. He offers himself as Savior; we acknowledge Him as Lord.

17

The language takes an unexpected twist, doesn't it? Historically, people have followed their lords into battle against their "present evil age," in whatever form that evil was perceived. They marched with eyes open, fully aware that many who marched out to war would never return. They would give their lives for their lords.

In the Bible, however, it is the Lord who lays down His life for His followers, which is like a general dying for his troops. That just doesn't happen in real life! We have read our histories; hundreds of thousands—yea, even countless millions have been slain for the sins of their generals. Who has ever heard of a general sacrificing himself to save his soldiers?

Yet it happened. We call the General who laid down His life for His followers, "Lord."

He sacrificed himself to free us from "the present evil age." This term needs no explanation. Today's headlines, screaming of murders and strikes and wars and drunkenness and disease prove that "the present evil age" did not go away in the first century. "The god of this age" (2 Corinthians 4:4) hasn't abdicated his hellish throne.

The troubles that headline our newspapers are not what God wants for us, however. If He gets His way, He will rescue us all from the clutches of the evil one. He is like the loving father of Jesus' parable (Luke 15) who paces impatiently until his errant son gets tired of his miserable condition and returns to the protective embrace of his loving—and liberating—parent.

God does more than wait. He sends His Son, the Christ of the gospel (good news), to save us.

The Greeting in the Gospel—the Gospel in the Greeting (1:3-5)

"Grace . . . to you" (Galatians 1:3). The typical Greek greeting, *charis,* connotes several things at once: gracefulness, attractiveness, kindness, graciousness, goodwill, thanks, favor, approval. From the pen of the apostle Paul, the greeting takes on a particular significance. He has in mind God's favor to us in spite of our obvious lack of deserving. Paul undoubtedly can never use the term without at least a flicker of remembrance. He had made a career out of fighting God. He hunted down Christians as if they were criminals, doing everything in his power to stamp out the pestilence. Then God stopped him short.

18

You could expect that much. Of course God would prevent His enemies from having the final victory. What so startled Paul—and continues to amaze the thoughtful reader of the Bible, is that God wasn't satisfied with merely stifling His enemy. He did something much more drastic: He converted him into an ally and friend. If ever anyone didn't deserve such treatment, it was Paul. Yet to him God offered "grace." He saved Paul in spite of himself.

One of the lasting benefits of Paul's conversion is that from that time on no one has honestly been able to protest, "I'm not good enough to become a Christian." Nobody is, of course, but that doesn't matter. If God could rescue Saul of Tarsus and transform him into the apostle Paul strictly on account of His grace and in spite of Saul's sin, then He can do that for anybody. And He will.

"Peace" is _eirene,_ the Greek equivalent of the Hebrew _shalom._ This large word began as a greeting that wished the recipient peace, but in time it came to encompass much more: it wishes nothing less than one's total well-being for time and all eternity. In light of Paul's constant thankfulness for forgiven sins and accompanying harmony with God, the greeting becomes a sign pointing to our newly peaceful relationship with the God from whom we were formerly (that is, before we were rescued by Christ) estranged. We don't have to fight with or flee from Him anymore.

In James Michener's _Hawaii,_ Nyuk Tsin Kee stands before the officer in her examination for United States citizenship. She has relentlessly driven herself to prepare for this exam. More than anything else, she wants to become a citizen of America. But now she is strangely silent. When the examiner asks who is the father of our country, Mrs. Kee does not answer. Michener explains that the old woman is overwhelmed by the import of the moment. She has so wanted to belong—first to her father, later to her Punti husband (who made fun of her big feet), then to her children (who had feared she might have had leprosy), then to America (which had turned its back on Orientals). Now that she is about to attain what she has so fervently hoped for, she has lost her tongue.

Finally, when the examiner asks her the third time, she begins to speak. Then she can't be stopped. She names the capitals of the states, she explains the three branches of government, she describes the Bill of Rights, and still she talks. But when she triumphantly leaves the immigration building as a citizen, she tells her family that when you are a citizen, even the earth beneath your feet feels different.

That's *shalom,* peace. You belong. You are a citizen of the nation of God. You have been brought back to God through the efforts of His Son.

From now on, you will give "glory" to God (Galatians 1:5). Three times in these short verses, Paul has referred to Him as "Father" (Galatians 1:1, 3, 4). That word suggests the kind of glory we can give Him.

One of my children said not long ago, "I want you to be proud of me." My mind quickly flashed back to my own youth. Nothing mattered more to me in those days than that my parents be proud of me. We don't outgrow that desire. I still seek to do right—so that they can glory in my achievements for them!

We do the same for our Heavenly Father.

Shortly after a young minister and his wife moved into a certain neighborhood, they became friends with the young couple next door. For several weeks, they visited in each other's living room, and the newcomers could hardly ignore the huge painting of a nude woman that dominated the neighbors' sitting area.

They never said anything about it, but one day, they noticed that the painting was gone. They never saw it again. In its place were hanging baptismal certificates. Their neighbors had become Christians. In fact, they later moved to a Christian college and are now preaching the gospel. The nude woman had to go, because Christ had moved in and made them citizens of His kingdom. They now displayed their citizenship papers. They had found grace and peace—and wanted everything they did to make their Father proud of them. To His glory.

CHAPTER TWO

The *Only* Good News of Freedom

Galatians 1:6-12

In a rare breach of etiquette, Paul skips the customary word of commendation. Proper letter-writing form dictated that the writer say something complimentary about the recipients of a letter. Instead of thanking them for their partnership in the gospel (as in Philippians) or their widely renowned faith (as in Romans), for example, Paul jumps abruptly from his greeting to a scolding. He's in a hurry; he's upset. His loved ones are gambling with their eternal salvation.

Although the letter trembles with the writer's excitement, however, Paul does not succumb to mere emotion. His logic is as rational as his argument is irrefutable. What is at stake is nothing less than the gospel itself. Since what he has preached to them was the good news of freedom, they must not abandon it for the bondage of religious legalism.

Let's trace his argument.

There Is Only One Gospel of Freedom

Paul had founded the churches he is addressing here. The Galatian believers had welcomed Paul's offer of freedom from pagan superstition with its multiple petty gods and from Jewish legalism with its hundreds of commands and prohibitions. Christ had set them free.

Unfortunately, not everyone can handle freedom, since an accompaniment of freedom is responsibility, a virtue that requires at least a modicum of maturity. It's easier to obey the dictates of another than to think for oneself; it's more comforting to measure your spirituality by your obedience to a set of rules and regulations than to act responsibly in freedom. Thus, when the Judaizers arrived from Jerusalem to persuade the Galatians that besides their faith in Christ they must adhere to the traditional Jewish

21

laws—circumcision for the males, dietary regulations, observance of certain religious holy days, and so on—some of the more insecure young Christians fell easy prey to them.

You remember Jim Jones, who led over 900 of his disciples to their mass suicide in Guyana. Somebody said that his slavish followers did not so much abandon their self-control, their judgment, or their competitive instinct when they turned all their thinking over to Jones. It was more that they traded them off for love, peace, community, and security.

Something of this trade-off must have been taking place among the Galatians. To the tiny handful of Christians, surrounded by a host of Jews and Gentiles who thought them crazy for their faith in this obscure prophet who was crucified in Jerusalem, the arguments of the Judaizers could have seemed overwhelming. They seemed so right, so strong, so sure of themselves. They were Christians like the Galatians, but they had something more. They could boast that they were also safely within Jewish tradition; they tempered the radical freedom that Paul offered with the more customary restraints of religious communities. All religions, the Judaizers must have argued, need to have rules and ceremonies and human authorities to be obeyed. The Judaizers made good sense to them, especially since they weren't mature enough in their own faith to handle their new freedom. As far as they were concerned, something seemed to be missing in Christianity. There weren't enough rules.

I think we can understand the Galatian mentality a little better if we will consider the popular appeal of today's religious cults. Well over 10,000,000 Americans now belong to these sometimes bizarre organizations. In many instances, they convert and hold their devotees by the same attractions that appealed to the defecting Galatian Christians.

At least eight characteristics describe the cults:

(1) An overpowering charismatic leader. Whether he be a Jim Jones, a Reverend Moon, or a Joseph Smith, cults are founded on a dynamic leader who claims direct access to the mind of God.

(2) The absolute authority of this leader. Sometimes he is called Prophet, sometimes President, often Father. His title is less important than the fact that by deed and word, he assumes a power superior to that of Jesus Christ.

(3) The use of Jesus' name but denial of His authority. Many cults ride on the Lord's coattails, even claiming to be Christian,

An informal, five-part series

Thru the Bible. J. Vernon McGee. Commentaries covering the Old and New Testaments in five informal, informative volumes. Recommended for lay people.

Volume I: Genesis-Deuteronomy 4973-2

Volume II: Joshua-Psalms 4974-0

Volume III: Proverbs-Malachi 4975-9

Volume IV: Matthew-Romans 4976-7

Volume V: 1 Corinthians-Revelation 4977-5

Five-Volume Set 4957-0

but then replace the Bible with their own holy books ("The Bible has mistakes in it," they explain) and usurp Jesus' sovereignty by so-called later "revelations" or "proclamations" handed down by the leader.

(4) **The presence of secret rites and doctrines.** If there are doctrines that are hidden from outsiders or if there are sacred rites in the temple or secret passwords that cannot be observed or learned by everyone, then the organization cannot be genuinely Christian. In Christ, there are no secrets. A Christian church has nothing to hide from the world. Its doctrines are found in an open book and can be examined by believer and non-believer alike. Its meetings are open to the world. Its rites are performed in view of anyone who wishes to see. Christ hides nothing.

(5) **The proliferation of rules.** I have been told that one prominent American cult has over 4,000 rules. Every aspect of its members' lives is governed by religious law. I don't know of any cult that can promise, as the Christian church promises in harmony with this Galatian letter, "In this church, there are no rules! You are free in Christ."

(6) **Salvation by works.** It only stands to reason, of course, that a religion of rules can offer salvation only to those who faithfully obey the rules. Break the law, and you lose your salvation. The Galatian appeal could not be more timely, could it? "A man is not justified by observing the law, but by faith in Jesus Christ" (Galatians 2:16).

(7) **A sense of spiritual superiority.** Strange, isn't it, how this happens? Rule-book religion specializes in producing Pharisees. These masters of ecclesiastical gamesmanship memorize the regulations and doggedly follow them. They also keep score. They can measure their spirituality by the number of points earned; their competitive spirit keeps them far ahead of their contemporaries who are less adept at playing by the rules of religious games. The Pharisees, having decided that spirituality consists in the abundance of good works, have every reason to congratulate themselves on their superiority. They have done a lot of good works! We Christians, on the other hand, have to admit that "all have sinned and fall short of the glory of God" (Romans 3:23). We have such a strong sense of our own sinfulness that we can't look down on anybody else. Our spirituality does not consist of our goodness, but of God's grace.

23

(8) All the answers. When you reduce spiritual things to rules, regulations, and rituals, when you have systematized and defined and delimited God into manageable categories, then you can bend all questions to fit your preset answers. Few if any cults admit the existence of any knowledge that their systems haven't fully accounted for and can explain away. By contrast, we Christians have to admit that while our Lord did say, "I have overcome the world," He never told us, "I have explained the world." There are lots of things we don't know.

As you can see from this list of characteristics, there is nothing new in them. We find almost all of them in the Judaizers. They would improve on the gospel that Paul preached to the Galatians, which fails to meet even one of the cult criteria. Let's review them one by one:

(1) Far from being a charismatic leader, Paul speaks elsewhere of his being unattractive, even weak (Galatians 4:13, 14; 1 Corinthians 4:8-13; 9:1-23; 2 Corinthians 11, 12). The appeal of the Gospel is not in the messenger, but in the message of freedom.

(2) Even as an apostle, Paul has no personal authority. An apostle is only a messenger or ambassador; the authority is in the sender, not in the one He sends.

(3) The only power a Christian has is in his Lord, not in himself. There is only one Lord and there is only one authoritative book, the Bible. For the Christian, these cannot be replaced or improved.

(4) As already noted, in Christ and in the Christian church, there are no secrets.

(5) And there are no rules.

(6) Our salvation is by the grace of God, to which we respond in faith (Ephesians 2:8; Galatians 2:16).

(7) Far from feeling superior, we humbly admit our sinful condition and gratefully accept the grace of God.

(8) We remain disciples ("learners," "students"); we admit we don't know all the answers.

Paul's response to the challenge of the Judaizers is completely straightforward: "I have preached to the Galatians the gospel that the Lord revealed to me. He has revealed nothing else. There is only one gospel of freedom. Your add-ons do nothing to enhance the gospel; as a matter of fact, they pervert it. The good news of Jesus Christ is unique and unalterable. Therefore, when you abandon it in favor of the confusion and legalism you escaped

24

when you accepted Christ, you are actually abandoning the grace of God. There is only one gospel."

Anything Different From What God Has Planned Isn't Good News

A different gospel "is really no gospel at all" (Galatians 1:7). The Judaizers are undoubtedly trying to be helpful as they sew the new unshrunk cloth of the gospel onto the worn-out garment of Jewish legalism (see Matthew 9:16, 17). Helpful, but misguided. To modify the gospel of freedom by tacking on the multitudinous regulations of Judaism is to deny any freedom at all. It is to return to prison. "It is for freedom that Christ has set us free. Stand firm, then, and do not let yourselves be burdened again by a yoke of slavery" (Galatians 5:1).

Strangely enough, there is something appealing about prison. Alexander Solzhenitsyn, in his novel *The First Circle* (New York: Bantam, 1976), records the conversation between the prisoner Nerzhin and his wife, who had come to visit him there. "It suits you here," she told him. He had to agree. He found that he wasn't at all sorry to have spent five years there. He had learned about people and about himself in his confinement. He mused about how many youthful hesitations and how many wrong starts he had been saved from by the iron path of prison.

True, but he was still in prison.

In spite of the fact that God has designed us fo are still those who prefer imprisonment. Such the seductions of the Judaizers.

The Judaizers certainly do not think of the or perverters of the gospel. They are merely are like Alexander Pope rewriting William S standards of eighteenth-century literary ta demythologizers throwing out most of the the "true" Jesus remains, or a modern re wording the Bible so that "sexist" langu intent is honorable but the results dam fanatic whom Peter Dunne describes in "A fanatic is a man that does what he he knew th' facts in th' case."

They are **the regulators.** Believing that most ill-prepared to handle complete freedom in Christ, these ple generously write up regulations to help keep them in line. The

25

improvements are their efforts at standardizing religious behavior—so it can be observed, examined, and evaluated. Then people can be cut and trimmed to fit. And judged if they don't.

They are **the legislators.** You have to get the regulations down in writing. The Jewish religion had its scribes (who became the lawyers of the land) and its Sanhedrin (the Supreme Court). Surely Christianity needed the same. In time, the Christian faith did indeed come to suffer the same fate, one so aptly described by the non-Christian Roman historian, Tacitus, who complained of Rome: "As formerly we suffered from crime, so now we suffer from laws."

They meant well, but improvers, regulators, and legislators always become, in the end, **perverters of the** gospel.

A scandal in the history of Western civilization illustrates how this can happen. In 1619, twenty black people were landed at the colony of Jamestown in the new country of America and immediately sold into slavery. They probably came from the Indies. If so, they were snatched away from their servitude to Spaniards there, only to be delivered into new slavery to the Englishmen in America. What is scandalous about this event is that the name of the ship that delivered them from slavery to slavery was the "Jesus."

Paul's horror arises from the fact that the very people he delivered from slavery to "the present evil age" through the Gospel of Jesus were now being returned to slavery. In the name of Jesus!

Let Him Be Eternally Condemned

The language is strong; the emotion is stronger. Paul is outraged that religious slave traders would perpetrate such a crime against his newly freed people. Of anyone guilty of such a crime he writes, "Let him be eternally condemned!" (Galatians 1:9). The word *anathema* is as strong as Paul could find. It means what it says: let him be delivered up to divine wrath. Let him be accursed by God.

Strong action is needed to counteract the psychologically powerful, persuasive enemy of Christian freedom. What the deceivers offer is covert slavery; what they deserve for what they are doing is Hell.

Obviously, Paul, who must have been charged with courting popular favor, is not doing so now. "Am I now trying to win the approval of men, or of God? Or am I trying to please men?" All

26

he cares about is being "a servant of Christ" (Galatians 1:10). It is the only slavery this lover of freedom will abide.

A clue to Paul's intensity is found in verses 11 and 12. He did not fabricate the good news he preached in Galatia, he insists. Indeed, he could never have even imagined it. It had to be *revealed* to this Hebrew of Hebrews, this Pharisee of the first rank (Philippians 3:4-6). If the Lord himself hadn't changed Paul's mind, he'd probably be right there with the Judaizers, leading the charge.

But he would have been wrong, just as he had been so wrong before. Now, with the anguish of a man who has so much to make up for, he cries out against his own former crime as he condemns the criminals who have come after him. They must not be allowed to perpetuate his former errors. People's lives are at stake.

CHAPTER THREE

What the Good News Is Like

Galatians 1:11-24

READ

The Judaizers who have been attempting to lure the Galatian Christians back into religious legalism have adopted a two-fold strategy. First, playing upon the insecurities of people too imma- ture to enjoy their new freedom in Christ, they have touted the certainties of the Mosaic law and the traditions of the Jewish elders. Second, they have discredited Paul by (a) casting doubt upon his apostleship and (b) charging him with seeking popularity with men instead of being strictly devoted to God (Galatians 1:10).

Paul defends himself by reminding them of the nature of the gospel itself. In so doing, he defines the gospel and shows its profound effect on life, on his life especially.

The Gospel Is Revealed Good News

"The gospel I preached is not something that man made up" (Galatians 1:11). Neither Paul nor any other human being in- vented or imagined the message the apostle preached to the Galatians. Nobody proposed it, no majority voted for it, no legis- lative or judicial body ratified it. It was not—and is not—subject to popular referendum.

Nor did it come through the dictates of important men (Galatians 1:16) who like to rule on such matters.

It was not the product of philosophers or theologians, nor even of scribes or Pharisees or the elders, whose traditions had been so revered by Paul and his fellow Jews for centuries.

In fact, as the apostle never tires of reminding his many corres- pondents, the gospel was something he could never have known or even guessed at apart from God's direct revelation. We appre- ciate Paul's candor here. It helps us to be more forgiving of Pharisees, Sadducees, Essenes, and all other first-century Jews who could not accept the Christian message of Jesus' resurrection and of the inclusion of Gentiles in God's general invitation for people of all races and persuasions to become a part of His people. Even Jesus' disciples did not fully understand the gospel until after His resurrection. The message of Christ crucified and risen has long remained "a stumbling block to Jews and foolishness to Gentiles" (1 Corinthians 1:23).

The story continues to challenge our credulity, doesn't it? What are we to make of a baby born out among the animals in a far-off outpost of the Roman Empire, who spent His first years with His parents as alien refugees, who then grew up in a humble carpenter's home where He learned the craft himself, and who later became an itinerant preacher among one of Rome's captive—and less illustrious—nations? This man wrote no books, established no political party, owned no property, and amassed no fortune. He was always poor. He cultivated the friendship of outcasts and seemed to spurn the attention of the powerful. He was tried as a traitor and was crucified as a criminal, deserted in the end by even his closest friends. Then, wonder of wonders, this apparent failure (by the world's standard of values) arose from the dead! When you add to this biography the essence of His teaching, which was that God loved everybody and was destroying the walls that separated Jew from Gentile, man from woman, free from slave (Galatians 3:28; Ephesians 2:1-22), and man from God (2 Corinthians 5:19), you can appreciate Paul's insistence that this message had to be revealed; it could never have been invented.

What is even more mind-boggling than the gospel message is the gospel purpose: Jesus, who had everything to lose, became a nobody in the world in order that we might become somebody (Philippians 2:5-11). This is not what we would expect—it is not even what we would want—of God. We would prefer our God to remain high and lifted up, uninvolved with the grubby affairs of the likes of us. An aloof God makes fewer demands. While He remains somewhere up there, we can go on our merry way, pausing to lift an occasional glance in His direction, or offer up the expected ritual sacrifice, but remaining basically uninvolved ourselves. A God who stoops to set us free has to be dealt with. You have two choices. You can let Him liberate you or *choose* to remain in bondage; you can't just ignore Him.

By the way, Jesus' decision to become a nobody for our sake makes good sense in light of the theme of Galatians. "It is for freedom that Christ has set us free" (Galatians 5:1) Christ himself could not have been free on earth had He come as a king or political or even religious leader. Had He been somebody, He'd have been shackled with all the inhibiting trappings of His office; being nobody, He was free to speak His full mind regardless of the consequences. He did not have to be afraid of anybody, because the worst His enemies could do was kill Him, and that was no problem, since they did not have the final say in matters of life and death. They just thought they did. Had He really valued position or status on earth, they could have controlled Him, but since He didn't and since He chose to be a nobody on the human scale of importance, He was absolutely free to complete His mission on earth.

How different was this Son of the living God from the gods of the Greeks and Romans. In *Hippolytus,* by the Greek playwright Euripides, the hero has dedicated himself to the service of the chaste goddess Artemis. This devotion has aroused the hatred of Dionysus, the god of wine, who therefore plots the death of Hippolytus. As he lies dying, you wait expectantly for the goddess to whom he has committed himself to do something for him.

Then she appears. The death sweat covers Hippolytus' face and death rattles in his throat with every tortured breath he takes. Overwhelmed with sadness, Artemis explains to her devotee that no dweller among the gods on Olympus can witness the physical death of mortals. Then she vanishes. That's it. He is dying for her, but the goddess can do nothing for him.

Thus Euripides offers his judgment of Greek religion, an opinion shared by many of his fifth-century B.C. contemporaries. Is it any wonder that the first century A.D., locked in between Greco-Roman fatalism on the one hand and Jewish legalism on the other, welcomed the good news of a Savior who rescues His believers from sin and death and delivers them by His grace to life and freedom? Such a message was totally unexpected and, to some, quite offensive, but "to those whom God has called, both Jews and Greeks, Christ [came as] the power of God and the wisdom of God" (1 Corinthians 1:24).

This revelation is special. It does not come as a body of facts to be mentally received but as a claim upon our lives to be acknowledged. There is an urgency about it. It is stated in the indicative mood, but an imperative question is always implied: Christ died

31

for you—now what are you going to do about it? The Son of God loves you—now what are you going to do about it?

In the closing moments of the famous movie *Star Wars,* the romantic hero, Hans Solo, is descending into a pit where he is to be frozen to death. As he is lowered away, the Princess finally lets him know her feelings: "I love you," she tells him.

"I know," he answers, and the audience laughs. Our laughter is a kind of protest. "That's just not how you treat love." A profession of love is not a fact to be registered, but an invitation requiring a response.

God has revealed His love and in so doing has challenged us to respond. We have to do something about it, about Him, or we fail both Him and ourselves. This is the nature of the gospel.

The Gospel Is Revolutionary Good News

T. R. Glover tells somewhere of the incisive little girl who, when asked to name the last book of the Bible, named Revolutions. She made a mistake and told the truth. The final chapter of God's Word is written in the lives of its readers. If they have comprehended what God has revealed, they will never be the same, for His gospel is revolutionary.

Paul offers, as the best evidence he has concerning the impact of the gospel, the change in his own life (Galatians 1:13-24). The story of Paul's dramatic conversion and subsequent career is told frequently in the New Testament, by himself and by others (See Acts 8, 9, 13—28, especially chapters 9, 22, and 26; Philippians 3:4-6).

Formerly Paul, who by nature is aggressive and dynamic, had been all-out in his service to God through Judaism. Born a Jew, he chose to belong to the strictest Jewish sect, the Pharisees, and among the members of that sect, he distinguished himself for his zealousness. When the followers of Christ became a threat to Jewish *status quo,* Paul became a leader in stamping out the movement. A student of "the traditions of my fathers" (a reference to the *Torah* [the first five books of the Old Testament] and the collections of traditions of the elders which Paul would have memorized), he could not abide the Christians' casual substitution of the teachings of Jesus for Jewish doctrine.

All this Paul says "I" was doing, but in Galatians 1:15, the subject shifts: "God . . . set me apart . . . called me by his grace." Again the language indicates that events and knowledge greater than his capacity to control or even know have taken over his life. He used to be in charge; now God is. It pleased God "to reveal his Son in me so that I might preach him among the Gentiles" (Galatians 1:15). Without the revelation, no revolution! But when God revealed both His Son and His purpose, Paul, convinced that his former self-directed life had been in vain, surrendered to God full control.

God is in charge—and God alone. When Paul went up to Jerusalem to visit the apostles, it was not to submit to their authority or even to consult with them (Galatians 1:17-21). He postponed his visit, opting instead to go into Arabia and back to Damascus first, and then going to Jerusalem only after three years had elapsed. He did not want to be dependent on any man. He did not need to consult with them, since God had revealed everything necessary to him and had wrought a revolution in Paul's life.

This, then, is Paul's best argument, the evidence of a changed life. ("What a wonderful change in my life has been wrought, since Jesus came into my heart."[2] The gospel hymn unconsciously echoes the testimony of the great apostle.) It is not the only argument, of course. There are theological, historical, and moral considerations to follow. Paul will always sing, "He lives within my heart,"[3] but he is too astute to rest his case on subjective or existential proof alone.

Paul's testimony refutes the "salvation by works" heresy that he is at such pains to stamp out in the Galatian churches. Even this cursory review of his career as a crusading Pharisee establishes this point: if knowledge or good works or the observance of religious rules could ever have been sufficient to save someone, Paul was a prime candidate. He had earned an A + in righteousness. But works couldn't do it.

We should also take note, by the way, that Paul was not converted from an evil life, but from a good one. He did not turn away from irreligion, but from religion. As Paul Scherer has written, "Everything inside of him had been swept and garnished, not to say starched and ironed, for years. There was not a demand which his devotion to the God of his fathers had lain on him that he had not done his best to meet."[4] Jesus revolutionizes the lives of very bad men—and of very good ones.

We could use more of the revolution. George Bernard Shaw, in the preface of his *Androcles and the Lion,* challenges his readers to give Christianity a trial, noting that for two thousand years, man has kept on calling for Barabbas instead of Jesus, but it is becoming apparent that Barabbas was a failure. He represents money and victories and empires and traditional moralities and political constitutions and even established churches, but he looks a failure nonetheless. Jesus, on the other hand, Shaw insists, has not been a failure yet, "for nobody has ever been sane enough to try his way."[5] G. K. Chesterton has added a little different twist: "Christianity has not been tried, and found wanting. It has been found difficult, and not tried."

But where it has been tried, it has led to revolution.

The Gospel Is God-glorifying Good News

The Gospel revolutionizes lives that can be changed in no other way. It took an act of God to change Saul of Tarsus into the apostle Paul. Only God could have done it—so "they praised God because of me" (Galatians 1:24). When the Christians heard the report that their former persecutor had become one of them and was now preaching the very message he had previously done everything he could to stifle, they congratulated God on His good work!

This raises a question for every Christian, doesn't it? Has anybody congratulated God recently because of me? Can other people see there evidence that He has been at work in me?

You probably remember that little fellow whose Sunday-school teacher was recounting the incredible escape of Moses and the Israelites from the clutches of Egypt's Pharaoh. Her young

---

[4]Paul Scherer, *The Word God Sent* (New York: Harper & Bros., 1965), p. 207.

[5]George Bernard Shaw, *Androcles and the Lion* (New York: Penguin, 1963).

charges were breathless as she told the story. When she came to the climax, with the parting of the Red Sea and the subsequent drowning of the enemy, the little guy couldn't contain himself any longer. "Good for God!" he shouted.

He was giving glory to God for what He did through Moses.

The resurrection of Jesus has caused people everywhere to shout, "Good for God!"

The revolution in the life of Saul of Tarsus has had the same effect.

The shouting goes on, because the Lord's disciples seek, in big things and little, to live so that others can see His good work in us and shout, "Good for God!" (1 Corinthians 10:31).

CHAPTER FOUR

What Kind of Freedom
Do We Have?

Galatians 2:1-10

As Paul continues his personal testimony, we notice a shift of emphasis between Galatians 1:13-24 and 2:1-10. In the former passage, he first described the dramatic change God effected in his life when He blocked his persecution of Christians and called him into His service. Then, and not incidentally, he defended his apostolic authority as coming by revelation directly from God ("I did not consult any man, nor did I go up to Jerusalem to see those who were apostles before I was," Galatians 1:16, 17).

In the present passage, his concern turns from authority as an apostle to his unity with the other apostles, from the assertion of his independence to assurance of his harmony and doctrinal accord with his apostolic peers.

The consultation in Jerusalem confirms that Paul's is not an heretical message. "Those men added nothing to my message" (Galatians 2:6). That should not surprise us, since the events of the gospel (specifically Jesus' death, burial, and resurrection), which the apostles had witnessed, were in turn made known to Paul by direct revelation (Galatians 1:16; 1 Corinthians 15:3-8). What were at stake, then, were not the facts of the gospel, but their implications for consistent Christian obedience (especially in relation to certain teachings of the Mosaic law like circumcision).

Paul reports that he, Barnabas, and Titus went to Jerusalem "in response to a revelation" (Galatians 2:2). He doesn't give us the details. In Acts 15, Luke describes the circumstances a little differently. He reports that some men invaded Antioch from Judea, insisting that the Gentile converts in the church at Antioch could not hope to be saved unless they were circumcised according to Mosaic law. Quite naturally, a sharp dispute broke out between them and Paul and Barnabas, since these two leaders had been teaching that salvation depended on faith in Christ alone and had nothing to do with the Mosaic law. In order to resolve the issue, the church dispatched their two leaders and a few other believers to Jerusalem to meet with the apostles and leaders there.

There is no real contradiction between Paul's account here and Luke's in Acts. God communicates His messages to us both directly and indirectly, individually and through group consensus, and the New Testament nowhere suggests that direct guidance is somehow more spiritual than indirect. Both Paul and the congregation as a whole must have fervently prayed for direction in resolving the divisive debate. Paul's claiming to go "in response to a revelation" is undoubtedly his way of asserting that even in this decision, he was under God's authority and not his fellow apostles'. He claims neither superiority nor inferiority to them: He is a *fellow* apostle, a peer.

The issue is the same as the theme of this letter: freedom in Christ. He has led Gentiles to a saving knowledge of Jesus Christ; he has convinced them that God loves them as much as He loves Jews, and that Jesus died for them, also. If the Judaizers from Judea had prevailed in their demand for circumcision, the whole gospel Paul has preached would have been rendered null and void.

In dealing with this controversy here, Paul in this passage makes four important statements about the freedom Christ gives us.

We Are Free From Those Who Would Enslave Us

The church is seldom left in peace from infiltrators who "spy on the freedom we have in Christ Jesus and ... make us slaves" (Galatians 2:4). Those who are themselves in bondage resent the freedom of the liberated. They themselves prefer to remain in their chains and want to lock up everybody else as well. Jean Jacques Rousseau cried in the eighteenth century, "Man is born free; yet everywhere he is in chains." He was wrong, of course. Man isn't born free, but comes into the world helpless, ignorant, dependent, and a slave at the mercy of the powers that be.

That he remains unfree is all too often by his own choice, because for the most part, he prefers easy dependency to the demands of liberty. In modern terms, he likes a powerful government that, with its bureaus and budgets, assumes responsibility for his welfare from cradle to grave. Socially, he conforms to the

38

tenets of etiquette published by the current arbitrators of taste. Religiously, he is drawn toward ecclesiastical organizations that lay down rules for him to follow, rituals for him to perform, and guidelines that make it possible for him to judge his own and everybody else's spirituality.

Nobody threatens him more than the person who has been truly reborn into freedom. This explains why Christians can never expect to be fully accepted by their peers. Such free spirits, by their lack of conformity to the standards of this world, have no right to expect praise or even toleration from the slave-mentality of a nation of sheep. They are, after all, disciples of Jesus, who said, "If the world hates you, keep in mind that it hated me first. If you belonged to the world, it would love you as its own. As it is, you do not belong to the world, but I have chosen you out of the world. That is why the world hates you" (John 15:18, 19).

We Are Free From Fear of Important People

How often in the debates in Antioch the Judaizers must have thrown the authority of the apostles and elders in Jerusalem up to Paul. Their taunts are echoed in Paul's three references to the Jerusalem leaders: "those who seemed to be leaders" (Galatians 2:2), "those who seemed to be important—whatever they were makes no difference to me" (Galatians 2:6), and "those reputed to be pillars" (Galatians 2:9). The Judaizers did not argue the issue, for circumcision on its merits alone; they couldn't keep personalities out of it. They felt compelled to attack Paul along the way, stressing his inferiority to the genuine apostles. Paul took his stand then and takes it now in this letter not on any personal superiority or achievement but (1) in the nature of the gospel and (2) in the call of God himself ("God does not judge by external appearance," Galatians 2:6). Men may accord higher honors to the Jerusalem leaders, but God judges on a different basis—conformity to the gospel. And by this standard, Paul has acquitted himself satisfactorily.

Modern ministers can profit from Paul's stand in this passage. As a young man, I was called to establish a new congregation in a suburb of Portland, Oregon. My relative youth made me easy prey to critics who could point to my inexperience and uncertainty as a leader. Since most of our members came from older congregations, some of them felt uneasy whenever we departed from "the way we used to do it back in our old church." The loudest protests, however, did not come from within the congregation but from the defenders of the faith outside.

What often discouraged me in those days—and still bothers me now—is that our critics never called us back to the gospel but to this or that ecclesiastical tradition. If we varied the worship hours or the order of service, or if we dropped evening service or the Wednesday night prayer meeting, or if we sang more contemporary music—or whatever, we were open to charges of departure from the faith!

Thank God I had an eldership wise enough to keep studying the Scriptures to discern the essence of the gospel and the nature of the church. Their faithfulness to the dictates of the Lord kept us free from unnecessary fear of so-called "important" people.

I wonder whether Paul was surprised at the warm reception he received in Jerusalem. It is apparent that the "important" people were gracious to the delegation from Antioch and in agreement with their preaching. They recognized that Paul's ministry among the Gentiles corresponded to Peter's among the Jews, and they added nothing to Paul's message. In fact, they extended "the right hand of fellowship" (Galatians 2:9), an act symbolizing genuine fellowship.

We Are Free From Ethnic Prejudice

Freedom in Christ is for Jews *and* Gentiles

The Jews had traditionally recognized only two classes of people: us, and everybody else. The term we translate "Gentiles" literally means "the nations"; the Jews used this term for all non-Jews. They treated circumcision of males as the essential mark of belonging to the people of God. The problem for the Judaizers in Antioch was their inability to accept the fact that God wanted to receive Gentile sinners into His embrace without first demanding them to be circumcised. As far as the Judaizers were concerned, God must make them Jews (as well as Christians) before He can save them.

No, Paul countered. Nothing more is required than that they become Christians. They are free in Christ, just as you are (see Galatians 2:15), because God intends for Jews *and* Gentiles to have the privileges of freedom.

40

Paul explains this a little more fully in Ephesians 2:14-18: ✳

> For he himself is our peace, who has made the two one and has
> destroyed the barrier, the dividing wall of hostility, by abolishing in
> his flesh the law with its commandments and regulations. His pur-
> pose was to create in himself one new man out of the two, thus
> making peace, and in this one body to reconcile both of them to God
> through the cross, by which he put to death their hostility. He came
> and preached peace to you who were far away and peace to those
> who were near. For through him we both have access to the Father
> by one Spirit.

So we are all free in Christ.

Paul's great doctrine has never been universally realized, however, even in the church. James Michener's *Chesapeake* speaks
directly to the problem in the scene in which a preacher, Reverend
Buford, has been summoned to a plantation to pacify the rest-
less slaves. Some of them had been devising a plot to run
away to freedom. Reverend Buford urges them to forget their
scheme. "And what is running away, really? Tell me, what is it?
It is theft of self. Yes, you steal yourself and take it away from
the rightful owner, and God considers that a sin." The preacher's
logic is watertight. If you accept his premise that the slaves are
Mr. Sanford's property, then running away *is* a sin. For this
abominable deed, Buford tells the slaves, "you will roast in
hell."[6]

For wanting their emancipation from slavery? No, Buford
hasn't read Galatians. Christ died for all—Jews and Greeks,
slaves and free, male and female. (See Galatians 3:28.) God did
not create any human being to be a slave—to a political or economic system, to social prejudices and barriers, to sin or habits or
customs. Nor did He create us to be slaves of any religious system.
From everything that would bar men and women from true fellowship with God, God in Christ has set us free. "It is for freedom that Christ has set us free" (Galatians 5:1). On behalf of this
message, Paul is willing to debate anyone, even the apostles in
Jerusalem, if need be. *Gal 5:1*

6James Michener, *Chesapeake* (New York: Random House, 1978), p.
619.

He doesn't have to. They are in complete accord. Freedom in Christ is for everyone.

Freedom in Christ is for Gentiles and Jews Everywhere

It's for Titus, a Greek. Converted (but not immediately circumcised) by Paul, Titus has become the center of the controversy. Should he submit to circumcision, as the Judaizers in Antioch insisted, or can he be considered a Christian without also allowing this rite to mark him as a convert to Judaism as well? Had Paul capitulated on this issue, Christianity would have become just another sect of Judaism (like Phariseeism or Sadduceeism) and could never have moved on to become a worldwide faith for people everywhere.

It's for Gentiles. This was a huge concession for the Jerusalem leaders to make. Nothing less than a revelation from God could have compelled them to cross national boundaries to fraternize with people they had always called "Gentile sinners."

It's for Jews. Equally significant, nobody at the Jerusalem conference called for Jews to adopt Gentile customs, either. Christian worship in the Holy City retained many of the characteristics of the Jewish synagogue, and prayers in the temple were offered up by Jewish Christians until its destruction in A.D. 70. The conference has found the essence of Christian church life. It is in the gospel, not in Jewish or Gentile traditions.

It's for Everybody. When Christ's commission is remembered, disagreeing Christians can settle their differences for the sake of winning the world to Christ. When it is forgotten, their gatherings disintegrate into petty arguments that distract from the real business of the church.

We Are Free to Liberate Others

The conference ends on this compassionate note: "All they asked was that we should continue to remember the poor, the very thing I was eager to do" (Galatians 2:10). How typical of the New Testament to conclude a doctrinal discussion with a call to get practical with your religion. In Galatians, this means translating the lofty concept of freedom into practical activities to set people free: evangelism, to liberate them from superstition, idolatry, and fear; education in God's will, to free them from ignorance and disobedience; direct financial assistance, to rescue them from poverty and hunger.

Because western governments have taken over so many welfare duties from the church, the Christians tend to forget this final charge to the Antioch delegation (and to all disciples of Christ). As far as the New Testament is concerned, the assignment for care of the poor was made to the church. James offers a good commentary:

> Suppose a brother or sister is without clothes and daily food. If one of you says to him, "Go, I wish you well; keep warm and well fed," but does nothing about his physical needs, what good is it? In the same way, faith by itself, if it is not accompanied by action, is dead" (James 2:15-17).

Paul demonstrated his concern for the poor when he and Barnabas traveled to Jerusalem with an offering from Antioch (Acts 11:27-30). In his subsequent ministry, Paul devotes great energy to raising money for the poor, once again specifically the poor in Jerusalem (Acts 24:17; Romans 15:26; 1 Corinthians 16:3, 4; 2 Corinthians 8 and 9).

In E. Stanley Jones' inspiring autobiography, the missionary tells us what he hopes to do when he dies and goes to Heaven. He'd like about twenty-four hours to visit with friends and acquaintances, he says; then he will petition the Lord—after expressing his appreciation for the grace that saved him—for the privilege of once more being an evangelist to a fallen world. "I know no heaven more heavenly than proclaiming the good news of Jesus Christ."[7]

He believes the good news of freedom is for everyone everywhere. So does Paul.

---

[7]E. Stanley Jones, *A Song of Ascents* (Nashville: Abingdon Press, 1968), p. 370.

CHAPTER FIVE

How Much Freedom Do We Have?

Galatians 2:11-21

So much is communicated over a meal. Businessmen don't schedule so many appointments in restaurants because they prefer mass produced food to their wives' home cooking, but because eating together with their clients has proved to be such an effective way to conduct business. Through common meals, friendships are solidified, romances are ignited, and barriers are broken down. To eat together is to treat one another as an equal.

That's the reason slaves have always been forbidden to eat with their masters. That's also why, in the first century, no self-respecting orthodox Jew would share a meal with Gentiles. As far as the Jew was concerned, Gentiles weren't equal.

Peter, a Jew for many years longer than he was a Christian, got himself into trouble with Paul in Antioch when he allowed his Jewish prejudice to overrule his Christian convictions.

Peter's Problem

Peter's problem was whether he should eat with Gentiles or not. Intellectually, he knew the answer. Acts 10 records the dramatic revelation he received that made God's will unmistakably clear. As he was praying, he fell into a trance and saw heaven open and an object like a large sheet descending toward him. On it were all kinds of four-footed animals, as well as reptiles and birds. A voice from heaven commanded him, "Get up, Peter. Kill and eat" (Acts 10:13).

Peter protested. He had never eaten anything impure and wasn't about to begin now. (See Leviticus 11; Deuteronomy 14.)

Again the voice spoke. "Do not call anything impure that God has made clean" (Acts 10:14).

This happened three times, following which the sheet-like apparition ascended into heaven.

It was only later, when Peter was summoned to assist in the conversion of the Gentile Cornelius (Acts 10:17-48), that he fully understood the implications of the vision. God was commanding Peter to allow Gentiles, whom the Jews considered "unclean," to enter the kingdom. As he explained to Cornelius and his household, "You are well aware that it is against our law for a Jew to associate with a Gentile or visit him. But God has shown me that I should not call any man impure or unclean" (Acts 10:28).

At the Jerusalem conference (Galatians 2:1-10 and Acts 15), Peter stood by this conviction. The Judaizers had applied great pressure in Antioch to force non-Jewish converts to Christ to add Jewish laws and traditions to Christian grace in order to be saved. They must have lobbied the Jerusalem apostles and elders just as fiercely, but Peter and his colleagues didn't buckle. They extended the right hand of fellowship to their Antioch brethren and refused to force Jewish practices on the Gentile Christians.

When Peter later visited Antioch, he acted consistently with the Jerusalem accord. At the most severe testing point for a Jew, actually sitting down to the table together, Peter graciously accepted Gentile hospitality and ate with his non-Jewish Christian brothers.

Then he abruptly stopped. Some Jewish Christians arrived from Jerusalem (they were associated with James, the Lord's brother, a leader in the church there), and in their presence, Peter would not eat at a Gentile table. Was he afraid of their criticism? Was he merely trying to keep from upsetting them? Was he uncertain of his convictions or his standing with his brothers?

Whatever his motive, as far as Paul was concerned, Peter's withdrawal from the Gentile Christians was an insult. Even worse, he was guilty of hypocrisy and of leading others (including the gentle Barnabas) into hypocrisy. He left an impression that Paul was at such pains to stamp out in his own ministry, that Jewish Christians believed themselves to be superior to Gentiles. "We Jews, even though fellow Christians with you non-Jews, are more Christian than you are," such a withdrawal implied.

It is an attitude prevalent today among believers who think with denominational, sectarian, or cultish minds. A leader of a prominent cult in our community spent a couple of hours vainly trying to persuade me that he and I were "fellow Christians." Having had some experience with his religion, I had to raise only two

46

questions to prove that he did not, indeed, consider us "fellows." The first question was this: "If we are *fellow* Christians, as you insist, why do your people try to steal my people?" His is a cult that is very energetic in proselyting from the membership of mainline Christian churches, claiming that we are in error and only his body has the truth. Members of orthodox churches, therefore, are lost, and his fellow cultists must save us.

The second question put forever to rest any hint of our being "fellow" Christians. "When we die," I asked him, "will I be in the same place in Heaven as you?" I already knew the answer. His group teaches that there are levels in Heaven. He would be on top, and I would be on the bottom. We weren't "fellows" at all.

Cults and sects and denominations thrive on their knack of dividing and separating and classifying all humanity into two groups: Us and Them, the Elect and the Damned, the Best and the Worst.

Peter knew better, but under the judgmental gaze of the eyes from his hometown, he caved in. He withdrew from the non-Jewish Christians, refusing to eat with them any longer. Paul would have none of this vacillation. He reprimanded the veteran apostle in front of everybody. "You are a Jew, yet you live like a Gentile and not like a Jew. How is it, then, that you force Gentiles to follow Jewish customs?" (Galatians 2:14). Paul says he confronted Peter for the sake of "the truth of the gospel," his second use of this phrase (Galatians 2:5, 14). The truth is that people become Christians solely on the basis of God's grace expressed in the death and resurrection of Jesus Christ, irrespective of their race or even of their religious traditions. Their acceptance of this grace erases distinctions among them, and they become fully united with one another. Peter is not guilty of a mere social snub; he has denied the power of the gospel!

He has been hypocritical. Until the Jews arrived from Jerusalem, Peter had no trouble living "like a Gentile," ignoring the complicated laws governing Jewish diet and dining behavior. He didn't demand kosher, and he didn't disdain to recline at table with non-Jewish Christians. Now, by his withdrawal, he seems to be implying that the Jews are right after all and the Gentiles should adapt themselves to Jewish demands.

For Paul, there could be no compromise on the issue, for which centuries of Christians can thank God!

47

Paul's Reprimand

In a nutshell, Paul's argument is this: "Since we are all saved by God's grace and not by our efforts, you must not erect legalistic barriers that God has torn down through the gospel." He has two specific quarrels with the legalism that Peter's action symbolizes. First, observing the law can't make you right with God. Second, freedom in Christ does not promote sinfullness.

Observing the Law Can't Make You Right With God

Jesus had already established this point in His ongoing disputes with the Pharisees about the meaning of the Sabbath. In our Gospels, we read of at least seven occasions when Jesus debated the observance of the holy day with religious leaders. On five of them, the discussion centered on His healing ministry in violation of their understanding of the Sabbath (He healed a withered hand, a woman badly bent over with what appears to have been severe arthritis, a paralyzed man, a blind man, and an invalid). On the other two occasions, His disciples' crime of plucking grains of wheat on the forbidden day was the issue. As far as Jesus was concerned, God intended the Sabbath for the sake of man, not man for the Sabbath (Mark 2:27).

Judaistic legalists had to have directions for the minutest perplexities. Do you have a toothache? You must not gargle with vinegar, although it is permissible to use an ordinary toothbrush dipped in vinegar. Do you have a job to do that just can't wait? You must not work on the Sabbath. You can't carry any burden then, either. A burden is defined as anything weighing as much as a dried fig. Don't cheat, now: you can't get around this prohibition by just carrying something weighing half the weight of a dried fig twice.

The debates go on today. Orthodox law forbids sewing on the Sabbath, and the prohibition against it includes pasting and gluing. This raises an issue unanticipated in the first century. Can you use gummed adhesive strips on disposable diapers? The argument seems to center around whether the tape is considered temporary or permanent, and whether removing it is seen as destructive or constructive labor. One rabbi has ruled that even if the practice is permissible, it really shouldn't be done in the presence of anyone who might misunderstand.

Such precise attention to minutiae can lead to some ludicrous conclusions, such as the breeding of rabbits by French monks in the Middle Ages, who strictly observed the church's injunction to eat only fish on certain special days. They found a way to bend the rule, though. They defined baby rabbits as fish, then proceeded to raise them in abundance so they could indulge their fondness for them and, thanks to the definition, still not violate the law.

Laws are always going to win. They are negative only. Observance of them can keep you from being locked up, but the most scrupulous attention to them can never set you free—for your scrupulosity is a form of bondage. The law can never liberate you from the law's demands.

It is this shortcoming in the law itself that Paul never lets us forget. He begins his argument here by reminding Jewish Christians that they and he became followers of Jesus for the same reason. They wanted to be saved. They had turned to Christ because He offered an alternative to the futility of a religion based on laws. Salvation is through a relationship with the Savior, not through slavish obedience to a complex code of behavior. In their desire to be saved, and in their reliance upon the Savior, there is no difference between the so-called righteous Jews and the "Gentile dogs," a disparaging term that the Jews commonly used to refer to non-Jews.

Freedom in Christ Does Not Promote Sinfulness.

The Judaizers fear that granting Gentiles total freedom from the law will foster lawlessness among them. Not true, Paul insists. "If, while we seek to be justified in Christ, it becomes evident that we ourselves are sinners, does that mean that Christ promotes sin? Absolutely not!" (Galatians 2:17). Paul may have two things in mind here. First, the closer we draw o Christ, the more aware of our sinfulness we become. We are like Isaiah, whose vision of God made him cry out in his comparative wretchedness (Isaiah 6:1-4). Second, if our behavior is less than exemplary, if we act like sinners, we are not to blame Christ for our abuse of our freedom. He's not the lawbreaker, but we are, because we are then not living a life filled with the Spirit but are instead still following the dictates of the flesh (Galatians 5:16-26).

The Larger Principle

There's something more important here than just freedom. Paul is discussing the basis for one's relationship with God. That basis is not law, but faith. "I live by faith in the Son of God, who loved me and gave himself for me" (Galatians 2:20). Here Paul becomes very personal even as he universally applies the doctrines of the grace of God and freedom in Christ:

I was brought up under the strict laws of my religion.

I tried to satisfy the law, but I couldn't. I realized that I could never find God's favor by trying to obey the letter of the law, since I kept failing. I fought myself even as I struggled to be good (Romans 7). Eventually I gave up.

Then something wonderful happened. When I gave up, I learned that there *is* a way to please God. It wouldn't be through all my vain efforts, but by believing in Jesus Christ and letting Him live in me.

So I am now dead to the law and it is dead to me. It no longer has any jurisdiction over me. According to its terms, I am an outlaw, a criminal. Since it has no power to give me life or help anyway, though, I have nothing to lose in ignoring it.

The law was responsible for the death of Christ. Legalists killed Him. I am a Christian, in Christ. Legalists would kill me, too.

The law did its worst to Christ, but it wasn't enough. It could kill Him, but it couldn't keep Him dead. It isn't enough to undo me, either, because of Christ.

I have only one hope, therefore. I hope in Christ. I live in Him. I don't trust intellect or religion or money or glamor or power or anything else to save me. I live in Him who alone can save me.

Only what Christ wants do I want. He lives in me, rules me, directs me. You see, I can't be bothered with the outdated rules of an outdated and powerless religion.

Christ lives in me. He's been resurrected. God lifted Him high above the power of death and the authority of any human law. He has lifted me along with Him (Romans 6:1-14). I'm not subject any longer to the rule of this world but am triumphant over it in Christ.

Cyril Connolly, in his *Evening Colonnade,* describes the fixation of Arthur Symons, a late nineteenth-century British poet of humble reputation. Symons' imagination was dominated by the French poet Baudelaire, to whom he devoted his forties and fifties, translating his poems and writing his biography. In his research, for example, he spent one entire summer tracking down all the hotels at which Baudelaire had stayed. The effect on Symons was not beneficial. Connolly opines that in some natures, the French poet is more a disease than an inspiration. He may have seemed a godlike youth, but in Symons' biography, he "crumbles before our eyes into the prematurely decrepit, shiftless parasite, driven out of his dignity by debt and out of his mind by syphilis." What is deplorable is that some of his readers come under his spell, imitating his decline or taking up his cause. Connolly concludes incisively, "He can set one back a lifetime."[8]

When Baudelaire moves in, the one under his spell dies. Symons had been "crucified" with Baudelaire, and it set him back a lifetime.

When Christ moves in, the one under His spell also dies, but is set *forward* an eternity. Christ lives in us; we live in Him. This is our freedom. We are above the law.

This is the extent of our freedom in Christ, when Christ lives in us:

(1) We are free to eat what we want to, with whomever we choose.

(2) We are free to love whom God wants us to love—and God loves the whole world.

(3) We are free to endure the criticism of those who don't understand us.

(4) We are free to oppose those who exclude or insult anyone in the name of their religion.

(5) We are free to become what God wants us to be. As Paul de Lagarde once said, "He is not free who can do what he wills, but rather he who can become what he should."[9]

(6) "It is for freedom that Christ has set us free. Stand firm, then, and do not let yourselves be burdened again by a yoke of slavery" (Galatians 5:1).

---

[8]Cyril Connolly, *Evening Colonnade* (New York and London: Harcourt, Brace, Jovanovich, 1973, 1975), p. 155, 156.

[9]Quoted in Helmut Thielicke, *The Freedom of the Christian Man* (Grand Rapids: Baker, 1963), p. 10.

CHAPTER SIX

Freedom in Faith

Galatians 3:1-14

So far, Paul has offered two defenses of his gospel of grace: one based on his own experience in Christ and the other on the nature of the gospel itself. Now he offers a third. He appeals to the experience of the Galatians themselves and then, to bolster his argument further, he has them consider the example of their national father Abraham.

His direct address ("You foolish Galatians!" Galatians 3:1) is more abrupt than earlier ("I want you to know, brothers, . . ." 1:11). He's getting more intense as he raises a series of questions that expose the weakness of their grasp on the gospel of freedom.

Questions for Slipping Saints (3:1-5)

"Who has bewitched you?" (Galatians 3:1). "Who has convinced you of a fantasy?" This is the only New Testament appearance of *baskaino,* which here connotes the seductive power of falsehoods (the word hints at black magic) to entice believers away from the truth. People who let themselves be seduced so easily are indeed "foolish" *(anoetoi).*

Paul won't allow the Galatian Christians to blame anyone else for their falling away; they have minds to think with, but in throwing away the riches of Christ for the poverty of legalism, they are acting stupidly. They have been hoodwinked, but willingly.

Paul is especially exasperated because they originally believed his message about Jesus Christ, whom he "portrayed as crucified." Paul was consistent here with his preaching everywhere: "For I resolved to know nothing while I was with you except Jesus Christ and him crucified" (1 Corinthians 2:2). The cross dominates Paul's theology of salvation by grace; if legalism could have saved the Galatians, then Jesus need not have died (Galatians

53

2:21). But laws can never save; they can at best merely control. The cross, however, dramatizes the love of God and the grace that saves. The Galatians heard Paul gladly when he preached this message to them then. What has happened to their faith now?

"Did you receive the spirit by observing the law, or by believing what you heard?" (Galatians 3:2). The answer will be obvious to Paul's readers. From Peter's Pentecost sermon (Acts 2:38) on through the life of the early church, the Holy Spirit was offered in Christ's name to those who believed and repented and were baptized into Him. Reception of the Holy Spirit, in fact, was what separated Jesus' baptism from that of John the Baptist (Acts 19:1-7).

The New International Version translates *ex akoes pisteos* as "believing what you heard." The New English Bible paraphrases it as "by believing the gospel message," and the Revised Standard translates it "by hearing with faith." Whatever words you choose to render this ambiguous phrase into English must hold *hearing* and *believing* together, since Paul obviously intends them to be joined. (See Romans 10:14-17.) He implies that when you hear the gospel, you will naturally believe it. Then, when you act on your belief, you will be given the Holy Spirit as God's response to your faith in Christ. (See Acts 2:36-41. The people heard Peter's sermon on the day of Pentecost. Because they believed what they heard, they then asked what they should do. Peter instructed them to "repent and be baptized" and they would receive forgiveness of their sins and "the gift of the Holy Spirit." Peter held these components together: hearing, believing, repenting, being baptized, being forgiven, and being given the Holy Spirit.)

The Holy Spirit is never given because of one's obedience to any laws. If He were, then good law-abiding Jews could have received the Holy Spirit at any time before the coming of Christ. But they didn't. They couldn't. That's not the way God gives the Spirit.

"Are you so foolish?" (Galatians 3:3). Paul won't let them forget their folly.

"After beginning with the Spirit, are you now trying to attain your goal by human effort?" (Galatians 3:3). "In the beginning you enjoyed a close personal relationship with God himself through His Spirit. Whatever He asked you to do He gave you the

54

power to accomplish through the Spirit. Will you throw away that assistance and go back to sweating out your salvation by your own uncertain merit and energy?"

Paul has already pointed to two opposing routes to redemption: grace and faith versus law and works. Now he says the same thing in a different way: the power of the Spirit versus human effort. The lineup now reads like this: either salvation is by grace through faith aided by the Holy Spirit; or it comes through careful obedience to the law of Moses and the traditions of the elders plus hard human labor (and the hope that you'll be good enough to make it). Another way of saying it: The supernatural way (initiated and supported by God) as opposed to doing what comes naturally (strictly human effort).

"Have you suffered so much for nothing—if it really was for nothing?" (Galatians 3:4). The Galatian Christians, like all early Christians, were persecuted for their faith in Jesus, so the word "suffered" may have a literal meaning here. On the other hand, since "suffer" sometimes means something more like "experience," the New English Bible could be right in translating the clause, "Have all your great experiences been in vain . . . ?" Whichever choice we take in rendering the Greek into English, we come out at the same place: Has what you have undergone so far in your life in Christ been to no avail? Difficulties are associated with walking in the Lord, to be sure, but tough times must be expected in any walk of life. You Christians may have had some troubles, but you have also been given the very best life has to offer; was it wasted on you? Were you like children, who don't know the value of a treasure when they receive it?

"Does God give you his Spirit and work miracles among you because you observe the law, or because you believe what you heard?" (Galatians 3:5). Here Paul shifts from the Galatian to the Heavenly point of view. "Why has God poured out His Spirit? Why has His power been unleashed in miracles for you? Hasn't it been in response to your faith? Surely you don't think it has been because you have been such extraordinary keepers of all the laws and traditions of formal religion?"

Paul's contrast here is between dutiful, respectable religion as observed in scrupulous attention to laws and an exciting, miraculous experience in a personal walk with the Lord, which can only be attained through trusting in His grace.

Behind each of these questions are some real concerns:

Paul's Concerns (3:1-9)

You must not confine yourself by rules nor cramp your personality by regulations or laws or injunctions. Christ has set you free. Martin Luther once asked a laboring man what he believed. The man replied, "What the church believes."

"That is not believing," Luther told him. "It is not your own." A religion that is little more than a canonized and codified legal system leaves no room for personal conviction and interpersonal relationship. A member of that religion may be obedient to its dictates and faithful in its meetings ("I believe what the church believes"), but he has substituted obedience to print on paper for the rewarding freedom of a hand-in-hand relationship with the Lord.

An employee who slavishly obeys the letter of the law in his job description may hold his position, but until he can rise above the contract to a genuine relationship with his employer, he will never enter into the joy of his calling.

A man who does just what the law expects of him as a lawfully wedded husband may satisfy the minimal expectations of his society, but he can never taste the bliss of a real blending of spirits in marriage.

A student who restricts his research to merely satisfying the teacher's instructions may get his A, but he deprives himself of the rich discoveries and relationship awaiting the one who becomes a partner with his teacher in the search for knowledge.

A Christian who confines his religious experience to "doing what is expected" according to law and ecclesiastical tradition can congratulate himself on his piety, but he has turned his back on genuine spiritual freedom.

You must walk by faith, in confidence and freedom and at peace with one another. Otherwise, for you there will be no more miracles, no more joy. The "spiritedness" of your walk with Christ will depart.

You would be well advised to follow the example of your father Abraham. ("He believed God, and it was credited to him as

56

righteousness"; Galatians 3:6). Abraham lived before the Mosaic law came into existence, yet God adjudged him righteous (in a right relationship with God and man). That means there must be a righteousness that isn't dependent upon that law. In fact, Abraham was really a Gentile, in the sense that he lived before the nation of Israel existed, so he was not in the strictest sense a Jew. Yet this Gentile was righteous, so there must be a righteousness not dependent upon one's Jewishness.

Further, Abraham received God's promise that all the nations of the world would be blessed through him (Galatians 3:8). Obviously, then, God did not intend to limit His blessings to just the biological offspring of Abraham. Whom will He bless, then? All who share Abraham's *faith* in God. "Understand, then, that those who believe are children of Abraham" (Galatians 3:7). "So those who have faith are blessed along with Abraham, the man of faith" (Galatians 3:9). "He redeemed us in order that the blessing given to Abraham might come to the Gentiles through Christ Jesus, so that *by faith* we might receive the promise of the Spirit" (Galatians 3:14).

Abraham accepted the rite of circumcision as a covenant sign. He performed it as an act of faith (Genesis 17). He believed God's promises that he would father a nation and rule Canaan. He believed so totally that as an old man, he obeyed God when He asked for him to sacrifice his only son Isaac, through whom he had thought God was fulfilling these promises (Genesis 22).

The Jews revered Abraham as their father (John 8:39), but Jesus chided them: "If you were Abraham's children, you would do what Abraham did." His point is identical to Paul's: the true descendants of the great man are not his biological descendants but his spiritual ones, and they are those who trust in God as Abraham trusted.

Here Paul appeals to the real basis for parental pride. When a baby is born, the parents delight in detecting their own physical characteristics in the baby, who is said to have the mother's eyes, the father's nose, and perhaps Grandfather's chin. When the baby becomes an adult, however, the parents don't care not so much whether the child now favors the parents in physical appearance as that he displays those attitudes and activities and values that the parents believe in. Specifically, does the offspring exhibit the "faith of the fathers"?

A Choice to Be Made (3:10-14)

The Galatian Christians have two choices, then. They can enjoy their status as offspring of Abraham in a walk of faith like that of Abraham, or they can anxiously devote themselves to a slavish attempt to satisfy the impossible dictates of the law and the traditions of the elders. If they choose the latter, Paul warns them, they must be prepared for the consequences:

"All who rely on observing the law are under a curse (Galatians 3:10)." Paul has in mind Deuteronomy 27:26, "Cursed is the man who does not uphold the words of this law by carrying them out," and the next verse, which makes the curse applicable to the breaking of any part of the law: "If you fully obey the Lord your God and carefully follow *all his commands* I give you today, the Lord your God will set you high above all the nations on earth." Hundreds of years separated the original declaration of these words from the time of the apostle Paul; in those intervening years the legalism that governed Judaism had fused the two verses into one, making the curse apply to the breaking of any of the commands. Since there were so many separate commands, no one could be certain to "continue to do everything written in the Book of the Law" (Galatians 3:10). The curse was inescapable.

This strong word alludes to God's original curse in the Garden of Eden (Genesis 3:14-19), to His curse in Cain's murder of Abel (Genesis 4:11, 12), and, as noted above, in failing to keep the law (Deuteronomy 27:16).

Even the Jewish Scriptures taught that righteousness did not come through the law, but through faith. To bolster his argument that God dealt with Abraham and his true descendants on the basis of their faith in Him rather than their obedience to a law, Paul quotes Habakkuk 2:4, "The righteous will live by faith" (Galatians 3:11). The law can't produce merit in the keeper of the law, but God can grant righteousness to the one who believes in Him. Here is the heart of the New Testament doctrine of salvation by grace. It appears again and again: Romans 1:17; Hebrews 10:38; Ephesians 2:4, 8.

"The law is not based on faith" (Galatians 3:12). You can satisfy the demands of the hundreds of commandments without ever genuinely trusting in God or enjoying any relationship with Him. Your relationship is with the laws, not the Lawgiver. Your reward is in believing you are a good obedient citizen rather than in experiencing the love of the King who wants to be like a Father to you.

Further, you are deluded if you think you can "live by" the commandments of the law. Remember the curse for breaking any one of them?

We Christians don't have to give another thought to that curse, because through Jesus' death on the cross, the Lord took any curse we might deserve on himself and set us free from it. The Scriptures have said, "Cursed is everyone who is hung on a tree" (Galatians 3:13; cf. Deuteronomy 21:23). This form of death was common among the Romans; it was less so among Jews, but it is mentioned in Deuteronomy as the type of death reserved for criminals already cursed by their society (and by God). Jesus willingly yielded himself to this ignominious death in order to release us from any curse we might deserve. "God made him who had no sin to be sin for us, so that in him we might become the righteousness of God" (2 Corinthians 5:21; see also Romans 8:1-4). (He also invalidated the law, leaving it powerless over those who are in Him; Colossians 2:13-15.)

In other words, He "redeemed us" (Galatians 3:14), "bought us back" from the clutches of the law and its curse, so that the promises God made to Abraham (Genesis 12:1-4) might be fulfilled in us, Gentiles and Jews alike. The Holy Spirit that you received (Galatians 3:2), you must surely understand by now, is not yours because of any merit you earned through painstaking adherence to the law's commandments, but simply because of your faith in Christ Jesus. It is in this faith that you are the true children of Abraham. God has kept His promise to bless all nations through Abraham. You are evidence that He has kept His word.

Do we still need this argument?

Yes.

A young man in his thirties, father of two children, attended our church for some time. He was troubled by the implications of belief and wanted to talk about them. He told me he believed in a Supreme Being, but he confessed he didn't know what he meant by that term. "I think I believe in Christ," he added, but he wasn't sure. "I know I want the church," he told me, but he said it was for the sake of his children and because it gave him a good social circle to be a part of. He had noticed that the church members seemed "to have it together."

He wanted to know how much faith was required. He couldn't agree with everything I preached. I told him that such agreement was unnecessary, since what mattered was his relationship with the Lord, not conformity to my thinking.

Our conversation ended inconclusively. He continued attending for some time, then dropped away. He had discovered that belief was not as easy as he wished. In fact, what he wanted was a religion that had more clearly stated regulations. He was a career military man, used to giving and following orders. He knew how to obey.

But he didn't know how to relate. After a while, it became obvious that he couldn't form lasting relationships with people. He rejected any attempt we made to draw him into a circle of fellowship, and he resisted every suggestion that he could find what he was looking for by simply trusting God. He would have appreciated the Judaizers. Human effort he was prepared to give; salvation by faith and grace he could not accept.

CHAPTER SEVEN

The Law and the Promise

Galatians 3:15-25

We now encounter one of the most difficult passages in all the apostle Paul's correspondence. In these verses, he draws on the debating skills he learned from his rabbinic teachers. His reasoning is that of a typical first-century rabbi who loves to take a single word and build his whole argument on its specific and sometimes previously hidden meanings. In this case, the word is "seed" or "descendant" (Galatians 3:16). Paul's reasoning does not seem very convincing to a twentieth-century reader, but its form would have satisfied the critics of his own day. Had he been writing specifically to us, he would have used more contemporary reasoning, but it's his conclusion, not his reasoning, that is important.

We'll find it more helpful to take the passage as a whole. As we do, we note that Paul makes use of four large concepts. By arranging them according to chronology and importance, we can quickly seize the essence of his argument.

Promise (3:15, 16)

Everything began with God's promise to Abraham. "The promises were spoken to Abraham and to his seed" (Galatians 3:16). Quickly review Genesis 12:7; 13:15; 17:7, 8; and 24:7. In each instance, the Lord makes specific promises to Abraham, who, in faith, takes God at His word and lives in expectation that He will keep His promise.

Paul argues that God's promise was to Abraham's *descendant,* not *descendants* (or *seed,* not *seeds*), so its fulfillment was in a particular person, not in all of Abraham's progeny. In other words, God had Christ in mind when He spoke to Abraham. Paul's critics will claim that citizens of the nation of Israel are the true descendants of Abraham. But Paul has already contended (see last section) that the Lord doesn't have Abraham's biological offspring in mind at all, but those who are like the patriarch in their faithfulness to the Lord. Now he adds that Christ (including, of course, those who are in Christ) is the true descendant of Abraham.

The Jews would have to admit that not all the descendants of their father Abraham would be among the elect, since the children of Ishmael (who was Abraham's son) had never been included. (See Genesis 17:19-21.) What is surprising to them is that Paul now excludes everybody but Christ (as *the* seed) because, he argues, only in Christ is the promise completed.

Covenant (3:17)

Abraham heard God's promises and acted on them, thus transforming one-sided promises (from God to Abraham) into a two-party covenant (God and Abraham), with both sides accepting the terms of the agreement. When Abraham and the males of his family were circumcised (Genesis 17), their special relationship with God was formalized, and the people of Abraham became God's covenant people.

The agreement is, of course, unequal, with the Lord establishing the generous terms and His people pledging to meet them. Circumcision signified the pledge of their obedience. But, as Paul takes pains to explain again and again, the sign of obedience must never be confused with the obedience itself, nor must slavish obedience be thought to suffice for faith in the promise. Otherwise, bondage to law replaces joy in relationship—which is exactly what has happened to the Jews.

Law (3:18-25)

When compared with the promise and the covenant, the law plays a relatively minor role in God's relationship with His people. It wasn't introduced until 430 years later, and when it appeared, it did not replace the covenant and certainly didn't affect the promise (Galatians 3:17). Our whole inheritance does not depend on the letter of the law, but on the grace (the unmerited favor) of the One who made the promise in the first place.

The law has been helpful. It has governed life among God's people. It has defined transgressions so that people would know right from wrong, acceptable behavior from unacceptable; it has given guidance to sinful people who haven't risen to a high enough level of conduct to be able to function without rules and regulations (Galatians 3:19). Thus, the law satisfies human needs, but it is powerless to take us to God.

It is inferior because it places itself between us and God. A covenant is a direct relationship, but the law forces us into an indirect relationship with God. It hasn't even come to us directly, but rather through a mediator and messengers ("angels"; Galatians 3:19, 20).

Paul's purpose here is not to diminish the role of Moses, but to demonstrate that the law, which requires an intermediary when it is first established and which then intrudes itself between the two parties so that they can no longer communicate except on the basis of its commandments, is obviously inferior to a covenant based on a promise and the direct relationship between the Promiser and the recipient of the promise.

Paul's criticisms should not be interpreted as any lack of appreciation for the law as such; he just wants it understood that the law operates on different level from the covenant. It can't substitute for either promise or covenant. It is a supplement (because of our sin—Galatians 3:19) or a caretaker (to get us ready for something better—Galatians 3:23-25), but never an adequate replacement for the real thing.

Of this fact we can be certain: the law cannot give life. "For if a law had been given that could impart life, then righteousness would certainly have come by the law" (Galatians 3:21). But law can't do that. Only a close, unmediated relationship between the sinner and the Life-giver can.

We resist this truth. Our natural reaction seems to be that of the Anglican clergyman who heard Charles Wesley preach on the kingdom of Heaven. "That [the kingdom] is what I am seeking," he told Wesley. "I realize now that I must seek it by a long course of devotional discipline, by years given to reading the Bible and years devoted to prayer." The clergyman made no reference to the Old Testament law; indeed, he would have been offended had he been called a legalist. Yet his approach to the Lord was very much in the Old Testament mode: he felt he must prove his worthiness by a careful regimen of stipulated disciplines. In his thinking, there was still something between him and God. He could only approach Him indirectly, by way of these spiritual exercises.

He was like the elder brother in Jesus' famous parable of the prodigal son (Luke 15). When the erring younger brother returns to the forgiving, graceful embrace of his Father, the elder brother is eaten up with jealousy. "Look! All these years I've been slaving for you and never disobeyed your orders. [I have kept your commandments, obeyed your law.] Yet you never gave me even a young goat so I could celebrate with my friends" (Luke 15:29). He is in bondage to rules and estranged from the deep relationship based on grace that the Father could have with him as well as with the younger brother. When he could be rejoicing in the life of grace, he is instead withering away in his obedience to the commands of sonship, rather than in freely offered trust in, and love for, his Father.

These "commands" do not lead to, indeed cannot give, life. H. L. Mencken has written in a much different context, "Injustice is relatively easy to bear; what stings is justice." From a purely legalistic point of view, the elder brother has a case; his insistence on the justice of his case, however, has kept him from the joy of life. The Father offers more than justice under law; He offers grace under love.

The Judaizers' demand for law to prevail will lead to the same barrenness as the elder brother exhibits, because "we were held prisoners by the law" (Galatians 3:23). Law imprisons; grace liberates.

Saul Bellow proves that this kind of bondage has not passed away. He recounts a conversation with his seat mate on a British Airways flight to Jerusalem. The author, a Jew, has deeply offended his Hasidic fellow traveler (Hasids are strict observers of Jewish laws, modern-day Pharisees), when he begins to eat his unkosher lunch. The Hasid first asks him how he, a Jew, could eat such stuff. Then he offers him one of his own kosher-beef sandwiches. When Bellow politely accepts it, the Hasid tries to extract a promise that he will never eat unkosher food again. He offers to pay him up to twenty-five dollars a week if he promises. When Bellow thanks him for his concern (although he has no intention of accepting the proposal), the Hasid tells him, "You are a Jew. I must try to save you."[10]

For this conscientious Hasid, dietary regulations have come between man and God. Now we understand why Jesus declared

---

[10] Saul Bellow, *To Jerusalem and Back,* (New York: Viking Press, 1976), pp. 3, 4.

all foods clean (Mark 7:19). He wanted nothing to come between us and God, even food. Paul is satisfied, then, that the law, which has got in the way between man and God, has been removed through Jesus Christ. His purpose was to break down every barrier separating man from God and man from man (Ephesians 2; 2 Corinthians 5:11-21).

Promiser (3:15-25)

What God started with a promise and formalized in a covenant cannot be replaced by a mere temporary law. The promise has endured until the present, and now it has been completely fulfilled in the arrival of the promised Christ (Messiah). The Promiser has kept His word.

Since what God wants more than anything else is a personal, unmediated relationship with His people, "without faith it is impossible to please God, because anyone who comes to him must believe that he exists and that he rewards those who earnestly seek him" (Hebrews 11:6). When the Philippian jailer asked what he had to do to be saved, he was told to "believe in the Lord Jesus, and you will be saved" (Acts 16:31). Whenever the apostle Paul returns to the theme of salvation, he stresses the grace of God and the response of faith (Ephesians 2:4, 8). Our redemption is not through obedience to law but through union with Christ (Romans 6:1-11). The Promiser has kept His promise in Christ; everyone who is in Christ shares the promise (Galatians 3:22-25). As the law was unnecessary for Abraham, who walked by faith, so it cannot be placed in charge of us, if we are in Christ (Galatians 3:24).

If we have only law, then "the whole world is a prisoner of sin" (Galatians 3:22), since it has already been established that from a strictly legal point of view, we deserve to be locked up for our sins. We have broken the law; we should pay the penalty.

But God is not interested in justice; He really wants us to enjoy the blessings He promised clear back in Abraham. That enjoyment is now ours, if we are among "those who believe" (Galatians 3:22).

CHAPTER EIGHT

The Difference Faith Makes

Galatians 3:23—4:7

The apostle Paul never tires of rejoicing over the revolutionary change that faith in Jesus Christ brings to the life of the believer. In this passage, he vividly contrasts pre-faith bondage with post-faith liberation.

The Days Before Faith Came (3:23, 24, 28; 4:3)

Law ruled before faith came. The law of Moses, with its hundreds of commandments, regulated every aspect of life: morality, society, and religion. Was the law evil in itself? "Absolutely not!" (Galatians 3:21). Its fault did not lie in any opposition to God's will but in its powerlessness to give life. It was negative, able to prohibit but unable to enliven. The law can lock you up, but it can't set you truly free.

A mischievous Mark Twain gives us a humorous illustration of the law's power to crimp our life-style. It certainly inhibited his writing style. His editor cautioned him never to state anything as fact unless he could verify it from personal experience. (If I were to follow this rule strictly, I couldn't tell you this anecdote, since I can't verify whether it actually happened. It may just be one of the many apocryphal stories that have attached themselves to this most fascinating of American authors.) Later, when he was sent out to cover an important social event, he wrote up this brief report:

> A woman, giving the name of Mrs. James Johns, who is reputed to be one of the social leaders of the city, is said to have given what purported to be a party, yesterday, for a number of alleged ladies. The hostess claims to be the first wife of a reputed attorney.

No libel suit could be filed against Twain on this one!

When you live in fear of breaking one of the law's hundreds of commandments, you hedge and hesitate and box yourself in so that you won't be found guilty.

Guardians ruled before faith came. Wherever law is in charge, lawyers are in control. "So the law was *put in charge* to lead us to Christ" (Galatians 3:24). The word is *paidagogos,* our *pedagogue* or *schoolmaster.* So long as we are under the law's tutelage, we take orders like obedient schoolchildren. But also like schoolchildren, we should one day be set free. That's where Christ comes in, as we shall see.

Paul is dealing here with the power of law in the abstract, but implicit in everything he says is the fact that to be in bondage to the law is to be under the sway of lawyers. Priests and scribes and rabbis, whose business it was to understand and interpret the law, became the final authorities in Jewish society. They claimed to speak in the name of the law, but in reality the law was subject to their translation of it. Chief Justice Charles Evans Hughes said of the American legal system, "We are under the Constitution, but the Constitution is what the judges say it is." So it was with the law of Moses.

Division ruled before faith came. When Paul writes, "There is neither Jew nor Greek, slave nor free, male nor female . . . in Christ" (Galatians 3:28), he alludes to the great mischief legalism inflicts on people. It divides them into arbitrary segments; it deals with them categorically and fails to respect them as persons. ("She's just a woman." "He's nothing but a slave anyway.") So humanity is fragmented into Jews and Gentiles, Romans and barbarians, masters and slaves, blacks and whites, the bourgeoisie and the proletariats, "good ol' boys" and "nigger-lovers," and on and on.

Some of the divisions are humorous. C. H. Spurgeon found a club in nineteenth-century London that catered only to small men. The qualification for membership was a height of five feet or less. The honored members believed—or pretended to believe—that of all mankind, they were the closest to perfection. They argued that since primeval men were gigantic ("there were giants in the earth"; Genesis 6:4, KJV), as the human race has progressed they have grown smaller. It's all perfectly reasonable, therefore: smaller is better, smallest is best.

The little men are absurd, of course, but only slightly more ridiculous than the rest of a race that divides itself into "us" and "them" and then declares "us" far superior to all of "them." Such divisiveness has to be abolished, or the race is doomed.

Alienation ruled before faith came. Division leads to alienation. Wherever the in group reigns, the outsiders will be treated as strangers and aliens. This is the condition Paul addresses in Ephesians 2:11f:

> Therefore, remember that formerly you who are Gentiles by birth and called "uncircumcised" by those who call themselves "the circumcision" (that done in the body by the hands of men)—remember that at that time you were separate from Christ, excluded from citizenship in Israel and foreigners to the covenants of the promise, without hope and without God in the world.

1 Peter 2:10 (RSV) summarizes the outsider's condition: "Once you were no people. . . ."

Superstition ruled before faith came. ". . . we were in slavery under the basic principles of the world" (Galatians 4:3). Those basic principles are the *stoicheia* of the world, the common set of beliefs and presuppositions by which a human culture governs and tries to save itself. They are enslaving principles that, like the law, can never set their people free. Although we don't know exactly which of the many "stoicheia" Paul has in mind as he writes to the Galatians, his words are relevant to all readers who have found themselves under the power of demons or astrologists or palm readers or godless philosophers of every stripe.

The Days After Faith Came (3:25-29; 4:4-7)

Then, when God saw that everything was ready, "God sent his Son, born of a woman, born under law, to redeem . . ." (Galatians 4:4). When the Jews were ready for their Messiah, and Rome was hungering for a higher morality, and the law had done its preparatory work, then God sent Jesus.

The rule of freedom replaced the rule of law. Concern for relationships replaced the constraints of regulation. Who knows this truth better than the adult who was reared in a repressive home governed by an endless list of arbitrary rules, or a former Christian who was driven away from the church by the unyielding legalism of older members who valued their regulations more highly than their young people?

Unfortunately, many adults are still rebelling against that legalism and hence, in their rebellion, are still subject to its commands. Whatever the "law" told them they must do, they devote themselves to not doing. They haven't achieved genuine freedom of choice or action. Their past still controls their present.

To just such people Paul writes in Galatians 5:1, "It is for freedom that Christ has set us free. Stand firm, then, and do not let yourselves be burdened again by a yoke of slavery." Freedom reigns in the hearts of Christians, the true freedom that is based on love and cherished by relationships and has pulled itself free from any form of rebellion.

The rule of faith replaces the tyranny of guardians. "Now that faith has come, we are no longer under the supervision of the law" (Galatians 3:25). Nobody else is responsible for us now. The law doesn't govern us (freedom in love does), so the lawyers can't tyrannize us. We have grown up. We are "no longer . . . infants, tossed back and forth by the waves, and blown here and there by every wind of teaching and by the cunning and craftiness of men in their deceitful scheming" (Ephesians 4:14).

In a real sense, then, each Christian walks by faith in the Lord and is responsible to no human authority for his ultimate salvation. He respects his earthly teachers and follows the lead of his pastors, but whenever he discerns a conflict between their guidance and the Lord's spoken will, he must throw himself on the mercies of the Lord. His faith is in Him, not them.

Unity replaces division. The old categories are abolished. Christ has wiped them out. "For he himself is our peace, who has made the two one and has destroyed the barrier, the dividing wall of hostility, by abolishing in his flesh the law with its commandments and regulations. His purpose was to create in himself one new man out of the two . . ." (Ephesians 2:14, 15). There is no room in the church of Jesus Christ, then, for racism or sexism or ageism or even the social distinctions of capitalism (or any other "ism" you might think of). No longer can the "us" against "them" polarity rule. All who are in Christ are in each other, for there is only one body.

Adoption has driven away alienation. God sent His Son "that we might receive the full rights of sons" (Galatians 4:5). Through Christ, He has taken us (who were once "no people") into His family and made us full heirs, just as if we had been biological sons. We have been adopted (Romans 8:23). As sons. Since there is no longer male or female in Christ, then all of us receive the same treatment. Jesus, Son of God, condescended to become son of woman so that we, all sons and daughters of woman, might now through Him become sons of God. We are no longer alienated because of our weakness, our sinfulness, or our humanness. We now belong to the family of God. He has adopted us.

So we are now heirs of all our Father has written into His will for us.

> For you did not receive a spirit that makes you a slave again to fear, but you received the Spirit of sonship. And by him we cry, "*Abba,* Father." The Spirit himself testifies with our spirit that we are God's children. Now if we are children, then we are heirs—heirs of God and co-heirs with Christ, if indeed we share in his sufferings in order that we may also share in his glory" (Romans 8:15-17; see also Ephesians 1:17-19; 3:6-8).

Therefore, **confidence** has overpowered our superstitions. We believe in the one true God who has the power to accomplish all things, even our salvation. We are "justified by faith" (Romans 5:1), so we have nothing to fear from anybody. "In him [Christ] and through faith in him we may approach God [and thus anybody else in the universe] with freedom and confidence" (Ephesians 3:12).

It is a confidence the world can't offer. My son and I visited the auto display at the Imperial Palace in Las Vegas. Two of the cars on display fixed themselves in our memory. The first was the 1942 Packard that once belonged to General Douglas MacArthur. He bought it in the fall of 1941, sending his personal check for $2600 to the company (which sent it back with their compliments). The Packard had the latest accessories: factory air conditioning, overdrive, electromatic clutch, radio, heater, defroster, and fender skirts. It was painted—including the trim—the standard (and ugly) olive drab. MacArthur had it shipped to Australia, and then it followed him to the Philippines and on to the occupation of Japan at the close of World War II. We were pretty impressed with this vehicle, until we saw the second one.

The second car also belonged to a wartime leader. It was a 1943-44 Mercedes Benz 770K, Adolph Hitler's last car. It was delivered to him on March 17, 1944, the only automobile built in 1943 and 1944. Crafted totally by hand over a period of fifteen months, the armor-plated vehicle was designed for Hitler's personal use, at a cost of $2,000,000. It weighs five and a half tons, and its eight cylinders develop 400 horsepower to a top speed of 120 miles per hour. Gas mileage is two and a half miles per gallon.

The car's wheels are bullet-proof, as are its two-inch-thick windows. The floor is mine-proof. The doors consist of one-inch armor plate and weigh approximately nine hundred pounds each. In the rear is a compartment for schmeiser submachine guns and lugers.

There is also a self-destruct mechanism that could be operated by the turn of a separate key on the dashboard. When activated, it would send a spark to the 66-gallon fuel tank, blowing the car to smithereens.

As my son and I admired the car, I found myself pitying the shell of the man who at one time terrified the world. "How scared he was," I thought. He had the very best this world offers; he worshiped the "basic principles" of this world, and they weren't enough. All his power, his prestige, his military success, his adoration from the masses could not erase the terror in his heart, so he was reduced to cowering behind an armored-plated car or hiding out in his specially equipped bunker.

When you have boldness of access to God, you don't have to be afraid of anything or anyone else. You live in confidence. Nothing can ultimately harm you, even death itself. You are a son of the King, heir to everything He wants for you. "You are all sons of God through faith in Christ Jesus, for all of you who were baptized into Christ have clothed yourselves with Christ" (Galatians 3:26).

"Through faith . . . who were baptized . . . clothed yourselves with Christ." It is fascinating that in a letter that denounces legalism and insists that only faith expressing itself through love matters (Galatians 5:6), Paul takes for granted that the Christians to whom he is writing have all been baptized.

We wouldn't even pause at 3:27 if it were not for the fact that we can no longer assume that Christians have been baptized. Baptism has fallen on hard times in some circles, for the understandable reason that so many voices have been raised against it. These voices equate any insistence on baptism with a kind of "salvation by works" theology, or they treat it as a symptom of a kind of legalism. Yet Paul, who could never be accused of teaching that salvation is by works and who is always the church's leading proponent of freedom, takes baptism for granted. He treats it as the convert's statement of faith in Christ and as the means through which he "puts on" and is "united with Christ." (See Romans 6:1-10; Colossians 2:12.) G. R. Beasley-Murray, in his *Baptism in The New Testament,* says that "baptism is the moment of faith in which adoption is realized."[11]

When we are certain of our adoption into God's family, we live with confidence.

---

[11] G. R. Beasley-Murray, *Baptism in the New Testament* (Grand Rapids: Eerdmans, 1973), p. 151.

ABBA - the Word PATER (FATHER)
GREEK - greek New Testament

WUEST'S
Word Studies
Galsher
Kenneth S Wuest

CHAPTER NINE

Living Free—As Sons of the King

Galatians 4:8—5:1

With almost a shout of triumph, Paul has just concluded, "So you are no longer a slave, but a son; and since you are a son, God has made you also an heir" (Galatians 4:7). The purpose, then, of God's sending His Son, of the Son's putting on humanity, and of His sacrifice to set us free, was to make us all God's sons and heirs!

We ought, then, to keep on living as sons of the King, celebrating our freedom and resisting any temptation to return to slavery. Unfortunately, what we ought to do and what we actually do are often not the same. So it is with the Galatians. They are in danger of tossing away their freedom in Christ. How could they?

Paul's appeal now becomes personal.

You Are Sons of God (4:8-11)

Building on Galatians 3:26—4:7, Paul reminds them of their former slavery ("you were slaves to those who by nature are not gods," Galatians 4:8). This is the third time (see Galatians 3:23f and 4:1f) that he speaks of the slavery they have escaped through Christ. What made their former condition so pitiful was their delusion that their masters were gods, when they were really nothing. The Galatians didn't know better then, perhaps, but they have no excuse now. Paul is astonished that they would even entertain the idea of returning to their past slavery. Peter would say of this reversion, "A dog returns to its vomit," and "A sow that is washed goes back to her wallowing in the mud" (2 Peter 2:22).

They actually *want* the old familiar restrictions; they used to feel secure under their "guardians and trustees" (Galatians 4:2) while they comfortably obeyed "the basic principles" (Galatians 4:3) of a godless world. They preferred law to grace and

75

immaturity to maturity. But God prefers them to be sons and heirs (Galatians 4:7).

God wants them to rise above the strictures of legalism to a relationship based on His grace: "But now that you know God—or rather are known by God ..." (Galatians 4:9). Paul uses *ginosko* here, the word that connotes knowing and being known intimately, on a personal level. God has taken the initiative, making the move to get acquainted with us first. Our "knowing God" is simply our response to His offer. (See 1 John 1:10, "This is love: not that we loved God, but that he loved us and sent his Son as an atoning sacrifice for our sins.")

Instead of enjoying their free access to the Father, however, the Galatian Christians are "turning back to those weak and miserable principles" from which Christ had rescued them (Galatians 4:9; see also 4:3). Paul's adjectives show his contempt: What governs most of the world's people is *weak* (powerless to set us free; it can point out what sin is but can't wipe out the sin to which it points) and *miserable* (poor, lacking buying power, not to be compared with the surpassing riches of grace that Paul lauds in Ephesians 1:7, 18, and 3:8).

These principles—whether religious, political, economic, or social—organize society, all right, but the effect of the organization is to diminish men and restrict their freedom. People then become slaves of the system (whether it is socialism or communism or capitalism or Judaism or spiritism or whatever). Even when a person breaks loose to "express himself" and "do his own thing," the effect is not freedom but enslavement to "created things" (see Romans 1:18-32), and their destruction is sure.

John Greenlee whimsically bewails his imprisonment to an apparently harmless hobby. He writes,

> It sounds ridiculous ... but it's true. I *am* being held captive by my yard. No, I'm not being held captive *in* my yard ... it's *by* my yard. To be completely accurate, it's the rose bushes, African daisies, tomato vines, yuccas, and the avocado tree, in a conspiracy with the snail army, the voracious beetles, and the bluegrass fungus who are holding me captive.
>
> What's worse is that I walked right into it. I practically invited it! It began two years ago when I first looked at this huge yard and, in my midwestern mind, loved the spacious expanse of grass, flowers and trees. I smiled in my naive delight. And the bugs and snails and

fungus all peeked out from behind their leafy hiding places and smiled back. They were plotting against me from day one!

Now they've got me. I started out thinking I owned this yard. Now I know that this fool yard owns me![12]

False religion takes over in the same way.

The Galatians may think they are simply returning to a few of the pleasant practices of their former religion, but Paul predicts that they are naively heading into slavery. The system will soon own them. Religions organize and systematize and dehumanize, but in Christ, Paul constantly argues, man is energized and actualized. He is liberated.

Unfortunately, something in us prefers being organized into a system to being truly free. Famous theologian-turned-prisoner, Dietrich Bonhoeffer, mused on this debilitating characteristic during the second spring of his imprisonment by the Nazis. He who had so cherished his liberty realized that something had happened to him he never would have thought possible. He confessed that he had become used to being a prisoner!

He isn't the first to make such a discovery. Every now and then we read in our newspapers of a prisoner who has petitioned to return to the secure life he knew behind bars.

It might seem that Paul exaggerates the danger. Why should he fear for the Galatians just because they are "observing special days and months and seasons and years" (Galatians 4:10)? Is there something inherently wrong with celebrating?

Not at all. The problem lies in substituting these structured "special times" for a living, vital relationship with the Father. Instead of being allowed to approach our loving Parent at all times, visits to Him are restricted to certain "sacred" occasions and by means of certain "sacred" rituals. So we must observe

—"Days" like the sabbaths and specific feast days.
—"Months" like those scorned in Isaiah 1:13, 14.
—"Seasons" like the annual Feasts of Tabernacles or Passover.
—"Years" like the Jubilee and sabbatical years.

For purposes of his argument here, Paul seems to be equating these Jewish holy times with pagan festivals and so-called lucky

---

[12]John Greenlee, *Conejo Caller* (July 19, 1978).

days. Even those times that God himself had appointed had been corrupted by men and had become means of separating from, rather than uniting with, Him.

That Paul is not exaggerating the enslaving effect of these special "times" can be documented by an examination of any legalistic religion today. Since the apostle has Judaism in mind, it is not amiss to mention a prominent twentieth-century Jewish novelist whose works faithfully to depict the heritage of his orthodox Judaism. In Isaac Bashevis Singer's *Shosha,* the protagonist describes the orthodox Jewish household in which he grew up. He and his brother had no toys to play with. Instead, they played among their father's books, which lined the walls of the otherwise nearly bare living room. There was no sofa, upholstered chair, chest of drawers, or anything else but a long table, some benches, and an ark for scrolls. It was a place for prayer on the sabbath, when their father stood at a lectern all day studying his commentaries. The boy's dominant memory of their father was his phrase, "It is forbidden." Whatever the boys wanted to do was a transgression. To draw or paint a person violated the second commandment; to laugh was mockery; to say a word against another boy was slander; to make up a story was to lie; to touch a candle or a coin on the sabbath was absolutely forbidden.

Religion like this, Paul argues, is a form of slavery. In Christ, we don't need rituals or sacrifices or magic or astrology charts or signs of the zodiac or anything else. Such superstitious behavior has been replaced by a personal relationship with the Father. Just as my children do not have to observe any standard ritual to approach me—or come to me only on stipulated hours or days or seasons, so Christians can enjoy the presence of their Father whenever. We are sons.

"I fear for you, that somehow I have wasted my efforts on you" (Galatians 4:11). Although Paul has written in Romans 8:35-39 that nothing can separate us from the love of God in Christ Jesus, here he acknowledges that he might have wasted his effort on the Galatians, if they choose to reject that love and replace it with law. They will be throwing away the closeness with the Father that Paul worked so hard among them to make possible.

They would be like a husband and a wife who prefer a marriage contract based on law to a marriage covenant based on love and grace; or like children who prefer to be governed by a handbook of rules legalistically applied rather than guided by a loving parental hand. They are sons. They should enjoy their sonship.

Paul deals with only these two conditions: You will be sons or you will be slaves. You will never be masters—that's not an option. God has not turned His universe over to us. He remains sovereign. We can either serve Him on His terms (and they are easy), or we can be slaves of another master (whose terms are much more exacting).

God has always placed such a choice before us. When Joshua renewed the Israelites' covenant with God at Shechem (Joshua 24:14f), he did not insist that everybody follow him in serving God. He let them choose God or any god, but he made it clear that no matter whom they chose, they would *serve* a master. So will we.

We Are Brothers (4:12-20)

With Galatians 4:12, Paul becomes very personal. He calls the Galatian readers "brothers," using the term for only the third time in this epistle. Later, in verse 19, he calls them "dear children," as he pleads with them like a pastor with a wandering flock. In verses 12-16, he reviews their past relationship, and in verses 17-20, he speaks to their present one. His heart is breaking over the rupture that separates them.

Eddie Elliston, a dear friend serving as missionary in Ethiopia in the days before the Communist takeover there, wrote of his own heartache in similar terms:

There has been quite a bit of harassment again recently across our whole area. As a result about fifteen churches have been temporarily closed—and people are afraid. [Whether the harassment comes from Communist rebels or Judaizers, the effect is the same, isn't it?] A few outsiders have stirred up nearly all of this. [Again, the situation parallels Paul's, doesn't it?] Also, please pray with us about the Tosse situation. We had to transfer Bob and Phil with their families out of there under threat of violence against them. George, Mickey and I were stoned in our cars after we had gone in to try to work through some of the problems. No one was hurt but that was just a miracle. *It really troubles me deep in my soul that people I've known, eaten with, prayed with, and counseled with would try to kill George and Mickey and me. They have just been poisoned by the growing influence of this small number of outsiders.*

From kindness to cruelty. In the beginning, the Galatians treated Paul royally. He "became like [them]" (Galatians 4:12). He had forsaken the security of his Jewish faith in order to be obedient to Christ's commission to go to the Gentiles. So he went. That's how he arrived in Galatia, doing everything he could, even becoming like them, in order to free them in Christ's name. (See 1 Corinthians 9:20-22.) He gave up what he was for them; they should not now return to what they were, or become what he had been, but should become as he is now—free in Christ and loving one another as brothers.

When he arrived, he was ill. We don't know the nature of his disability. Scholars have offered many guesses: malaria, eye disorder (ophthalmia—suggested by Galatians 4:15), or bruises from physical abuse. Paul's use of *exeptusate* (Galatians 4:14, "treat with ... scorn"; literally, "spit out") has suggested to some that Paul was epileptic (although there is no evidence this was so), since it was the practice to spit at an epileptic to ward off any evil spirits (epileptics were thought to be demon possessed). Jews and Gentiles alike considered an illness or physical infirmity as a sign of God's punishment for sin. Yet the Galatians, instead of shunning him, warmly welcomed him as an "angel of God" (Galatians 4:14), even as they would have received the Lord himself.

But that was yesterday. Today, they are turning on him. "Have I now become your enemy by telling you the truth?" (Galatians 4:16). That wouldn't be surprising, since the simple gospel is "a stumbling block to Jews and foolishness to Gentiles" (1 Corinthians 1:23).

He knows the answer. The Judaizers have pestered them to leave Christ and return to the law. Paul doesn't condemn the zeal of the proselytizers, but does raise the question of motive. Zeal is the expression, but envy is the force that drives them.

Paul is zealous also, but for their good, not his own. He cares about them "always and not just when I am with you" (Galatians 4:18). He loves them as a father loves his children (and as God loves us). If he were with them, he'd use a different tone of voice (but his love would be the same). Nowhere else in his letters does Paul use this tender term, "my dear children" (Galatians 4:19). If he has spoken harshly earlier, they must understand that it is because of the pain he feels on their account (like that of a mother in childbirth); they are his loved ones and he is "perplexed" about them.

We Are the Free Children of Promise (4:21—5:1)

Paul abruptly turns from his personal appeal to another persuasive argument. Putting aside his pastoral and fatherly role, he now adopts the stance of a trained Jewish rabbi as he allegorizes a well-known incident in the life of their father Abraham (from Genesis 16, 17, 21). There are three parts in his presentation: (1) the Bible story itself (Galatians 4:21-23), (2) the allegorical development (Galatians 4:24-27), and (3) the application (Galatians 4:28—5:1).

All Jews were proud to claim descendancy from Abraham, but they conveniently forgot that Abraham had two sons (actually, he had many others as well—Genesis 25:1, 2), so to claim Abraham as father was not enough to prove that you were rightly related to God through him. If you traced your lineage through Hagar instead of Sarah, you could not claim membership in the people of God.

Paul is arguing like John the Baptist and Jesus here. The Pharisees boasted of their ties to Abraham, but their claims to superiority were quickly dismissed (Matthew 3:9; John 8:33-41). Paul notes that even the descendants of Hagar and Ishmael can claim Abraham as their father, but that does not place them on a par with Sarah's and Isaac's offspring.

In Paul's allegory, Ishmael represents all those Jews who are under the law and outcast because of it. They are natural-born, and born into slavery. Isaac stands for Christians, who are born because of God's promise; their birth is supernatural (as was Isaac's, conceived by a father in his nineties and a mother long past childbearing years; only God's intervention made this birth possible). Paul's allegory comes to the same conclusion as the prologue of John's Gospel: "Yet to all who received him [Christ], to those who believed in his name, he gave the right to become children of God—children born not of natural descent, nor of human decision or a husband's will, but born of God" (John 1:12, 13).

Here is how Paul interprets the story (Galatians 4:24-26):

Hagar, the slave woman	Sarah, the free woman
Ishmael, a natural birth	Isaac, a supernatural birth
The old covenant (Mosaic)	The new covenant (Christian)

Mt. Sinai	Calvary (implied)
Earthly Jerusalem	Heavenly Jerusalem
Jews under law	Christians free by grace

So Jews and Christians alike can argue that Abraham is our father, but the pivotal question is, "Who is our mother?"

Isaiah 54:1, quoted in Galatians 4:27, was not originally associated with the story of Hagar and Sarah. It is a prophecy of the restoration of Jerusalem following the years of captivity in Babylonia (586 B.C. to 458 B.C.). It predicts that the blessing of the latter years will be much greater than that enjoyed in the years before the exile. Paul borrows the verse to further his allegory, setting up a contrast between pre-exilic and post-exilic Jerusalem to represent earthly and Heavenly Jerusalem.

He applies the allegory to his fellow Christians in Galatia. They are "children of promise," descendants of Sarah. Now they need to follow the precedent of their spiritual mother in driving out Ishmael's descendants as she banished Hagar and her son for mocking the son of promise (Isaac—see Genesis 21). The proper way to deal with the Judaizers, Paul implies, is to dismiss them from the fellowship of Christians.

It has been pointed out that, in a sense, the Genesis story deals with two kinds of freedom: Ishmael's is the freedom of a nobody, and Isaac's is the freedom of the son. By Paul's time, however, even Isaac's freedom has been lost through Israel's addiction to laws that bind. Israel has given up its rights as true descendants of Abraham.

Old habits change slowly. Judaizing Christians keep on acting as if they were still chained by the complications of religious law, when in fact Christ has set them free.

Oswald Hoffman of *The Lutheran Hour* illustrates what is happening in Galatia through a helpful story about his dog Mack. One night, Hoffman and his wife were sitting outside when Mack began barking loudly at them. They realized what had happened. Mack was off his chain, but he didn't know it yet. He would run to the spot where the chain usually yanked him back. Then he'd stop, turn, and run in the other direction. As they watched, it took him over ten minutes to realize he was free. Until then, he remained in bondage, even though he had been set free.

Christians can be just as foolish, if we let the law that no longer applies to us yank us up short. So we need Paul's reminder: "It is for freedom that Christ has set us free. Stand firm, then, and do not let yourselves be burdened again by a yoke of slavery" (Galatians 5:1). No longer are we under any schoolmaster or guardians or trustees. We are free.

When I received my Ph.D., a dear friend awarded me a specially engraved trophy. The inscription reads, "Free at last." He understood my feelings. For fourteen years, I had worked steadily toward that degree. I had sacrificed almost everything to attain it. It cost me more money than I care to mention even now; it made my wife and children do without any luxuries and some of the necessities. I followed the prescribed regulations, observed the essential rituals, and attended diligently to every precept of academic law. But finally, gloriously, I was "free at last."

There is no way I would submit again to that yoke of slavery.

Nor to a religious yoke. Christ has set me free.

I feel like Xerxes' general in the Persian war against Greece. The general sent an ambassador to Athens to offer most generous peace terms. Everything good, in fact, except freedom. "Tell the general," the answer came back, "that the Athenians say, as long as the sun moves in his present course, we will never come to terms with Xerxes."

They would not submit to a yoke of slavery.

Neither will we.

CHAPTER TEN

The Only Thing That Counts

Galatians 5:1-6

As we have constantly reminded ourselves, Galatians 5:1 states the theme of the entire letter. Christ has set us free. Paul wants more than anything else for us to remain free. We nullify the Lord's redemptive work if we allow ourselves to be enslaved again to the same stultifying religious strictures from which He has liberated us.

Besides, nothing else matters. "The only thing that counts" is neither an external religious act like circumcision, nor any other outward observance of the law (unless we are prepared to obey every miniscule jot and tittle of it), but "faith" (Galatians 5:6).

Faith

Not just faith, either, but faith in Christ. Central to everything Paul has written is the gospel, which he clearly spells out in 1 Corinthians 15:1-8. John Calvin, writing centuries later, defines faith as "a firm and certain knowledge of God's benevolence toward us, founded upon the truth of the freely given promise in Christ, both revealed to our minds and sealed upon our hearts through the Holy Spirit." Jesus defines it more simply. When asked, "What must we do to do the works God requires?" Jesus answered, "The work of God is this: to believe in the one he has sent" (John 6:28, 29). The gospel is the good news about Jesus (His life, death, resurrection, and life-saving ministry). Christian faith is faith in Christ.

This faith is far removed from Dwight Eisenhower's famous explanation (in 1954) of the foundation of American democracy: "Our government makes no sense unless it is founded on a deeply felt religious faith—and I don't care what it is." Paul cares—and is convinced God cares. The faith that expresses itself is faith in Christ.

85

At a ministerial meeting in Stockholm some years ago, a speaker strongly urged his colleagues to preach the actual resurrection and actual life after death as the hope of man and the world. Following his presentation, a friend asked him in astonishment, "I didn't think you believed in life after death, from what you have told me personally. Why are you so insistent on this message in the pulpit?"

"Oh," he replied, "I do not preach my personal faith, but the faith of the Church."

He wouldn't feel very comfortable with Paul, would he? The only thing we can preach is a personal faith, since lip service to traditional doctrines can no more save us than acceptance of physical circumcision can. What matters is honest faith in Christ. The outward paraphernalia of religion—circumcision, dietary laws, sabbath observance, or the mere mouthings of doctrine—can't save us. To trust in such things is to be alienated from Christ, "fallen away from grace" (Galatians 5:4) and having no right to hope that the Lord will declare us righteous one day.

Faith Expressed

"The only thing that counts is faith expressing itself . . ." (Galatians 5:6). If the Galatians submit to the rite of circumcision, they are demonstrating more faith in Jewish law than in the redemptive work of Jesus Christ. They are expressing faith, but not in Christ. Since "in Christ Jesus neither circumcision nor uncircumcision has any value," for anyone to require the ritual is to grant Jewish law a higher authority than the teachings of Jesus. They don't really believe in Jesus as much as they believe in the ritual. So "if you let yourselves be circumcised, Christ will be of no value to you at all" (Galatians 5:2). You have chosen law over Christ.

Beware. If you make that choice, you need to realize that "every man who lets himself be circumcised . . . is obligated to obey the whole law" (Galatians 5:3). You can't pick and choose; it's all or not at all. If your faith is in the law, it is in all the law. You are obligated to obey all its commands.

When Paul speaks of "faith expressing itself," he assumes the obvious: faith cannot help expressing itself. In this respect, he is in accord with James, who argues that faith and works cannot be separated (James 2:18).

A letter to the editor of *Time* magazine (October 8, 1984) betrays a common misguided belief that faith exists in some never-

never land that's out of touch with daily behavior. "Believing in God," the writer asserts, "has nothing to do with a person's moral values. Morality flows from an understanding of life's potential grace and beauty. When a person's conduct is influenced by a bribe of heaven or a threat of hell, his actions are merely an involuntary result of force and fear." The first part of the statement has little to do with the second part, although the writer is quite unaware of the lapse of logic here. In fact, the paragraph contains three fairly unrelated and quite unsupported dogmatic statements. You either accept them or reject them.

(1) "Believing in God has nothing to do with a person's moral values." That's the opinion of the writer, but certainly not of the Bible.

(2) "Morality flows from an understanding of life's potential grace and beauty." How? Who says so?

(3) "When a person's conduct is influenced by a bribe of heaven or a threat of hell, his actions are merely an involuntary result of force and fear." Is Biblical teaching of Heaven and Hell to be considered mere bribe or threat? Couldn't it be an objective statement of reality? Is one's response necessarily involuntary?

This isn't the place to argue with a magazine's correspondent, of course, but I did want to indicate the extremes to which some people will go to avoid admitting the inseparable link between faith and behavior. The inescapable truth is this: what I believe, I do. What I do expresses my faith. Morality is faith expressed in word and in deed.

George Whitefield is still recalled, two centuries after his amazing preaching ministry in the United States and England, as an exemplar of this union. So powerful was his preaching that thousands were won to Christ by his words. Benjamin Franklin is reported to have said that he wanted to hear Whitefield preach, but he left all his money home before going because he had been told that the man's speaking was so persuasive he would get all Franklin's money, if he had any with him. Then, the story says, midway through Whitefield's sermon, Franklin turned to his neighbor and asked to borrow some money to give to Whitefield!

His power, however, was not in words only, but in his deeds. An asthmatic, Whitefield struggled through his days gasping for breath. Even his last night expressed his marriage of faith and deed. In Newberryport, villagers came in the middle of the night and asked his host to awakened him, so that he could preach to them. Whitefield came downstairs and stood on the bottom step and spoke until his candle went out. He made his way back upstairs to his room, lay down, and died. The deed was as powerful as the sermon.

Words *and* deeds, preaching *and* practice.

President Franklin Roosevelt, after the leaders of the Allied Nations met together at Yalta in February, 1945, went to Warm Springs, Georgia, to prepare his speech for the inauguration of the United Nations in San Francisco. On the twelfth of April, he succumbed to a cerebral hemorrhage. The last words he wrote were on our subject. "The only limit to our realization of tomorrow will be our doubts of today. Let us move forward with strong and active faith." The Christian would alter the words slightly: "Let us move forward with strong and active faith *in God*." He can do what we can't.

A supreme example of the way faith expresses itself comes from the Winchester House in California. William Wirt Winchester, the son of the Winchester Rifle investor, died of tuberculosis in 1882, leaving his young widow Sarah twenty million dollars plus an allowance of one thousand dollars a day for the rest of her life. She could never be at peace, however, because she felt this was tainted money. She consulted a spiritualist in Boston, who told her that the spirits of those killed by the Winchesters were angry. A month-old daughter had died fifteen years earlier, and now her husband was dead. Would Sarah be next?

She moved west and began a new life. She dedicated herself to building a house in Santa Clara Valley for the spirits. She wanted to please the good ghosts who would protect her, deter the bad ones that would do her harm. She believed that if construction ever stopped, she would die. Beginning with an eight-room farmhouse, Mrs. Winchester hired carpenters, plumbers, masons, electricians, gardeners, and servants. For 38 years, day and night, 365 days a year, her crew worked to build her house.

You can see it today, a magnificent, patternless, quite ridiculous house exhibiting the finest quality workmanship. Mrs. Winchester considered thirteen her lucky number, so her house has thirteen bathrooms with sinks having thirteen drain holes; rooms with thirteen windows and thirteen panels; staircases with thirteen steps, a seance room with thirteen hooks that held thirteen colored robes that she wore in communicating with her spirits. Her will had thirteen parts and was signed thirteen times.

Mrs. Winchester spent five and a half million dollars on her house. She believed in staying alive; she believed in spirits. Her faith expressed itself.

Faith Expressed Through Love

"The only thing that counts is faith expressing itself through love" (Galatians 5:6). Belief in Christ leads naturally to love, the perfect love that casts out fear (1 John 4:18). Paul never ignores the new commandment Christ has given his disciples, "Love each other" (John 15:12). There is a popular missionary story of some Americans on a world tour. Visiting a leprous area, they observed a missionary stooping over a wretched leper covered with open, oozing sores. As the missionary gently wiped away the infectious, stinking, yellow-white liquid, one of the Americans watched for a few minutes and then walked away: "I wouldn't do that for a million dollars."

The missionary heard him and replied, "Neither would I."

But he would do it because he believed in Christ. He was simply expressing his faith through love.

Hans Kung, writing on the subject of Christian freedom, calls it "a mystery to the world" because it harmonizes such opponents as "independence and duties, power and renunciation, autonomy and service, dominion and slavery." He finds the solution to the mystery in love, and cites Galatians 5:6 as his source. "To be available for others, to exist for others, to live in selfless love is the only way to realize freedom."[13]

An important example of this kind of love was reported in Philadelphia in 1980. A twelve-year-old boy in Greece developed a benign tumor that began pressing against his brain and causing difficulty in the lad's breathing and frequent nosebleeds. He had undergone several surgeries, but the tumor kept on growing and threatened to leave him brain damaged.

His people were quite poor, his father a fisherman trying to eke a living out of the uncertainties of the sea and the little oil he could get from a few olive trees. In spite of his poverty, though, he managed to save enough to take his son to America for a successful surgery at the Children's Hospital in Philadelphia. The father scarcely left the boy's side. He slept in a cot in his hospital room

---

[13] Hans Kung, *The Church* (New York: Sheed and Ward, 1967), p. 156.

and, when the surgeon announced the operation's success, the father couldn't stop hugging the doctor and tried his best to kiss him. Casting aside restraint in the fullest expression of his gratitude, the father whose love compelled him to sacrifice everything for the sake of his son now abandoned himself in showing his love for his son's surgeon. His is a faith (in God, in his son, in the surgeon) "expressing itself through love"—and enjoying the freedom that is the result of such an expression.

The writer of the AP article on this event, Mrs. Kosak, concluded: "You've got to know these people. They work hard, they laugh hard, they cry hard, and *they love hard* [italics mine]."[14]

I value a letter from a friend in New Jersey. At the time, she was a social worker, and her letter describes the impressions of her new job. She says,

> It is a fairly emotionally-draining job, but I love the contact with the people. The first month on the job I came home in shock because of the intensity of the suffering of some of the families. One of the examples that I remember most vividly is a case in which the family requested an alternate living arrangement for their son who was 24 years old, having taken care of him all those years. He was profoundly retarded, epileptic, cerebral palsied, blind, born without a backbone and had a degenerative bone disease. Yet, for all these years, they had taken care of him without too much outside help, and without bitterness.

This is love expressed.

"The only thing that counts is faith expressing itself through love."

---

[14]Quoted by R. David Roberts, ed., "Preacher Ponders," *Trader's Point Christian Church Tidings* (March 3, 1981).

CHAPTER ELEVEN

Don't Lose Your Freedom

Galatians 5:7-26

Don't Listen to Your Critics (5:7-12)

Having repeatedly warned his readers to hang on to their freedom in Christ, Paul has specifically reminded them of the bondage imposed by the law (Galatians 5:2-6) and now cautions them to resist anyone who would force them back under the law (Galatians 5:7-12).

They had been doing so well before the Judaizers got ahold of them ("You were running a good race," Galatians 5:7); why had they let themselves be talked into changing? Paul does not seem to be dealing with a large body of Judaizers, but a few very persuasive ones. ("A little yeast works through the whole batch of dough," Galatians 5:9.) One can't help guessing that the Galatians are going along with them more out of a desire for peace than because of real conviction. Christians are always, indeed, out of step with orthodox Judaism, and it's always easier to follow the lead of the traditional dictators of religious taste than to chart your own course.

Further, the Judaizers came in the guise of friendship. They were acting only in the best interests of the Galatians, they assured them. In the name of friendship, then, they have been turning young Christians away from grace and freedom in Christ toward the binding strictures of legalism. (They call to mind that helpful old prayer, "Lord, deliver me from my friends; I can take care of my enemies myself!")

They may sound persuasive, but "that kind of persuasion does not come from the one who calls you" (Galatians 5:8). We know where it comes from.

Paul's also refers to the effects of yeast in 1 Corinthians 5:6, where he speaks of the penetrating power of immorality; here he alludes to the leavening influence of legalism. Jesus likewise warned His disciples to beware of the yeast of the Pharisees (Matthew 16:6). On the other hand, He also compared the kingdom of Heaven to yeast (Matthew 13:33), for it, too, has the power to penetrate and expand—but its effects are benign.

It takes courage to stand up against the criticism that Christians must take; Paul uses a stronger word: "Why am I still being persecuted?" (Galatians 5:11). Thornton Wilder, in *The Eighth Day*, says that faith and hope are nothing if they are not courageous; nothing, in fact, if they are not ridiculous. To persons of a Judaizing mentality, clinging to the apparent certainties of their prescribed religion, claims of freedom in Christ seem ridiculous. To withstand their ridicule and to cling to the hope that is in Christ, Christians must draw on courage that does not come naturally. They have to trust in a final judgment in which "the one who is throwing you into confusion will pay the penalty" (Galatians 5:10), and the Lord who sees all will judge righteously.

Criticism is inevitable. Paul identifies with the pressure the Galatians are feeling from the Judaizers, because he is suffering the same. Since he can no longer promote circumcision, he receives some very rough treatment at the hands of his persecutors. In fact, he points to his persecution as proof that he does *not* preach circumcision or the law ("Brothers, if I am still preaching circumcision, why am I still being persecuted?" Galatians 5:11.) He *isn't* preaching it, so he *is* being condemned, just as they are (or will be, if they remain faithful to the gospel Paul preached).

In a famous conversation between Henry David Thoreau and Ralph Waldo Emerson, we see some of the pride Paul took in this persecution. Emerson was visiting Thoreau in jail. He had been incarcerated for failure to pay his taxes, a stand Thoreau took in order to protest the use of tax money for what he considered to be immoral purposes.

"Why, David," Emerson asked him, "what are you doing in there?"

"Why, Waldo," Thoreau shot back at him, "what are you doing out there?" Far from feeling embarrassed by his imprisonment, Thoreau believed there should be many more in jail with him. His cause was just. He was willing to suffer for it.

The question is not whether you will be criticized (or persecuted) for your convictions, but for which of your convictions you will be willing to suffer. The Christian can always count on "the offense of the cross" (Galatians 5:11) to alienate him from certain groups, especially those groups of people who cannot comprehend that salvation is by grace and faith and not by merit and works.

When John Bunyan was serving time in Bedford jail for his preaching of the gospel, he was offered release on the condition that he would promise not to preach the gospel on the streets any more. Bunyan was tempted to succumb to the bargain, especially when he thought of his wife and children, particularly his blind daughter Mary. But when he thought of God, he had to reject the terms. "Unless I am willing to make my conscience a continual slaughtershop and butchery, then, God Almighty being my witness, the moss shall grow upon these eyebrows before I surrender my principles or violate my conscience!" He stayed in prison.

You don't have to give in to your critics. (But they can severely trouble you—even if you are an apostle. Paul confesses that by his outburst in Galatians 5:12: "As for those agitators, I wish they would go the whole way and emasculate themselves.") If they care so much about taking the skin in circumcision, let them go ahead and castrate themselves! Strong language, expressive of strong feelings. What the Judaizers are attempting, of course, is little less than the castration of the gospel itself. They would rob it of its potency, strip it of its power to give new birth in Christ, and thus wipe out genuine Christianity in its first generation.

Do not submit to such agitators.

Freedom, Not Self-indulgence (5:13-26)

All of Galatians 5 traces the implications of the letter's theme (5:1): "It is for freedom that Christ has set us free. Stand firm, then, and do not let yourselves be burdened again by a yoke of slavery." Do not submit again to the dictates of Jewish law (Galatians 5:2-6). Do not submit to those who are trying to talk you into returning to legalism (Galatians 5:7-12).

Now Paul turns in the other direction. In these verses (Galatians 5:13-26), he urges his readers not to go to the opposite extreme from legalism, wanton self-indulgence. That would naturally be an easy temptation, since so many people, even some Christians, define liberty as the license to do whatever they want.

This was true of the Beghards, or Brethren of the Free Spirit, who flourished in fourteenth-century France. One of the sects of voluntary poverty that appeared from time to time in medieval Europe, the Beghards claimed to be in a state of grace that required neither priest nor sacrament. They believed that God was in them, therefore they had achieved perfection. Since they were without sin, they were perfectly free to do all the things that for ordinary men would be considered sin. So they practiced free love and adultery and even group sex; they encouraged nudity (as an expression of their freedom) and freely took what belonged to others (tavern meals or market chickens) without paying. They could even kill anyone who interfered with them. Yet they considered themselves very religious. They were living, in their voluntary, poverty-stricken state, in imitation of Christ. They were free.

To combat just such a mentality, which can be found in every century, the apostle addresses these verses.

Do Not Use Your Freedom to Indulge Yourselves

Paul sets up a polarity here, with freedom at one pole and self-indulgence at the other. Some of his readers must have been surprised that he couples service with freedom and that he who has just been arguing so disparagingly against "the law" now writes, "the entire *law* is summed up in a single command: 'Love your neighbor as yourself'" (Galatians 5:14). He is not contradicting himself. His appeal is to a higher law, of course. Moving from the law of Moses, with its circumcision and other commandments, Paul ascends to the new commandment in the law of Christ, the command to love.

Martin Luther, in his famous propositions that sound contradictory at first, captures the essence of Christian freedom and love:

> "A Christian is a perfectly free lord of all, subject to none.
> "A Christian is a perfectly dutiful servant of all, subject to all."

Both statements are correct. They can only be resolved in love.

The opposition of freedom with love on the one hand and self-indulgence on the other is remarkably similar to the contrast drawn by the Historian Arnold Toynbee. "In human life as we know it from experience," he writes, "there is a perpetual struggle between love and conscience on the one side and self-centeredness and sin on the other side."[15] Toynbee, like Paul—to the perplexity

[15] E. W. F. Tomlin, ed., *Arnold Toynbee: A Selection of His Works* (Oxford University Press, 1978), p. 261.

of less thoughtful men—would locate freedom on the side of "love and conscience" rather than of "self-centeredness and sin."

There is a great deal of such confusion about the essence of true freedom. Gail Sheey tells of a man whom she interviewed on the recommendation of a psychiatrist, who called him "one of the most highly evolved adult males" in the United States. Ms. Sheey said she found it hard to endure interviewing the fifty-seven-year-old. He spoke nonstop for four hours, obviously thrilled with his post-divorce self. "Yes, I'm devoted to No. 1," he told her. "I have nothing to lose at this stage, except maybe money. So I don't give a . . . *what* I do as long as it pleases me or gives me strokes." He boasted of running marathons. He showed her he could stand on his head and curl his body like a cobra. It was obvious he thought of himself as some kind of superman. He was, he thought, free.[16]

Robert Frost didn't require as many words to expose his egotism. When invited to share a platform with other poets, his response was ready: "I only go / When I'm the show."

My friend John Greenlee summarizes this modern form of narcissism (which parades under the name of "freedom"). Agreeing with a current saying that our society lives by the three phrases—So what? Who cares? I got mine!—John adds that there are also three questions that we have to answer before we can act: Is it easy? Is it fun? and What's in it for me?

If I am free, then I am free to deliver myself over to what is free, fun, and self-satisfying. *Freedom* in its most widely applied definition means *doing what I want when I want where I want— for me.* Yet Paul, the great apostle of freedom, warns that freedom is not self-indulgence; in fact, it must not be used "to indulge the sinful nature" (Galatians 5:13). Rather, he will say in 6:2, "Carry each other's burdens." You don't live only for yourself. Living for yourself leads naturally to "biting and devouring each other" (Galatians 5:15).

Do Not Be Ruled by "the Flesh"

This is another way of saying the same thing, that is, "Do not use your freedom to indulge yourselves." "Do not be ruled by 'the flesh.'" "The flesh" is an older translation of the Greek word

---

[16]Gail Sheey, *Pathfinders* (New York: Bantam Books, 1970), pp. 56, 57.

(sarki) here rendered "the sinful nature" (see Galatians 5:13, 16, 17, 19, 24). The NIV phrase is in some ways an unfortunate translation, since it might mislead us into putting the emphasis on "sinful" rather than "nature." The contrast Paul is making is between the Spirit, which is of God, and the flesh, which is human nature, earthly existence, in its natural state apart from God. As far as Paul is concerned, what really matters is our relationship with God; only in Him are we complete. To live without Him is to be mere flesh. The flesh is not of itself either good or bad; it just *is*. If it is made an end in itself, however, and its impulses rather than the will of God take charge, self-indulgence is the result and destruction is our destination. Living after the flesh, whether by flagrant sexualism at one extreme or pious Phariseeism at the other, or anything in between, can never save one. Only God can.

Pagan moralists were if anything more severe than Paul when they discussed morality, because they regarded immoral behavior as unnatural, contrary to human nature. Paul doesn't. He treats it as quite in harmony with a human nature that is untouched by the Spirit. "The sinful nature desires what is contrary to the Spirit" (Galatians 5:17) but not what is contrary to itself. What ethicists call immoral behavior, then, is quite in keeping, according to Paul, with unregenerate human nature. To expect more of the flesh is unrealistic. We need the Spirit to help us rise above such conduct.

Further, "if you are led by the Spirit, you are not under law" (Galatians 5:18). In the Spirit, you ascend above rules and operate on a higher sphere, where your concern for relationships governs instead of your self-centered lusts.

Of course, we must recognize that there are limitations of the flesh from which there is no escape. As George Buttrick has pointed out, no man is "as free as a bird." There are some things we can't do:

> "No man can pitch a tent on the sun, or grow lollipops on cactus plants, or give way to sadism and still be welcome at children's parties, or fly to the fabled isles by using the breaststroke. He is within the necessities of his nature."[17]

---

[17] George Buttrick, *Christ and History* (New York: Abingdon, 1963), p. 87.

There are additional restrictions. We live today and not in the thirteenth century, and a time machine hasn't yet been invented that can transport us back to taste of medieval culture. We are born into a specific culture, on a specific continent, on a particular planet, and into a given language. We are free to imagine many things but not free to experience all of them. As long as we are in these bodies, we live with the constraints they impose.

These limitations we can take for granted. But these are not the ones Paul has in mind. He appeals in this passage for Christians not to restrict their Christ-given freedom by allowing their mere humanness to dominate their lives. If they give way to their sinful nature, letting it have its way, it will take over entirely. To indulge themselves is to invite slavery. Historian Edith Hamilton, commenting on the decline of Athens, has written somewhere that when the freedom the Athenians wished for most was freedom from responsibility, then Athens ceased to be free and was never free again. They succumbed to the flesh.

The flesh, then, refers to man limited by his physical constitution, his culture, his moment in history, the impulses of biology, stimuli of the senses, instinct for self-preservation, drive for power, and lusts for self-satisfaction. To resist his own propensity to indulge himself to the point of self-destruction, he needs supernatural help. Freedom apart from the Spirit is not possible, Paul argues. Determinists like the psychoanalyst Sigmund Freud, the economist/socialist Karl Marx, the psychologist B. F. Skinner, and others of their ilk may argue that man can never be truly free of the forces that shape him (that is, he can never escape his humanness), but the apostle Paul offers a divine rebuttal. When one lives in the Spirit, he can be free indeed.

If the freedom I want, though, is the freedom to be myself, I remain chained. What is needed is freedom *from* myself, the freedom that love expresses and the Spirit grants.

Otherwise, if I put myself first, I'll "bite and devour" (Galatians 5:15) anyone who gets in the way of my self-interests. I'll be as unreasonable as the Mississippi soldier captured in Pennsylvania during the Civil War.

"What are you fighting for?" an officer of General Meade's staff asked him.

"Fightin' for ouah right," the soldier answered.

"But friend, what earthly right of yours have I ever interfered with?" the major asked him.

"I don't know. None that I know of, suh. But maybe I've got rights I haven't heard tell 'bout, an' if so, I'm fightin' for them, too."

So we fight—for our sexual rights, our religious rights, and our social and personal rights. The result is anarchy.

We may not speak as crudely as the soldier nor fight as brutally, but scratch the veneer of polite society and the same self-serving can be found. John Galsworthy depicts it in *The Country House* in the creed of the Pendyce family.

> I believe in my father and his father and his father's father, the makers and keepers of my estate, and I believe in myself and my son and my son's son. And I believe that we have made the country, and shall keep the country what it is. And I believe in the Public Schools, and especially the Public School that I was at. And I believe in my social equals and the country house, and in things as they are, for ever and ever. Amen."[18]

Such arrogance is obviously in conflict with the Spirit.

All veneer of social etiquette has been stripped from "the acts of the sinful nature" (Galatians 5:19), as Paul describes them, and we behold them in all their ugliness. Shakespeare's Prospero in *The Tempest* may call man "such stuff as dreams are made of," but the dreams turn to nightmares when "the sinful nature" is unrestrained. Consider the current popular war (any one of the several armed conflicts bedeviling the earth at any given time), or the daily headlines announcing the latest atrocities: murders, rapes, child abuse cases, highway slaughter by drunken drivers. Consider also the neighborhood orgies and business larcenies and political deals that never make the papers. These are the works of the flesh. Was it Robert Louis Stevenson who referred to humanity as a disease on the face of the earth? For certain, it was Josh Billings who lamented that if man was created a little lower than the angels, the angels should reform.

> "I'll walk where my own nature would be leading.
> It vexes me to choose another guide."

---

[18] Quoted in Robert E. Luccock, *Halford Luccock Treasury* (New York: Abingdon, 1963), p. 233.

Emily Bronte has spoken for the multitudes in these lines, but in this way lies grave mischief.

Some of the mischief is sexual: "immorality, impurity and debauchery" (Galatians 5:19). All kinds of illegitimate sexual conduct are included in these three words. God gave the sex drive, so it is not inherently sinful. But when it takes command, it drives you right out of the kingdom of God.

Some of it is religious: "idolatry and witchcraft" (Galatians 5:20). Where the true God is ignored, false gods are worshiped. Man is a worshipful being. The question is never whether he will bow down, but before whom or what.

And the rest of it wrenches relationships asunder: "hatred, discord, jealousy, fits of rage, selfish ambition, dissensions, factions and envy; drunkenness, orgies, and the like" (Galatians 5:20, 21).

The list recalls the description Paul gives of humanity that has rejected God and is in turn abandoned to their lusts (Romans 1:24-32). Being merely human renders humanity inhumane! Since the kingdom of God is comprised of people in relationship with one another and with God, and since the works of the flesh finally make such relationships impossible, "those who live like this will not inherit the kingdom of God" (Galatians 5:21).

We must turn, then, from flesh to Spirit, remembering Francis Bacon's aphorism that "they that deny a God destroy a man's nobility, for certainly man is of kin to the beasts by his body; and if he be not of kin to God by his spirit, he is a base and ignoble creature."

He is also an unhappy one. Blaise Pascal puts the case in his usual forthright manner: "If man is not made for God, why is he only happy in God? If man is made for God, why is he so opposed to God?"

It is quite apparent from Paul's description of "the fruit of the Spirit" (Galatians 5:22, 23) that in the Spirit of God and in the Spirit alone does man become fully himself and enter into his joy.

Cultivate the Fruit of the Spirit

"So I say, live by the Spirit" (Galatians 5:16), for that is the way to salvation and true freedom. "But the fruit of the Spirit is. . . ." (Galatians 5:22). There are many, many individual, conflicting works of the flesh, but there is only one uniting fruit of the Spirit. The qualities that Paul lists here are inseparable; you can't have one without the others. The Spirit integrates one's life with God and man. To "live by the Spirit" is to be in harmony with God and at peace with oneself and other people.

Henry Ward Beecher explains that walking by the Spirit means that He leads us into such an appreciation of higher things that we no longer desire the inferior.

> Do you suppose that a bird, seeing a man in the muddy road toiling up the long ascent, when he can shoot through the air on even wing and go quicker and easier, would envy the man, or would stoop to use his legs instead of his wings? No. A man as respects his lower nature may be said to walk; he touches the earth at every step, man in his higher nature lifts himself above the morass, above the ravine, above the mountain, and goes by the shortest course to the noblest things.[19]

Beecher's symbol of the dove for the Spirit is a helpful one. We soar above the petty things of our "mere" humanity.

The Spirit expresses the qualities of God himself through our personalities. We experience and express "love, joy, peace, patience, kindness, goodness, faithfulness, gentleness and self-control" (Galatians 5:22, 23). These are all above the law. Can you imagine any government passing laws against love? or patience? or kindness? or goodness? These are the qualities without which no government can long endure, but which no amount of legislation can guarantee. (Law can't do anything to improve human nature. In fact, as Ortega y Gasset has wisely observed, law is born from despair of human nature. Law merely serves to keep us from each other's throats.) But where these spiritual qualities (the fruit of the Spirit) prevail, law is unnecessary. And where law is unnecessary, there is freedom!

The person who lives in the spirit, then, will be above conceit; he will have no desire to provoke or envy anyone else (Galatians 5:26). He will bear the whole fruit of the Spirit. And the Spirit will bear *him* up.

---

[19] Henry Ward Beecher, "The Fruits of the Spirit," *Twenty Centuries of Great Preaching*, Volume IV. Edited by Clyde E. Fant, Jr., and William M. Pinson, Jr. (Waco: Word, 1971), p. 319.

During World War II, the Allies drove the Italian forces out of Eritrea in North Africa. The departing Italians did their best to delay their enemy's advance, though, by filling great barges with concrete and sinking them across the entrance to the harbor.

They failed to take into account the ingenuity of the Allied engineers. The barges were removed in a brilliantly simple manner. The Allies requisitioned the huge empty tanks that oil refineries store their fuel in. They sealed them airtight, then floated them in the sea above the barges. Then at low tide they chained the gigantic floats to the submerged barges and waited for high tide. When the tide was full, the buoyancy of the fuel tanks lifted the barges off the harbor's floor—and away from the entrance.

The engineers could never have lifted such weights by themselves. Instead, they harnessed the power of the tides.

Paul insists that we cannot raise ourselves above the pull of sinful nature by ourselves, but we *can* be filled with the Spirit that lifts us Godward, above both the sinful nature and the law that sinful nature requires. There, in the purer air in which the fruit of the Spirit can flourish, is true freedom.

CHAPTER TWELVE

We've Got Each Other
on Our Hands

Galatians 6:1-10

There is an African tribe whose members, instead of saying, "My brother is sick," say, "I am sick in my brother." This same strong sense of identifying with each other in the family of God characterizes the church. Paul draws on this mutuality in his final portion of the letter. The spiritual family, exhibiting the fruit of the Spirit (Galatians 5:22, 23), cares for and protects every member. To this end Paul gives several specific directives.

Restore Sinners—Gently (6:1)

"Brothers, if someone is caught in a sin, you who are spiritual should restore him gently" (Galatians 6:1). Paul may still have the troublesome Judaizers and their Galatian victims in mind. If they heed his instructions and turn from their errors, their fellow Christians should accept them again in full fellowship. And even if they do not repent, the Christians who are attempting to deal with them should be gentle, remembering that their goal is reconciliation. They will not be vindictive. They will not give way to "hatred, discord, jealousy, fits of rage, selfish ambition, dissensions, factions" or any of the other works of the flesh (Galatians 5:20), but will instead exhibit the fruit of the Spirit (Galatians 5:22, 23).

This is but another of Paul's many reminders that the church is in the restoring business. It's the same advice he gave the church at Corinth. Having urged the Christians there to purge their membership of an immoral brother (1 Corinthians 5:1-5), he subsequently asks the church to forgive and restore the penitent sinner (2 Corinthians 2:5-11).

"But watch yourself, or you also may be tempted" (Galatians 6:1). You may find yourself lording it over your erring brother, and thus be no good to him while you yourself fall into the pit of spiritual pride. "It is as rare an achievement for the pious man to be charitable as for the rational man to be 'reasonable.'"[20] No wonder the little girl was led to pray, "Lord, please make all the bad people good and all the good people nice."

"Watch yourself" or you may give way to attitudes as uncharitable as your erring brother's, or may try to fight fire with fire, countering his Judaizing legalism with a Christian legalism of your own. Don't descend to the level of your opponent.

Carry Each Other's Burdens (6:2-4)

"Carry each other's burdens, and in this way you will fulfill the law of Christ" (Galatians 6:2). Paul has spoken earlier of the only law the Christian need concern himself with in Galatians 5:14. "A new command I give you," Jesus had instructed His disciples. "Love one another. As I have loved you, so you must love one another" (John 13:34). He lays this down as the world's test of true discipleship: "All men will know that you are my disciples if you love one another" (John 13:35).

Christ has set us free so that we will be able to help someone else. In a society that has been organized for the diminishment of others, Christians labor to build up others. "Dog eat dog" and "me first" may express the prevailing ethic, but the Christian offers a counter ethic: Brother help brother, and You first. It is what Denis Waitley calls "double winning": When you win, I win.

This verse takes its place with a host of New Testament Scriptures that hold up the priority of interpersonal relationships. There is no such thing as private Christianity. Our spiritual quest always requires social expression. We are urged to do the following with "one another":

Love one another (John 13:34; Romans 13:8).
Be devoted to one another in brotherly love (Romans 12:10).
Honor one another above yourselves (Romans 12:10).
Live in harmony with one another (Romans 12:16; 1 Peter 3:8).
Instruct one another (Romans 15:14).
Welcome one another (Romans 15:7).
Greet one another (Romans 16:16).

---

[20] Reinhold Niebuhr, *Pious and Secular America* (New York: Charles Scribner's Sons, 1958), p. 6.

Have equal concern for each other (1 Corinthians 12:25).

Serve one another in love (Galatians 5:13).

Bear with one another (Ephesians 4:2).

Be kind and compassionate to one another (Ephesians 4:32).

Forgive each other (Ephesians 4:32).

Speak to one another with psalms, hymns and spiritual songs (Ephesians 5:19).

Submit to one another (Ephesians 5:21).

Encourage each other (1 Thessalonians 4:18; Hebrews 3:13).

Build each other up (1 Thessalonians 5:11).

Spur one another on toward love and good deeds (Hebrews 10:24).

Confess your sins to each other (James 5:16).

Pray for one another (James 5:16).

Practice hospitality toward one another (1 Peter 4:9).

Because we are members of each other (Romans 12:5) and "have fellowship with one another" (1 John 1:7), there are some things we should not do:

Pass judgment on one another (Romans 14:13).

Take pride in one man over against another (1 Corinthians 4:6).

Go to law against each other (1 Corinthians 6:6).

Bite and devour and destroy each other (Galatians 5:15).

Provoke and envy each other (Galatians 5:26).

Lie to each other (Colossians 3:9).

Slander one another (James 4:11).

Grumble against each other (James 5:9).

There are other "one another" passages, but these are enough to establish the fact that a Christian lives constantly with others on his mind. We "carry each other's burdens." It's "the law of Christ."

The essential requirement for such reciprocal relationships is humility. "If anyone thinks he is something when he is nothing, he deceives himself" (Galatians 6:3). "Do not think of yourself more highly than you ought, but rather think of yourself with sober judgment, in accordance with the measure of faith God has given you" (Romans 12:3). Don't be intoxicated with self-love.

I was looking at a magazine photo of the inauguration of Brazil's new president when my little daughter, staring at the puffed-up posture of the man with the presidential sash across his chest, dismissed him curtly. "That looks silly, doesn't it?" I had to admit, it—and he—did look pretty funny. The geegaws of office and all the posturing that goes with it invite ridicule. There is also the possibility that the poseur may make the mistake of thinking the praise is actually for him!

That same daughter turned her sharp eye—and tongue—on me the first time she saw me strutting in my new doctoral robe. "Why are you wearing that dress?" she asked me. Then, without waiting for my reply, she gave me her assessment, in the same words. "You look silly." (She wasn't alone. The first official occasion in which I wore it was for the inauguration of the new president of a sister college. As we lined up outside the building for the processional, a disapproving bird flew overhead and splattered its opinion on my brand new gown. At that moment, it was impossible for me to think more highly of myself than I ought!)

Don't deceive yourself. Instead, "test [your] actions" (Galatians 6:4). And your test is of yourself according to yourself—your abilities versus your achievements; your performance against your goals. God never allows us to take our measurements against anybody else (see Luke 18:9-14); He will judge us on the basis of our own potential alone. So must we.

Carry Your Own Load (6:5)

". . . For each one should carry his own load" (Galatians 6:5). This calls for tough love. I must carry my brother's load without asking or expecting that he should help me with my own. I help you, but I don't take advantage of you or grumble if you don't help me.

I must carry my own load as far as faith is concerned. I can't expect anybody else's faith to save me, even Abraham's, as Paul proves in this letter. (Neither, we could add, can we expect to be saved because of a grandfather who was a circuit-riding preacher or because of a saintly mother.)

I must carry my own load as far as my contributions to the body of Christ and loving my neighbor are concerned as well. As a gifted member of the body, I use my spiritual gifts for the common good (see Ephesians 4:1-16; Romans 12 and 1 Corinthians 12).

A warning here. It is possible to push this single verse too far, using it to justify the common virus of false pride that goes before many a Christian's fall. Americans especially, who are beguiled by the myth of the self-made man, tend to fall for a kind of "do-it-yourself" religion. They don't realize that throughout Christian history "salvation-by-your-own-bootstraps" has always been treated as a heresy, as indeed it is. It denies the grace of God, renders the cross of Jesus irrelevant, and, worst of all, propagates a lie. And the lie leads to spiritual pride of the type Jesus condemned in the Pharisees.

Paul does not imply here that you can carry your own burden and all by yourself achieve salvation. Salvation is not the subject, but mutual Christian love. His point is that we Christians do all we can to help our fellow believers without demanding or even expecting any help in return. Whatever is given is given by the love and grace of our brothers and sisters, and we are appropriately thankful. It is boorish of us to demand or expect assistance from others, and to refuse it or deny the need of it is arrogance.

A backpacking trip in Havasupai Canyon, Arizona, taught me exactly what Paul has in mind here. A group of around twenty of us made the trek, which, I was told, was ten miles in and down the canyon. We took the same path back, which had stretched then to about 100 miles up and out! We were a mixed group, including several teenagers and young adults and four of us who were old enough to know better. As we climbed up the canyon wall, the youngsters passed up us oldsters with unseemly haste. They appeared not even to feel the weighty packs on their backs. We felt them. And we paused—frequently—to rest. (We called it "viewing the scenery.") The farther we climbed, the more frequently we viewed the scenery.

Our younger teammates reached the top well ahead of us. Instead of congratulating themselves on their vitality, however, or mocking the miniscule advances their elders were making down below them, they raced back down the trail to meet us. Then they graciously lifted the burdens from our backs and headed upward once more. They had "carried their own loads" and then "carried each others' burdens" as well! They had experienced the joy of self-sufficiency, then added to it the even more rewarding joy of helping the weak.

Thus it is in the body of Christ.

Pay the Preacher (6:6)

"Anyone who receives instruction in the word must share all good things with his instructor" (Galatians 6:6). Paul undoubtedly needed to add this admonition, since his own practice of supporting himself could have misled the church into expecting all leaders to do the same. He had boasted that he did not have to depend on offerings of the Christians. He worked as a tentmaker to pay his own way (Acts 20:34). But just as Jesus relied on offerings to conduct His ministry (Luke 8:3), so Paul realized that all Christian leaders could legitimately look to the churches they served to make their ministries possible. Churches are obligated to support those who serve them as teachers of the Word. It is an expression of carrying each other's burdens.

This verse needs no further explanation, although when one examines the salary schedules of full-time Christian workers, he is led to conclude that the verse does need further application. A church can hardly be said to "share all good things" with its instructor when the members enjoy a standard of living substantially higher than the teacher. *Sharing* means having in common, or being in fellowship, or participating together in.

Please the Spirit (6:7, 8)

"The one who sows to please the Spirit, from the Spirit will reap eternal life" (Galatians 6:8). This paragraph rests on Paul's earlier discussion of the works of the flesh and the fruit of the Spirit (Galatians 5:16-26). "Do not be deceived" (Galatians 6:7). You cannot sow in pursuit of the flesh and reap a harvest of spiritual fruit. God's ways are consistent. Just as in nature you plant wheat seeds to reap a harvest of wheat, so in the spiritual realm "a man reaps what he sows" (Galatians 6:7). So the question before us is quite simple: What do you want to reap? The appropriate advice is equally straightforward: Then plant the right seeds.

It is obvious by now in Paul's discussion that sowing "to please the Spirit" (Galatians 6:8) means to invest in other people rather than to indulge one's selfish appetites. The Holy Spirit works on earth to save men and women and reconcile them to God and each other. The spiritual person, then, is other-directed.

He is also Heaven-bound, and for that reason he invests his assets in what will last beyond the grave. "Do not store up for yourselves treasures on earth," Jesus taught, "where moth and rust destroy, and where thieves break in and steal. But store up for yourselves treasures in heaven, where moth and rust do not destroy, and where thieves do not break in and steal. For where your treasure is, there your heart will be also" (Matthew 6:19-21). Jesus wipes out everything material, since nothing material can accompany us to Heaven. Foolish, indeed, is the man who spends his life pursuing money or possessions or even fame or power. The grave robs us of them all.

It's a hard saying for Christians. We prefer the immediate rewards of this life to the dim virtues of our distant life. Cotton Mather, writing over three centuries ago, noted that "religion begat prosperity, and the daughter devoured the mother." In the eighteenth century, John Wesley bemoaned the impact of things on Christians. His revivals had the effect of turning beggars and thieves into honest, self-respecting, prosperous citizens. The conversion was so complete that the neighbors of these former roustabouts entrusted their own valuables to them so they wouldn't squander them themselves.

Unfortunately, as these Christians prospered, they had more and more worldly worries, and their Christian faith in time was crowded over by more practical concerns. Wesley decried the tendency.

> Wherever riches have increased, the essense of religion has decreased in the same proportion. Therefore, I do not see how it is possible, in the nature of things, for any revival of religion to continue long. For religion must necessarily produce both industry and frugality, and these cannot but produce riches. But as riches increase, so will pride, anger, and love of the world in all its branches. . . . Is there no way to prevent this—this continual decay of pure religion?[21]

There is only one way, and that is sowing "to please the Spirit" (Galatians 6:8), which means using everything at our disposal, including our wealth, to accomplish the Spirit's will. William Barclay illustrates the principle from the life of the Japanese Christian Kagawa. He reports that when Mr. Okamura, the secretary of the Kobe YMCA, informed Kagawa of the Association's debts, the latter man put his hand in his pocket and took out a letter containing the payment he had received that morning from his publisher for a book that was soon to be published.

---

[21] Quoted in Dean M. Kelley, *Why Conservative Churches Are Growing* (New York: Harper and Row, 1972), p. 55.

The check was for one thousand pounds. Kagawa handed it to Okamura.

"I can't possibly take it," Okamura protested.

"You must."

When Okamura returned to his home, he wrote a letter to his friend, trying to give him his money back. "You mustn't give money away like that," he wrote.

Kagawa wrote back, "Why shouldn't I? When your friend is dying, there is only one thing to do—give him your lifeblood."[22]

That is how you please the Spirit.

Never Give Up (6:9)

"Let us not become weary in doing good, for at the proper time we will reap a harvest if we do not give up" (Galatians 6:9). Encouraging words from a man who surely must himself have contemplated quitting. He certainly seems to have had reason enough to. (See 2 Corinthians 11:16-29.) He returned often to the theme of perseverance: Romans 2:6, 7; 8:35-39; 1 Corinthians 15:58; 16:13; Galatians 5:1; Ephesians 4:14; 6:13; Philippians 1:6, 27; 4:1; Colossians 1:23; 2:7; 1 Thessalonians 3:8; 5:21; 2 Thessalonians 2:15; 2 Timothy 1:12; 2:1-3, 12; 3:14.

Peter Gillquist found the meaning of perseverance when he was sixteen. He became a member of his high school's cross-country track team. On the first day of practice, his coach took the team by bus to a course that ran up and down several hills over four miles. When they arrived, he told his recruits that the object of the practice race that day was to finish the course. If anyone didn't plan to finish, he shouldn't start. "But if you start, then you *will* finish. You may slow down, or even stop for a bit, but you will not quit. Once you start, I want you to cross this finish line—no matter what."

Gillquist breezed through the first mile. At one and a half miles the joy began fading and by the second mile it had disappeared completely, replaced by sheer drudgery. He developed cramps in his thighs and his breath came in painful gasps. The last mile and a half were sheer torture, with his body screaming "quit." But he couldn't quit. He had promised to finish. He could hardly

---

[22]*Ethics in a Permissive Society* (New York: Harper and Row, 1971), p. 169.

remember crossing the finish line. He was surprised to learn that he came in fifth or sixth. It didn't matter. What mattered was that he hadn't quit.[23]

> When things go wrong, as they sometimes will,
> When the road you're trudging seems all uphill;
> When the funds are low, and the debts are high,
> And you want to smile, but have to sigh;
> When care is pressing you down a bit,
> Rest if you must, but don't quit![24]

Do Good to All People (6:10)

"Therefore, as we have opportunity, let us do good to all people, especially to those who belong to the family of believers" (Galatians 6:10). This is the sum of the matter. We are to love our neighbors (Galatians 5:14) with the full power of the fruit of the Spirit (Galatians 5:22, 23).

Paul may have his abiding concern for the poverty-stricken saints in Jerusalem in mind here (see 2 Corinthians 8, 9), although his exhortation has a much broader application. Paul's vision takes in the whole world: "all people." He is always mindful of his commission to take the gospel to the Gentiles. There's a world full of them! He and all his fellow Christians can only accomplish their God-given task by doing good to as many people as they possibly can.

It is so easy to be blind to the world. I was reading a *Time* magazine account of the sufferings in Kampuchea (Cambodia) during the civil turmoil that has destroyed that nation. Famine conditions in 1978-80 followed close on the heels of the internal war that kills three million of its seven million citizens earlier in the decade. By 1983, the reporter wrote, "the entire issue had been eclipsed in the world's short memory by newer and more fashionable tragedies."[25] With wave upon wave of human disasters bombarding our sensibilities, the world has developed a short

---

[23] "The Christian Life: A Marathon We Mean to Win?", *Christianity Today,* (October 23, 1981), p. 22.

[24] Tom Wallace, "Don't Quit," *Fundamentalist Journal* (March, 1983), p. 41.

memory as a form of self-protection. We can only do so much, we protest. We blot our yesterday's famine to concentrate on today's war. In the meantime, the people starving from yesterday's famine are forgotten.

Yet disciples of Jesus must not forget. Even if our ability is limited, the Christian's response is always, "I will at least do what good I can, to as many people as I can, wherever I can."

"Let us do good to all people."

---

[25]*Time* (July 30, 1984), p. 84.

CHAPTER THIRTEEN

Something to Boast About

Galatians 6:11-18

Coming to the close of his letter, Paul now takes the pen from his amanuensis (stenographer, scribe). His custom probably is just to sign his name at the bottom of a letter; in this case, he adds more than his name as proof that he is, indeed, the author. His writing in *large* letters fuels the speculation among some modern scholars that Paul's illness (Galatians 4:13) was eye-related.

In a few brief, words he summarizes his argument, once more contrasting the positions of the Judaizing Christians and what we might call "just plain Christians," or "Christians only," or what C. S. Lewis would term "mere" Christians. What the Judaizers boast about is very different from what simple Christians take pride in.

It's an effective conclusion, isn't it? Nothing gives us away more completely than the things we boast about. We all want to be the best at something, even in religion. Every denominationalist brags that his group is better than all the others in this or that trait. You probably remember the old joke that Baptists love to tell on themselves. "When it comes to dignity, we can't be compared to the Episcopalians. As for rituals, the Lutherans have it all over us, and in regard to singing, the Nazarenes have us beat. But when it comes to humility, we're tops!"

Let's look at what makes the Judaizers proud.

They Want to Make a Good Showing by Human Standards (6:12, 13)

Paul says they "want to make a good impression outwardly" by compelling the Galatians "to be circumcised" (Galatians 6:12). They hope to force the Galatians to conform to this requirement of the law. If they do, the Judaizers themselves will be praised by God and by religious leaders. But theirs is a human desire to gain

113

human applause by reaching human goals. Their standards may be very understandable, but they aren't what Christ wants, since circumcision has nothing to do with submission to Him (Galatians 5:6).

I once had an enlightening conversation with a middle-aged man who boasted, literally, of his "flesh." Not his human nature, but his physical body. He bragged about his weight (perfect for his height), his muscular tautness, his physical agility. The longer he talked, the more embarrassed I became for him. He was trying so hard "to make a good impression outwardly." He made an impression, all right, but not what he wanted. I walked away, pitying him for his emptiness. All his attention was paid to his body and none to his inner self. A man's worth can't be measured by the inches around his biceps any more than by his tattoos or his scars or any other extension of his ego. What matters is the essence of the man, his relationship with God and with others.

Equally pitiful is the person who believes his salvation is found in external rites like circumcision and a corresponding submission to law. To suggest that this is the essence of Christianity is to teach a lie.

"The only reason they do this is to avoid being persecuted for the cross of Christ" (Galatians 6:12). Paul charges the Judaizing Christians with cowardice. He believes that they are insisting on conformity to the Jewish practice of circumcision as a way of escaping persecution by the Jews (who would then accept them as their own) and the Romans (who recognized Judaism as a legitimate religion and accepted circumcision as evidence of membership). When Christians broke with their Jewish practices and entered into Christian fellowship with Gentiles, they placed themselves outside the protection of both Judaism and Rome.

If Paul's charge is justified, then the reasoning of the Judaizers is not far removed from today's nominal Christians who believe that it is a good thing to be a disciple of Jesus so long as you don't become fanatical about it. Be cool; don't do anything to attract attention to your differences from other nice people. You don't want to invite ridicule or persecution; go along with society's mores and you'll enjoy society's applause.

Paul's call is for complete conversion. There is no room for indifference or casualness in the body of Christ. Dwight L. Moody, in speaking of backsliders in one of his sermons, complained that

114

One backslider will do more harm than twenty Christian men can do good. Unconverted people say, "Here are some men who have tried this way. If there is as much joy in it as you make out, how is it that so many people are dissatisfied and go back into the world?" It's a hard argument to overcome.... A great many people are not true backsliders. As the old chaplain in the army said, they never slid forward. They have been clinging to some minister, some church, some choir; they never were converted at all.

That may be the affliction of the Judaizing Christians. They were never truly converted. They did not fully accept their freedom in Christ. Nor did they accept the fact that in accepting Him, they would have to accept others as equal to them in Him—others like the Gentiles!

"Not even those who are circumcised obey the law, yet they want you to be circumcised that they may boast about your flesh" (Galatians 6:13). They want to take credit for your conversion to their teaching. They do not keep the law themselves (it is too complex, too demanding), but they want you to be counted on their side. You'll become just so many more notches on their gun handles, more scalps to show off with. "They can boast that you are their disciples," is the way the *Living Bible* translates this clause.

But "mere" Christians can be disciples of only one Lord, and His name is Jesus. To be a disciple of the Judaizers, or of Luther, or Calvin, or Thomas Aquinas, or any other human leader is to limit yourself to the leadership "of the flesh" (that is, of someone as confined by human nature as you are).

I attended a college in my undergraduate days in which I was forced to declare myself to be either a Calvinist or an Arminian. I refused, since I didn't know enough in those days about either Calvin or Arminius to make such a choice. I still refuse, but on other grounds. I realize now that to be forced to claim a denominational loyalty or to join the camp of Calvin or Arminius or any other great Christian leader is to be just that much less a disciple of Christ. My hope is in Him, not in someone else who hoped in Him. (I'm not being very original here, of course. This is Paul's argument in 1 Corinthians 3:4, 11, "For when one says, 'I follow Paul,' and another, 'I follow Apollos,' are you not mere men? ... For no one can lay any foundation other than the one already laid, which is Jesus Christ.")

We Have Nothing to Boast About
Except What Was Done *For* Us (6:14)

"May I never boast except in the cross of our Lord Jesus Christ" (Galatians 6:14). The Christian has a great deal to brag about, but he can't take credit for any of it! Nothing he does can effect his salvation or render him righteous. Everything depends on what Christ did for him on the cross. His boast is in Christ.

The Cross Crucified the World to Us

The cross has helped me see, once and for all, the truth about the world. All that glitters in it is *not* gold. The world can't tempt me any more. It's dead to me.

The Cross Crucified Me to the World

Like my Lord, I am now judged by the world that judged Him. I, too, am a criminal, an outcast, a misfit. I am unimportant to the world. In choosing Christ, I have rejected the world as my master; the world has retaliated by rejecting me.

The blessing of this rejection is that I now have nothing to lose in the world. I am free to risk everything for Christ, since nothing the world does to me matters and I don't matter to the world. As far as the world is concerned, I am like my Lord, a criminal, offensive and repugnant. I can't be manipulated by its commercials and advertisements, controlled by its governments, or persuaded by its fads. I don't fit. The only place I really belong and am considered important is in the body of other misfits, the church.

We may not be the kind of company the world likes to hang around with, but we outsiders are the kind of people it relies on for its survival. Where would our society be if there weren't lawyers who are more interested in justice than in simply playing judicial games? Without politicans who refuse to become slaves of power? Without businessmen who have higher motives than profit alone? Without teachers who don't view their profession as a job but as a vocation? Christians are, as Jesus said, salt and light and yeast in the world, never fully identifying with their society, but everywhere improving it.

The cross was God's instrument for turning the world upside down. He took a symbol of criminality and transformed it into the means of rescuing the very people who rejected the Rescuer.

Our boast is only in that cross.

Thanks to the Cross, We Have Become New Creations (6:15-17)

That's what really matters. Unable to pull ourselves up by our own bootstraps, we have submitted to the grace Christ has offered through the cross. And He has pulled us up.

Rose DeLorenzo understands how this works in a physical body. A victim of Apert's Disease, Rose suffered from a malformation of her skull's bone structure that prevented its shaping itself to conform to her growing brain. It left her with ugly deformities. She underwent six operations to re-form her cleft palate, her webbed fingers and toes, and the fused bones in her head. Then she went under the knife once more to reconstruct her face.

The surgery was a success. She was "a new creation." She couldn't remake her appearance by herself, but the skilled surgeon could. Similarly, we can't remake our broken selves either. We require a Great Physician's help.

When Caril Fugate was fourteen, she accompanied Charles Starkweather on a murder rampage that left ten Nebraskans dead. She was apprehended, convicted of complicity in the crimes, and imprisoned.

When she became eligible for parole at thirty-two, Caril had spent more than half her life in prison. It was not lost time. There she gave her life to Christ, affiliating with the Nazarene Church. She worked in the church nursery on Sunday mornings, taught Vacation Bible School, and even preached some sermons to the congregation. She underwent training as a geriatric aid and became involved in the work-release program in a nursing home on Sundays.

She calls herself a new creation. She couldn't have done this herself, but in the depths of her disgrace in prison, she was re-created by Jesus.

Rose and Fugate both bear on their bodies the results of those who transformed them, as Paul writes, "I bear on my body the marks of Jesus" (Galatians 6:17). Like Jesus, Paul does not fit in this world. Like Jesus, Paul has been rejected by his fellow Jewish leaders. Jesus was literally crucified; Paul was so figuratively (Galatians 2:20). He has the stripes from his beatings and the fatigue marks from his exhausting labors to prove it. But he also has a light in his eyes and a spring in his step and an ever-renewing Spirit within.

He has been re-created, not through something done to his body, but through the transformation of his whole being.

It has become a cliche among believers today to refer to themselves as "born-again Christians." It's a term the apostle Paul wouldn't use, at least in precisely the same way. For him, being a Christian is the equivalent of being born-again. To say "born-again Christian" is to repeat yourself. If you are a Christian, you have been born again. If you want to use the term, you probably should refer to yourself as a "born again human being." You are a new creation. That's what counts.

"The grace of our Lord Jesus Christ be with your spirit, brothers. Amen" (Galatians 6:18). The doctrine of grace that has permeated the letter now becomes Paul's final word of greeting. It's what this letter has been all about.

For many years, the following story has been making its rounds of church papers. The author is unknown, and the event described is fanciful, but what it teaches about our reliance on the grace of our Lord Jesus Christ captures the essence of Paul's theme in this letter.

An active, dedicated, hardworking church member passed away after a long and satisfying life. As he approached the Pearly Gate, he noticed a sign posted on it, which read: "Entrance requirement 1,000 points."

When St. Peter appeared, the man asked him, "How do you accumulate these points?" St. Peter asked, "Well, what have you done, and why do you feel you should be admitted?"

"Oh," the man answered with enthusiasm. "I was an immersed believer in Christ for thirty-two years and I did not miss a Sunday in fourteen years. Also, I taught a Sunday School class for more than twelve years."

"Wonderful," replied St. Peter, "that's worth one point."

The man gulped, and anxiously went on: "And I tithed. More than that I served on the Finance Committee, the Building Committee and I was an elder in the church and a member of the Board of Trustees. If there was a fellowship supper, they knew they could count on me. I set up chairs, painted and ran errands for the preacher."

He looked expectantly at St. Peter, who smiled benignly, and answered politely, "Fine, fine. That's worth another point!"

The man was perspiring: "I recruited many people for our church. I took the kids to camp; my car always was available if transportation was needed; and I always gave strong support to the missions program."

"Wonderful," was the soft-spoken reply from St. Peter. "That's still another point. Now you've got three!"

Futility showed clearly on the man's face. Worried, and with a note of resignation, he said, "That entrance requirement is awfully tough. Why, I don't believe anyone could get in without the grace of God!"

"Ah," said St. Peter warmly, "that's worth 997 points."face. Worried, and with a note of resignation, he said, "That entrance requirement is awfully tough. Why, I don't believe anyone could get in without the grace of God!"

"Ah," said St. Peter warmly, "that's worth 997 points."

Part Two:

Ephesians

INTRODUCTION TO
EPHESIANS

You'll find this commentary quite old-fashioned. It accepts Ephesians as is, in its entirety, without worrying nervously over conflicting scholarly opinions. I've read the scholars, and I appreciate the tedious care with which they seek to solve questions of authorship, sources, literary forms, and so on. Sometimes, however, their attention to detail can destroy the reader's appreciation for the unity and relevance of the epistle as a whole. That danger I hope to avoid by calling attention to the major themes and implications of Ephesians and leaving the intricacies of scholarship to others more qualified than I.

So we'll read Ephesians in the traditional way, digesting several verses at a time, applying the principles one uses for studying any great piece of literature. But, of course, there is a difference. This literature is inspired by God (2 Timothy 3:16), so we shall listen carefully to hear the eternal Word of the Lord. My hope is that this Bible study will help you, as the preparation of it has helped me, to find instruction and inspiration for today's living.

I have used many illustrations in my comments on the Scriptures. I hope they help. My defense for this procedure is quite personal. As a boy, I listened every Sunday to a master preacher-teacher, Aldis L. Webb, as he preached for nearly an hour to his small-town congregation. His method was to read a large portion of Scripture, then deliver a thoughtful, provocative, and always persuasive message explaining the passage. A gifted story-teller, he used illustrations from wide-ranging sources to make the Scriptures come alive to his congregation. To this day, I remember many of his stories and the points he was illustrating. In later years, I was impressed to discover that Jesus used the same story-telling technique with His congregations. I have adopted it as my own, although I can't claim to be as astute in using it as either my mentor or my Master. I hope, though, that the material you find in these pages will be as helpful to your understanding as Dr. Webb's illustrations were to mine.

Ephesians is a letter (epistle). While we shall ask questions such as when it was written and by whom, we shall be quickly satisfied with brief rather than exhaustive answers, because we are much more concerned about the epistle's content. I am convinced that this letter, although nearly 2,000 years old now, was written as much to us as to its first-century recipients.

It is addressed "to the saints in Ephesus" (Ephesians 1:1), but we have reason to believe that even in the beginning, it was intended for a broader readership than merely the Christians in that city. The earlier manuscripts we have don't mention Ephesus. William Barclay explains that this omission shouldn't concern us, since in those days before postal systems, letters were written on papyrus (writing material made of the stalks of reeds or rushes, looking something like very heavy wrapping paper), then rolled, tied with a thread, and hand-delivered. Addresses weren't necessary. Thus, our New Testament letters did not originally have any titles; they were added later. So it was with this letter.

There are some other reasons for doubting that this letter went originally just to Ephesus. Paul ministered in that city for up to three years, yet makes no mention of his Ephesian friends. Further, his references to his readers seem quite impersonal. (See Ephesians 1:15; 3:2; 4:21). In addition, the letter's close resemblance to Colossians has caused some students to speculate that this may be "the letter from Laodicea" mentioned in Colossians 4:16.

My guess is that the letter was written for circulation among churches in Asia Minor (Western Turkey today) and that the name of Ephesus, being the major city of the area, later became attached to it. Ephesus may have even been the first stop on its circuit.

Ephesus, situated at the mouth of the Cayster River, began as a Greek trading post. It grew to rival Alexandria and Syrian Antioch as major Mediterranean cities, a busy, prosperous port during the Roman era. It also achieved prominence religiously as the capital of the worship of Artemis (Diana), who was represented as a many-breasted goddess of fertility. Artemis was served by hundreds of prostitute priestesses; in turn, she served the thriving industry of silversmiths who manufactured idols and other

124

religious trinkets for pilgrims who made their way to her shrine. (See Acts 19.)

The infant church of Jesus Christ challenged Ephesus and the other cities of Asia Minor with the exclusive claims of the gospel. Since the appearance of Jesus, no city could boast of its religions; now it must receive or reject the grace of God offered through Christ. Now it must recognize that in Christ, God wants the whole world united (Ephesians 1:10) and that God's agency for unity is the church of Christ (Ephesians 3:10). The letter of Ephesians was written to make this fact very clear, and to instruct young Christians in the way they should now live as members of the church, God's unifying agency.

What strikes the attentive reader is that the writer's instructions to the first-century readers are so relevant to us that the letter could have been written last week. Even the second half of the letter (chapters 4-6, the so-called practical section) seems to have been written in response to twentieth-century problems. Surely the author had to be inspired.

I don't doubt that inspiration, nor do I doubt that the author was the apostle Paul. I mention my opinion up front, since one of the continuing debates about the epistle is, "Who wrote it?"

Scholars who doubt its Pauline authorship have some pretty sound reasons for their questions. Although doubts did not seriously arise until the end of the eighteenth century, since then they won't go away. It is pointed out that more than eighty words in this letter are unique to Ephesians (in other words, not found elsewhere in Paul's vocabulary, at least as we know him in his undisputed letters). It is not really written like a letter, either. At least it doesn't read like Paul's other letters, in which he addresses concrete situations and answers specific questions for particular congregations. Even the style and subject matter seem different.

No one really suggests that the teaching contradicts Paul, however. Some have even thought that the letter seems to be a collection of Paul's thoughts, compiled by somebody else to be a kind of introduction to Pauline theology.

It is this last suggestion that makes me think we have argued too much about authorship. If it sounds so much like Paul that we think it could be an anthology of Paul's thoughts, then it is in fact Pauline, isn't it? I like the conclusion that Markus Barth comes to, that Paul wrote the letter and that he probably wrote it to the church at Ephesus, but more particularly to the newer Gentile

125

members there who became a part of the fellowship after Paul had left his ministry with the congregation.

At any rate, throughout this commentary, you'll find that I believe we are studying the inspired writing of the apostle Paul. I also accept the usual dating of around A.D. 60-61, and I assume (because there are no conclusive arguments to the contrary), that his references to being a "prisoner of Christ Jesus" mean that he is writing the letter during his imprisonment in Rome. He then will send it and the letters to Philemon and the church at Colossae (Colossians 4:7, 8; Ephesians 6:21, 22) along with Tychicus as he travels to Asia Minor.

As we have already noted, Ephesians does not read like a typical letter. Its style is more elevated, its development more systematic. It could be studied as a sermon, or as a doctrinal treatise. Paul's thought divides neatly into two sections. The first three chapters are primarily doctrinal, as Paul presents the grand theme of God's purpose in Christ (to unify all things) and Christ's purpose in the church (to act as His agency for unity).

The second half, the practical section, details the manner in which members of the church are to live in order to fulfill the church's purpose.

CHAPTER FOURTEEN

A Christian Hello

Ephesians 1:1, 2

How you greet another person is important. Whether yours is a breezy, "Hi ya," a formal, "How do you do?" or a macho, "Howdy, Ma'am," tells a great deal about you—where you live, how you view yourself, what you think of the person you are greeting, and even the nature of the occasion.

What is true in person is equally telling in a letter. The form of salutation you use betrays something about you, although perhaps less so today than in former years, when letter-writing was more of an art and more subject to formal guidelines than it is today.

The apostle Paul's letters follow the usual conventions for correspondence in the first-century Mediterranean world, but with some noteworthy differences. It was customary for an epistle to name the sender first, then say a word of thanks for the recipient before moving into the letter proper. Since the writer often employed an amanuensis (stenographer) to whom he dictated, these formalities were observed by the penman if not the author of the letter. A strong-willed correspondent like the apostle Paul, however, had no difficulty imposing his own character on the conventions, even though he seems to have dictated most of his letters. (In Galatians, he adds a few words in his own writing as proof of the letter's authenticity. See Galatians 6:11 and our comments, above.)

The Writer

More formal than Paul's other letters, Ephesians is like them in following the accepted letter format by beginning with the name and authority of the writer. Paul moves quickly to establish his credentials.

He is "Paul, an apostle" (Ephesians 1:1). He thus writes with authority, although the title indicates that his is a derived authority. We have already discussed the title *apostle* in our comments on Paul's greeting in Galatians, but a few brief words by way of reminder are appropriate here. An apostle is a commissioned messenger or ambassador, a person under orders. Whatever power he has he possesses only because it has been delegated to him. He is nothing in himself, but he is everything in the One who commissioned him.

The title was originally given to the twelve disciples who were closest to Jesus during His earthly ministry, but was later applied to others in the early church. Paul received a special appointment when the risen Jesus appeared especially to him ("as to one abnormally born"; 1 Corinthians 15:8-10), and he would never allow others to view him as anything but a full-fledged apostle (2 Corinthians 10-12). Let there be no doubt, in Paul's mind, his apostleship is a high calling, a supreme gift, and an awesome responsibility. He never forgets that Christ, not Paul, founded the church. As the Father had sent Jesus (John 20:21), so Jesus in turn has sent Paul.

This commission to be an apostle of the Messiah (Christ) came "by the will of God" (Ephesians 1:1). Ephesians has more references to God's will than any other New Testament book except the Gospel of John. It is God's will that Jesus be accepted as the Messiah (the Christ, the Anointed One of God). It is God's will that Paul serve Christ as His ambassador. Paul may labor in a field fraught with danger and discord, but he is secure in his relationship with God in Christ; he has no doubt that his work is what God wants him to be doing.

Is this assurance available to everyone? Can we, too, know that we are in God's will? Yes, and by the time we finish this study of Ephesians, we'll have no doubt what it is. For now, it is sufficient to say that God's purpose has not changed. He sent Jesus to seek and to save the lost (Luke 19:10). Everything Jesus did in His ministry was to keep anybody from being lost; that was His Father's will (John 6:38-40). When Jesus concluded His earthly ministry, He commissioned His disciples to carry on His saving work (Matthew 28:18-20) and left behind Him a church as the agency to accomplish the task. He equipped the church with leaders and workers who would be able to function as His body, doing His work (Ephesians 4:11-16). Whenever we let the Lord use us as members of His body to help in His saving work, we are doing God's will.

And if my personal experience means anything, the longer we let the Lord so use us, no matter how weak and ineffective we seem to be, the more convinced we become that we are what we are "by the will of God" (Ephesians 1:1).

The Readers

Having established his identity and credentials, Paul now names the recipients of his letter. As the introduction has pointed out, some early manuscripts omit *in Ephesus* from Ephesians 1:1, leaving a question about its original destination. That should not disturb us, however, because this tightly reasoned epistle is universal in its application, as relevant for our day as it was in the first century.

"To the saints" (Ephesians 1:1). Today's reader might be tempted to put the Bible down right now. This letter was written to saints, and if there's one thing we know we're not, this is it. Everybody knows what a saint is—it's a plaster of paris idol that sits on a fireplace mantle or in a special place in some homes or in a niche in a church building. A saint is somebody who lived a long time ago and did something miraculous so the church honors him or her with the title *saint*. Or a saint is a super-Christian, usually an old person, who never does anything wrong and is always helping other people; or one whose very appearance shows he's suffering for Jesus, the kind of person Samuel Butler had in mind when he noted, "How holy people look when they are sea-sick!" Everybody knows who a saint is and everybody knows he's not one! Right?

Wrong! Basically, the word *(hagios)* simply means "dedicated to God; set apart by God as holy or sacred." It makes more sense if we approach it historically, for its roots are deep in the Old Testament. Here is the Word of God to the nation of Israel:

> Now if you obey me fully and keep my covenant, then out of all nations you will be my treasured possession. Although the whole earth is mine, you will be for me a kingdom of priests and a holy nation (Exodus 19:5, 6).
>
> For you are a people holy to the Lord your God. The Lord your God has chosen you out of all the peoples on the face of the earth to be his people, his treasured possession (Deuteronomy 7:6).

129

In the New Testament, 1 Peter 2:9 and 10 picks up this same theme and applies it to Christians:

> But you are a chosen people, a royal priesthood, a holy nation, a people belonging to God, that you may declare the praises of him who called you out of darkness into his wonderful light. Once you were not a people, but now you are the people of God; once you had not received mercy, but now you have received mercy.

"Saints," "holy ones," "God's very own people." That is who we Christians are. What a privilege, yet what a discomforting thought! As we shall see, God's people will often feel uncomfortable in a world governed by the "powers of this dark world" (Ephesians 6:12); even more, we tend to make others around us uncomfortable. We don't intend to, but since our values are in stark contrast with those of most people, we cannot help putting them on the defensive. Even the Christian's thoughts are to be different (Philippians 2:5-11; Romans 12:1, 2). A secretary was typing a well-known quotation from the Roman emperor Marcus Aurelius. She just made one mistake, substituting a *k* for a *g,* but it made all the difference: "Examine men's ruling principles," Aurelius said, "especially those of the wise, what kind of thin*k*s [the secretary typed] they avoid, and what kind they pursue." A saint, having been dedicated to God, pursues different thinks, so he stands somewhat apart from his peers.

Saints, then, are both chosen and choosing. They have been chosen by God; in response, they are choosing God. They pursue different thinks!

A saint looks like just about anybody: he may be rich, he may be poor; he may be male, he may be female; he may be black or white or red or yellow; he may be learned or he may be illiterate. What makes him a saint is not his appearance, but the fact that God has set him apart as one of His special people. He is, in other words, a Christian. There were saints in Ephesus; there are saints in our pagan country. They are the faithful in Christ Jesus.

A child admiring the stained glass windows in her church one morning asked her mother about the people pictured in them.

"Those are God's saints," her mother explained. "They are people who proved their love for Him."

In her Sunday-school class some time later, the girl's teacher asked the class to explain what a saint is. "Saints are people the light shines through," the child wisely replied.

130

Saints are people the light of Christ shines through. The key thought of the entire letter is "in Christ Jesus." It is Paul's favorite phrase, occurring some 164 times in his letters. In the following verses (3-11) alone, he uses it eleven times.

"In Christ" is so rich a phrase it almost defies precise definition. It specifically denotes the relationship between God and His people that Christ has bonded through His earthly life, death, and resurrection. Those who accept Jesus as the Messiah and Savior and serve Him as Lord are "in Christ." They have been invited into the community of believers and remain faithfully there.

"In Christ" suggests even more. A few years ago, a Paris perfume company, Parfums Lagerfeld, ran an advertisement in some American magazines. The ad was a photo of a beautiful woman dancing inside a perfume bottle. The caption read, "A woman does not put on my fragrance. She enters it." She is *in* the perfume. Its aroma transforms the air around her.

Saints in Christ walk in a special atmosphere; even more, they are themselves atmosphere makers. "Be such a man," someone has said, "and live such a life, that if every man were such as you, and every life a life like yours, this earth would be God's Paradise."

"In Christ" suggests that once you've said this about someone, you know all you need to know. When someone tells you, "I'm in business," or, "I'm into sports," or even, "I'm in love," you don't have any trouble understanding the meaning, do you? The business or sport or love dominates the person's existence, giving unity, wholeness, and meaning to life. It is in this sense that Dietrich Bonhoeffer has written that being a Christian "does not mean to be religious in a particular way, to cultivate some particular form of asceticism ... but to be a man."[26] The Christian's whole life is "in Christ" and thus more whole, more complete.

You don't get "into Christ," then, simply by attendance at worship or by the performance of some ritual alone or even through memorizing God's Word. We remember with horror that at the Village Church in Kalinovka, Russia, the priest increased Sunday-school attendance by handing out candy to peasant children. One little pug-nosed lad did especially well; in fact, he won a special

---

[26]Dietrich Bonhoeffer, *Letters and Papers From Prison,* Eberhard Bethage, ed. (New York: Macmillan, 1972), p. 361.

prize for learning all four Gospels by heart and then reciting them non-stop in church. But for all that, Nikita Khrushchev could never have been said to be "in Christ."

No, being in Christ has more the nature of a love affair. Paul, who so loved this phrase, even more loved his Lord. His was not a formal relationship, like a sterile but proper marriage; his was a quite proper, but much more passionate, union of everything he had to offer (soul, body, brains, energy, and all) to the One without whom he could no longer live.

But there is no jealousy in his love. He wants all men everywhere to be "in Christ." He writes to the "faithful in Christ" (Ephesians 1:1) in the constant hope that their numbers will increase. He has written elsewhere, "Therefore, if anyone is in Christ, he is a new creation; the old has gone, the new has come!" (2 Corinthians 5:17). He wants to fill the world with such new creations.

The Greeting

"Grace and peace to you" (Ephesians 1:2). This is Paul's typical—and unique—greeting. He borrows from Greeks and Jews. Greeks greeted each other with the word, "Rejoice" (*chairein*); Paul alters it to a similar form, *charis,* with a broader meaning. It suggests the favor of a superior to an inferior, such as a special dispensation from a master to a slave. It also connotes kindness, mercy, good will, and, by extension, that which brings joy, pleasure, or loveliness. It's a big word. *Grace* refers to the favor God bestows of His own goodness upon unworthy recipients, to the beauty that brings delight to the beholder, and to the charm to which we allude when we call someone gracious. Paul had already received the grace of God in his salvation. When he was the chief of sinners (1 Timothy 1:15), God did him a favor and rescued him through Christ Jesus. When he was anathema to the Christians in Jerusalem, Barnabas graciously befriended him and championed his cause with the other members of the Jerusalem church (Acts 9:26, 27). He therefore lives with the overwhelming sense that God has blessed him far beyond his deserving. It is no wonder that grace becomes the foundation of Paul's theology.

John Newton's "Amazing Grace" captures Paul's gratitude for God's grace. After wasting his youth as a hard-drinking, hard-cursing sailor, slave, and ne'er-do-well, Newton was rescued from a storm at sea and a stormy life by his merciful God. When he returned to England, he forsook the sea and became a minister of God, never forgetting that

> Amazing grace! How sweet the sound
> That saved a wretch like me!
> I once was lost, but now am found,
> Was blind but now I see.

As an old man, Newton met a longtime friend on the streets of London. He told him, "My memory is gone. But I remember two things: I am a great sinner. And Jesus Christ is my savior."

Newton even expressed his gratitude for God's grace on his memorial stone:

> John Newton
> Clerk.
> Once an infidel and libertine,
> A servant of slaves in Africa
> was by the Mercy of our Lord and Savior
> Jesus Christ
> Preserved, restored, pardoned,
> And appointed to preach the faith
> he had so long
> laboured to destroy.

Paul elsewhere devotes large sections of his letters to discussing the theological doctrine of salvation by grace as opposed to works, but here the word is just a greeting—but a greeting with a difference! Here he asks God, the source of everything good, to favor you beyond your (or Paul's) deserving.

He also wishes his readers' "peace," which is the Jewish *shalom*. This greeting does not call for an absence of war or for ease and tranquility. *Shalom* (in the Greek, *eirene*) is the gift of God, which leads to your total well-being, in your family, your person, your physical being, your economic situation, your political environment, everything. "May everything in your life be good."

It will be, if you are "in Christ." In fact, you will then receive the peace Jesus mentions: "Peace I leave with you; my peace I give you. I do not give to you as the world gives. Do not let your hearts be troubled and do not be afraid" (John 14:27).

A former village woman in Pakistan, who later worked as an evangelist, gave her own explanation of this peace. "You cannot imagine the terror in which I lived as a girl. I was afraid of the priests, the landlords, the moneylenders, kidnappers, wild people, robbers, and most of all the evil spirits, devils and angry gods and goddesses." Bishop Pickett, who recounts this story, adds that when over 4000 village people in India were asked to tell what Christ Jesus had done for them, seventy per cent included, "He took fear out of me."[27]

The source of all this goodness is "God our Father and the Lord Jesus Christ" (Ephesians 1:2). The two are inseparable, since Paul knows God through Christ. Before meeting the risen Christ, Paul thought he knew God, but he was grievously mistaken. Now his every reference to God is by way of Jesus Christ.

Paul has mentioned his Lord in all three parts of this brief greeting. Jesus Christ commissioned him an apostle, calls and unifies the saints who are faithful in Him, and confers with the Father grace and peace. "In Christ" saturates Paul's letters. He writes as one whose identity has so merged with his Lord's that he no longer can think of himself separately. For him to live is Christ (Philippians 1:21); it is no longer he who lives but Christ who lives in him (Galatians 2:20).

---

[27] J. Waskom Pickett, *The Dynamics of Church Growth* (New York: Abingdon, 1963), p. 59.

CHAPTER FIFTEEN

What God Has Done for Us

Ephesians 1:3-14

Ephesians is a difficult letter, complex and compelling. One of its themes is the work and importance of the church, a vital subject for any Christian's consideration. But there is an even larger theme:

> And he made known to us the mystery of his will according to his good pleasure, which he purposed in Christ, to be put into effect when the times will have reached their fulfillment—*to bring all things in heaven and on earth together under one head, even Christ* (Ephesians 1:9, 10).

The uniting of all reality under the lordship of Christ is the subject that dominates the letter, but we'll postpone our consideration of these two verses until we have discussed the tone that permeates Ephesians 1:3-14.

The tone is the sound of thanksgiving. The apostle writes as one filled with gratitude for what God has done for us in Christ. Omitting, for the time being, verses 9 and 10, we discover eight sources of Paul's overwhelming appreciation. When we fully comprehend what God has done for us, then nothing can dampen our joy in Christ.

The form in these opening verses resembles both a Jewish blessing and the usual thanks a Roman writer would express for the recipient of his letter. Paul conforms to the convention of his day, but then he imposes his own style. He gives thanks as expected, but then goes quickly to the source of all he has received. He praises God for what He has done in Christ—for us. The agent of God's goodness to mankind is Jesus. As far as Paul is concerned, God gets the praise for Christ, but we get the blessings because of Him.

135

Let us see the eight specific acts of God for which we join Paul in giving thanks:

(1) God Has Blessed Us

"Praise be to the God and Father of our Lord Jesus Christ, who has *blessed* us in the heavenly realms with every spiritual *blessing* in Christ" (Ephesians 1:3). We cannot miss Paul's point here: Christians are God-blessed persons.

In a personal evangelism class a few years ago, our teacher cautioned us against using certain "churchy sounding" words as we presented Christ to non-Christians. He gave us a list of forbidden words, which sound foreign or peculiar to non-believers. High on the list was this word *bless*.

The teacher was right. It is a "churchy" word, all right. Who else but Christians use it in its fullest meaning? Others may offer a "God bless you" to cover the embarrassment of someone's sneeze, or mutter a near-curse, "Bless you!" or use some other trite variation, but it is seldom used in its Biblical sense outside the church.

To the Christian, however, *bless* is an almost indispensable word. There is no adequate translation, no equivalent synonym. To say *happy* isn't quite the same, nor is *joyful*. One Bible translator tries *supremely fortunate* in the Beatitudes (Matthew 5:3-12), but even this is misleading, since fortune rests on luck, and our sense of being blessed rests upon the sure hand of God, not upon blind chance.

Just as there is no good synonym, there is also no easy way to explain *blessed* to a stranger to God. But for the Christian, it is a treasured word. Gladly we sing, "Blessed assurance, Jesus is mine," or, "Blest be the tie that binds our hearts in Christian love," or "Blessed be the name, blessed be the name, blessed be the name of the Lord."

Because we can't substitute any other word for it, we go on using it, thankful that God has blessed us. That blessing is "in the heavenly realms." Paul uses this phrase *(en tois epouraniois)* elsewhere in Ephesians:

> Christ is exalted "in the heavenly realms" (Ephesians 1:20).
> We are exalted with Christ "in the heavenly realms" (Ephesians 2:6).
> Wisdom of God is made known "in the heavenly realms" (Ephesians 3:10).

We struggle against powers and forces "in the heavenly realms" (Ephesians 6:12).

The blessings we receive, like the life we live in Christ, are not to be measured by any earthly standard. God has elevated us above what is normal existence for this world's people. We think, feel, decide, and fight on a higher plane. We have already begun to live in Heaven; eternity has begun for us, so eternal values and the blessings treasured in Heaven are now real to us. "Our citizenship is in heaven" (Philippians 3:20), so we obey its laws and enjoy its beauty even on earth.

(2) God Has Chosen Us

"For he chose us in him before the creation of the world to be holy and blameless in his sight" (Ephesians 1:4). In his greeting, Paul addresses "the saints." Saints are, quite simply, God's chosen ones. He has selected us to be special to Him; His choosing makes us different from ordinary humanity. He has picked us out from among the masses for His own purposes, just as He chose the nation of Israel before us (Deuteronomy 7:6-8; 1 Peter 2:9). We Christians are a select group, then, not left to wander aimlessly through life, as is the wont of most of mankind, but challenged to a vocation: "to be holy and blameless in his sight."

"To be holy" is just another way of saying, "to be saints," to "live like God's people." Jesus put it this way: "Be perfect, therefore, as your heavenly Father is perfect" (Matthew 5:48). Christians are not people who have been saved because of their moral perfection ("For it is by grace you have been saved"— Ephesians 2:8), but having been saved and chosen "to be holy and blameless," we then seek to call attention to God by the quality of our lives. Like unblemished lambs offered for sacrifice (Leviticus 1:3, 10), we wish to be blameless for God and man, acceptable sacrifices in His service (Romans 12:1, 2).

To hardened secular thinkers, this talk of "sainthood" may sound peculiar, but more than one modern writer has concluded that only here is fullness of life to be found. Frederick Buechner couples two novels, one by a Roman Catholic and the other by an atheist, that arrive at the same conclusion. Graham Greene's moving story of a whiskey priest *(The Power and the Glory)* traces his flight from and eventual capture by the revolutionary Mexican government. Condemned to be shot, the priest spends his last evening in his cell, fortified by his brandy bottle, recalling what he admits is the dingy failure of his life. He's not afraid of damnation, or even of pain, but he cries with "immense disappointment"; he doesn't want to face God empty-handed. If only he could say he had done something worthwhile, if only a little more courageous, if only some self-restraint. Greene writes, "He felt like someone who has missed happiness by seconds at an appointed place. He knew now that at the end there was only one thing that counted—to be a saint."

Albert Camus's *The Plague* includes a bit of conversation between two atheists, one a journalist and the other a doctor working desperately to check the plague that has been decimating the population of their northern African city. "It comes to this," one of them says. "What interests me is learning to become a saint."[28]

What both the priest and the atheist misunderstand is that sainthood is not something earned but something conferred. God "chose" us. His grace (of which more will be said later) and not our sweat is what matters.

(3) God Has Destined Us

"In love he predestined us to be adopted as his sons through Jesus Christ . . ." (Ephesians 1:5). We have an appointment with destiny. "In him we were also chosen, having been predestined according to the plan of him who works out everything in conformity with the purpose of his will . . ." (Ephesians 1:11). God, motivated by His love for us, had already determined that He would adopt us as His sons. Here, then, is our security. We have been adopted, God thereby giving us all the rights of natural children. (Roman law made no distinction between adoptive and natural-born sons.) Our destiny is set. If we are in Christ, we are God's sons (whether we are male or female—see Galatians 3:28 and our comments on that passage above), heirs of everything He owns. We who are receiving so much, then, naturally respond with "the praise of his glorious grace" (Ephesians 1:6). We have something to live for.

When I was teaching high school, one of my colleagues was out for a day, and a substitute taught his senior social studies class. He

---

[28]Frederick Buechner, *The Magnificent Defeat* (New York: Seabury Press, 1966), pp. 118, 119.

assigned the students to write an essay, "The Purpose of My Life." We were discussing that topic later in the teachers' room, and the girls' physical education teacher strongly objected to the topic. "It's too difficult for high-school students," she protested. "They don't know the purpose of their lives. Why should they?" She paused for a moment, then added, "I couldn't write that paper, either. I don't know the purpose of my life." The woman was in her fifties.

Contrast her confusion with the sense of purpose the Christian has because he knows he has been destined to be a child of God and to live to praise Him.

The Westminster shorter catechism asks, "What is the chief end of man?" The expected answer is the simple but profound, "To glorify God, and to enjoy Him forever." What greater goal is there to live for? This purpose gives meaning to the job, to the home, to existence itself. What joy there is in this appointment with destiny.

"He predestined us to be *adopted*." This makes us privileged persons. After Americans withdrew from the Vietnam conflict, many Vietnamese orphans were airlifted from the war-torn country to new homes in the United States. Controversy whirled around this action, because some people believed it wrong to take these youngsters from their native culture. No one could deny, however, that a child needs parents and a home to live in, whether in Vietnam or America. Though political and humanitarian implications had to be considered, most objections were overcome when critics saw the deserted children being welcomed into homes that genuinely wanted them. What a moment it must have been for the frightened children when they realized that someone was saying, "I love you. I have chosen you. I want you."

Adopted. The orphan who has lived without a Divine Parent, when he feels the everlasting arms embracing him and hears, "I have chosen you because I love you and I want you to be my child," experiences the same inexpressible thrill. Do you wonder why a Christian is full of joy and thanksgiving?

(4) God Has Redeemed Us

"In him we have *redemption* through his blood" (Ephesians 1:7). At first, this sounds like another "churchy" word, doesn't it? It shouldn't, though, to a nation that was held in thrall as its hostages languished in Iran during the Khoumeini madness. When they were finally released, the word "redeemed" appeared in print. They had been delivered from captivity into freedom. The word suggests liberation from slavery, captivity, or danger and deliverance to safety.

One of the great events of British history occurred at Dunkirk in 1940. The Nazis were sweeping the European continent and breathing threats against Great Britain. By May, they had most of Europe under control and England was in extreme peril. Neville Chamberlain had resigned and Winston Churchill had just assumed command as Prime Minister. One of his first decisions was to evacuate hundreds of thousands of British citizens and soldiers still on the continent. But how was it to be done? Churchill sent out the word to British citizens to inform the government of all available boats at least thirty to one hundred feet in length. The purpose wasn't disclosed immediately, but it soon became obvious to the world what was happening. Within nine days in May, 1940, 887 vessels (sailing boats, tug boats, pleasure craft, whatever would float and could haul human cargo) rescued 338,000 people from Dunkirk. They *redeemed* Britain's citizens from their captivity.

"In him we have redemption *through his blood.*" A price had to be paid to release us from captivity to sin. The Son's life was given for our lives, the greatest possible price paid for persons whose value is not in their accomplishments but in God's estimate of their worth. (See 1 Peter 1:17-21; 1 Corinthians 6:20; Romans 5:6-11, Revelation 5:9.) We Christians are thus like Israel, who was also redeemed from captivity by the blood of a lamb (Exodus 12).

(5) God Has Forgiven Us

"In him we have ... the forgiveness of sins ..." (Ephesians 1:7). This seems to be a peculiarly Christian word, too, doesn't it? After the Watergate scandal, President Gerald Ford further scandalized the nation by pardoning former President Nixon. Newspapers shouted the indignation of journalism's instant theologians: "A pardon can only be granted after there is an admission of guilt and a request for forgiveness," they insisted, complaining that neither was offered by Richard Nixon. The pundits cited Bible chapter and verse to bolster their case. Ford's action is still being questioned, but most debaters agree that pardon should be made available only to one who confesses guilt and asks forgiveness. The pardon God offers through the blood of Jesus Christ is within the grasp of anyone who desires it, but what God graciously offers must be accepted on God's terms. (See Matthew 6:12-15; 18:21-35; Acts 2:38; 1 John 1:8-10; 2:12.)

We do not have to say much about forgiveness. When adults think seriously about becoming Christian, they become dreadfully aware of their sins. Even though they may wear faces that mask their guilt, and though they protest that they are "just as good as the next fellow," they remain unconvinced. They know that being as good as the next fellow is not being good at all, since nobody else they know seems to be terribly virtuous. To say, "I haven't been any worse than anyone else," is no compliment; we have only to glance around to acknowledge that "all have sinned and fall short of the glory of God" (Romans 3:23). After a while, the honest soul finally tires of carrying his load of guilt and asks for relief. And relief is available through Jesus Christ.

(6) God Has Lavished His Grace on Us

This relief is undeserved. It is "grace": "to the praise of his glorious *grace,* which he has freely given us in the One he loves" (Ephesians 1:6). Paul goes on to add, "In him we have redemption through his blood, the forgiveness of sins, in accordance with the riches of God's *grace* that he lavished on us" (Ephesians 1:7, 8). We have received favor upon favor and haven't deserved any of it.

> You see, at just the right time, when we were still powerless, Christ died for the ungodly. Very rarely will anyone die for a righteous man, though for a good man someone might possibly dare to die. But God demonstrates his own love for us in this: While we were still sinners, Christ died for us" (Romans 5:6-8).

Six times in Ephesians, Paul speaks of the mind-boggling wealth that God lavishes on us.[29] He does not merely give according to our need, but out of the super-abundance He possesses. He "lavishes" it on us (Ephesians 1:8).

---

[29]Here; 1:18; 2:4, 7; 3:8, 16. (See Ephesians 2:4 and 2:8 for further discussion on "grace.")

(7) God Has Marked Us With a Seal

"Having believed, you were marked in him [Christ] with a seal, the promised Holy Spirit" (Ephesians 1:13). In ancient times, letters were sealed. Wax was dropped onto the scroll, then a signet ring would be used to stamp an identifying seal in the wax. Similar seals were used on official documents to guarantee authenticity, on packages in transit to show that the goods had not been tampered with, and to identify governmental offices. Certain religious cults tattooed their adherents with an identifying emblem; then the devotees were "sealed," just as Jews viewed circumcision as a seal or mark of belonging (Romans 4:11).

The word always makes me think of a practice in the wild west: cattle branding. Every year, range cattle are rounded up, and cowboys and ranch hands heat a branding iron and sear the owner's mark on the cattle. From that moment on, whoever finds those cattle on the open range knows whose they are by the brand in their hide.

Christians are branded by the evidence of the Holy Spirit in our lives. Wherever we are, our Owner's mark should be in evidence. The mark of the Holy Spirit is "love, joy, peace, patience, kindness, goodness, faithfulness, gentleness and self-control" (Galatians 5:22, 23). This is not the world's brand. The fruit of the Spirit marks a Christian as belonging to the Holy Spirit's herd. God has sealed us with His Spirit. When we "heard the word of truth, the gospel of [our] salvation" (Ephesians 1:13), and when we responded in belief, God made good on His promise and gave us His Spirit (see Ezekiel 36:26; 37:1-14; Joel 2:28; John 14 and 15; Acts 1:4-8; 2:1-4, 38).

(8) God Has Guaranteed Our Inheritance

The Holy Spirit "is a deposit guaranteeing our inheritance until the redemption of those who are God's possession—to the praise of his glory" (Ephesians 1:14). So we have no anxiety about the future. We know who we are; we know where we are going; we have an appointment with destiny; and God has given us an earnest deposit on the riches to come. That earnest is the Holy Spirit. The word is *arrabon,* which is similar to our business term, "earnest money." When you buy a piece of property, you deposit in an escrow account an amount large enough to convince the seller you are "in earnest" about the purchase. It is your guarantee that your word is good.

In the same way, God has "deposited" His Holy Spirit in us so that we can be certain He means what He promises. The Spirit is just a foretaste of the magnificent future God has in store for us.

During his tenure as Secretary of State in pre-Civil War America, Henry Clay counseled, "I cannot at this juncture clearly foretell the outcome, but I counsel you to cultivate calmness of mind and prepare for the worst." The Christian cannot clearly foretell the future either, but he enjoys calmness of mind because he is preparing for the best. A glorious outcome is certain: God's Spirit is an irrevocable guarantee.

Three times Paul says that all God has done for us in Christ leads us "to the praise of his glory" (Ephesians 1:6, 12, 14). We have no reason to withhold praise when we add up what we have received: God has blessed, chosen, destined for adoption, redeemed, forgiven, and lavished grace upon us, even while sealing us with His Spirit and guaranteeing us our eternal home. What more could we want? Who but an ingrate would withhold praise?

All this has been accomplished "in Christ."

> Every spiritual blessing is ours "in Christ."
> He chose us "in Him."
> He destined us to be adopted "through Jesus Christ."
> He freely lavished grace on us "in the One he loves."
> He redeemed us "in Him."
> He revealed the mystery of the will He purposed "in Christ" (vs. 9).
> We hope "in Christ."
> We were included "in Christ."
> We were marked "in Him" with a seal.

Whatever else a Christian is, of this there is no doubt: he is "in Christ"!

CHAPTER SIXTEEN

God Has Told Us His Secret

Ephesians 1:9, 10

The word is *mystery,* but a more accurate translation for modern readers would be *secret.* God's disclosure of His unsuspected secret is the theme of this amazing letter.

We read this sentence very carefully: "And he made known to us the mystery of his will according to his good pleasure ..." (Ephesians 1:9). There is so much we cannot understand about the purposes of God. For us, *mystery* is the key word, even though we do not use this word in the Biblical sense anymore. We frequently speak of God's mysterious ways. We are baffled by the unsolvable puzzles that have confused mankind throughout history: Why do the good suffer while the bad prosper? Why does God allow the innocent to die? Why are some people healed through prayer while others linger in agony? We don't understand, and we squirm in the presence of anyone else who talks too authoritatively about God's plans or purposes. "It's not that simple," we cry out.

Yet here Paul claims to know God's secret. Even more, he asserts that God has made His purpose known to us all. If Paul is right, then Christianity should never be thought of as a "mystery religion." While God hasn't told us everything we would like to know, He has not kept us in the dark about why He is doing what He is doing in the universe. That mystery is a secret no longer.

The word *mystery* has a technical meaning whenever Paul uses it (as he does frequently in Ephesians: 3:3, 4, 6, 9; 5:32; 6:19). It doesn't mean "puzzle" but refers instead to a truth once hidden but now made known—specifically, made known in and through Christ.

So-called "mystery religions" were popular in the first century. Adherents to these cults prided themselves in the fact that they knew information that was mysterious to outsiders. Only the initiated were allowed to learn the secret rites and obtain the esoteric knowledge of the in-group, knowledge that lay beyond the grasp of ordinary people, information available only to the select few.

What Paul is boldly announcing in these two verses is that now that Christ has done His work, there is nothing hidden in the Christian faith. What God has told Paul He wants everybody to know. What was hidden is now information available to anyone who wants it. (See Colossians 1:26; 2:2; 4:3; and Romans 16:25, 26.) Anybody claiming to be Christian but who boasts of its secret rites or its esoteric knowledge, then, does not belong to orthodox Christianity. A religion of secrets is by definition something in violation of the purpose of God.

For God does have His purposes: "which he purposed in Christ" (Ephesians 1:9).

This simple statement makes us pay attention. Our world seldom seems to be following any plan or premeditated strategy. In chaos it began and to chaos it seems always to be returning. Each week's headlines scream of tragedy upon catastrophe upon disaster. If there is any purpose to human existence, most of the world's population has concluded, it is simply to survive.

But God is working out His purpose. And He has disclosed that purpose in Christ. If we can't see it, perhaps it is because we are too close to the action to see the pattern. You must not look at some paintings too closely; if you do, you see only a confusion of color. Step back a few paces, however, and these colors cohere into a meaningful pattern—a landscape, a flower, a group.

When the painter approaches a blank canvas, he begins with a few bold strokes, then adds detail, then shading. To the casual observer, the meaning is a long time appearing; he sees only the disconnected lines and blotches. To the painter, however, the meaning was there from the beginning; he just needed time to bring all of the elements into harmony.

When I first became a college administrator, a new office had to be prepared for me. A classroom was appropriated and divided into two offices, one for me and one for my secretary. The business manager invited my wife, an interior designer, to design and decorate the rooms. For quite some time, he and other administrators feared he had made a terrible mistake. First she ordered one ceiling painted black and the other rust. Then she purchased "shag" carpeting, the only floor cover of its kind on campus. She installed bookshelves to hide the old radiator and pipes; she selected some new furniture and retrieved some old library chairs from the campus warehouse. At first, there was no apparent meaning in her separate decisions. The academic dean was heard mumbling something about the "black hole of Calcutta" as he surveyed the damage. When she finished, however, I moved into the most beautiful, most sensible office on campus. She had done everything according to her far-seeing purpose.

God has proceeded according to His purpose, designing and administering an infinitely vaster project. His is not so much a fixed blueprint as ongoing administration that fulfills His overarching purpose. Paul uses the word *oikonomia,* which we usually translate as management, stewardship, or administration. While we cannot always discern all the administrative details of God's operation, we do not have to be in doubt about His management principles because He has revealed these to us through Christ.

Paul's great excitement comes from the fact that God has taken us into His confidence. He has made His purpose known "to us."

Do you remember the moment when your father first took you into his confidence? When he treated you like a grown-up? It meant that he felt you were ready to receive more insight into him and his purposes. Wasn't that a special day for you?

That's how Paul feels. His Father has taken him into His confidence. Furthermore, God has assured him that He is on schedule: "to be put into effect when the times will have reached their fulfillment" (Ephesians 1:10). If everything doesn't seem quite in order right now, don't worry. When the time comes, God will complete what He has set out to do in Christ. It is a matter of timing (*kairos*—the term refers to specific times or seasons, as opposed to *chronos,* the simple measuring of time by minutes, hours, days, etc.).

Here's what God told him: "[I will] bring all things in heaven and on earth together under one head, even Christ" (Ephesians 1:10).

"I am working toward unity for this strife-torn universe."

"I do not want division; I desire peace."

This still comes as a surprise to people unfamiliar with God's Word. They've heard about all the wars in the Old Testament. They have lived through many wars in their own century, the worst that human history has ever experienced. It has seemed to them as if God himself has been the author of these wars, or at least the bemused spectator. They have puzzled over the question of how these horrible atrocities could be God's will.

147

They can't. They aren't. If Paul is telling the truth here, no war is God's will. War is not His purpose—unity is. His plan in sending Christ to earth was—and is—to unite all things in Christ, thus bringing an end to conflict, division, and war.

This is no easy task, of course. Charles DeGaulle of France once asked in mock despair, "How do you govern a nation that has 246 varieties of cheese?" A real problem, as the history of France has demonstrated. How then do you unify a world that numbers hundreds of nations, thousands of tongues, and billions of persons?

Obviously, *we* don't. We certainly haven't, with our world wars, our civil wars, our national wars, our racial wars, our labor wars, our economic wars, even our generation wars. If there is to be peace, it will be the peace envisioned by that old war-horse General Douglas MacArthur, who spoke on the deck of the battleship *Missouri* at the close of World War II:

> We have had our last chance. If we will not devise some greater and more equitable system, ARMAGEDDON will be at the door.

Asserting that the problem is basically spiritual, MacArthur insisted, "It must be the spirit if we are to save the flesh." His words agree with those of Albert Schweitzer, this century's most famous missionary. Wondering what the human race will do with the power modern science has placed in our hands, Schweitzer concludes that "our only hope is that the Spirit of God will strive with the spirit of the world and will prevail."[30]

That keen observer of human foibles, George Bernard Shaw, who does not write from a traditionally religious perspective, nonetheless has the devil say in *Man and Superman:*

> And is Man any the less destroying himself for all this boasted brain of his? Have you walked up and down upon the earth lately? I have; and I have examined Man's wonderful inventions. And I tell you that in the arts of life man invents nothing; but in the arts of death he outdoes Nature herself, and produces by chemistry and machinery all the slaughter of plague, pestilence, and famine.

---

[30]Charles R. Joy, ed., *Albert Schweitzer: An Anthology,* (Boston: Beacon Press, 1947), pp. 301, 302.

But, the devil so correctly observes, "In the arts of peace Man is a bungler."[31]

So far, even Christianity has not fulfilled its potential as the unifying agency of the world. Harry Emerson Fosdick, noting how successfully we have blended Christ and warfare, quotes a missionary who was told by a national in an underdeveloped country, "You must know that the educated people of this country look upon Christianity as a warring, blood-spilling religion."[32]

The fault lies with us, however, and not with God's purpose. He wants unity. He sent His Son to bring together the warring elements of mankind (indeed, of the whole universe—Romans 8:22). He will bring harmony to all reality through the love and blood and ultimate rule of Christ (1 Corinthians 15:24-28; Philippians 2:10, 11).

When the United Nations was founded in San Francisco in June, 1945, the founders were clear concerning its purpose, as they expressed it in the charter: "To save succeeding generations from the scourge of war." In the next four decades, the world saw over one hundred armed conflicts, including more than three dozen major wars, and the deaths of over ten million people. The UN's plan obviously isn't working.

Before the United Nations, there was the League of Nations. That League initiated the signing of 4,568 peace treaties between 1920 and 1939, the year World War II broke out. Of this number, 211 of the treaties were signed in the eleven months just before the start of World War II.[33] How valuable, do you suppose, are international treaties in the cause of peace?

If there is going to be peace on earth, it must be brought from above. Paul will develop this thesis in detail in the second chapter. God has set into motion His plan for peace through Jesus Christ, who can tear down the walls that divide peoples and create new persons in Him (Ephesians 2:14-17). Herman Melville wrote more than a century ago that "all wars are boyish." What is needed for

---

[31]George Bernard Shaw, *Man and Superman,* Act III.

[32]Henry Emerson Fosdick, *The Modern Use of the Bible* (New York: Macmillan, 1942), pp. 204, 205.

[33]Fulton J. Sheen, *Life Is Worth Living* (New York: McGraw-Hill, 1953), p. 12.

peace, then, is that the playground games of little boys give way to the serious business of mature men and women.

As we shall see in our study of Ephesians, God's revealed secret has a profound impact on the church. As the body of Christ, the church's mission on earth is to carry out the unifying purpose that God started in the ministry of Christ. That is why every local congregation must take its purpose so seriously. Churches don't exist to attract attention to themselves as fine institutions or pleasurable social organizations. They are God's continuing agents of reconciliation and peace on earth (2 Corinthians 5:18, 19; Romans 5:10; Ephesians 2:15-18; Colossians 1:20-22).

It is for this reason that preachers tremble as they approach their pulpits. They are not delivering speeches; they are announcing the terms of peace on earth. They are God's change agents. They are essential instruments in God's plan to bring unity to divided humanity.

What can be said of preachers must be said of all Christians. Every part of the body contributes to the work of the whole (1 Corinthians 12; Romans 12; Ephesians 4), and the work of the whole is to participate in fulfilling God's purpose on earth.

When men and women come to Christ, they come to each other. The real key to peace on earth, then, can never be found in church mergers or denominational loyalties or international conferences, but in losing our individual self-importance in submission to the One in whom God has placed the hope for all history. Where Christ rules supreme, there can be no petty individualism, no bitter partyism, no hateful racism, no social injustice, no numbing comfortableness. There will be mutual acceptance, common helpfulness, and humble submission to one another in unity and love.

The business of the church is therefore the most important activity in the world. It is God's business.

CHAPTER SEVENTEEN

What God Can Do for You

Ephesians 1:15-23

"And *you* also were included in Christ . . ." (Ephesians 1:13). With these words, Paul subtly shifts attention from what God has done for "us" to what He has done and can do for "you." He is moving from praise for God's blessings to prayer on behalf of his readers. The shift from "us" to "you" indicates more than the natural distinction between writer and reader; it reflects the typical Jewish division of all humanity into two categories: Jews (the people of God) and Gentiles (everybody else). Paul, a Jewish Christian, is writing to Gentile Christians. His letter reflects his continuing amazement that God now intends for "you" non-Jews to belong to His people along with "us."

This is "the mystery" that God revealed to Paul. (See Ephesians 1:9, 10.) Ephesians 1:15-23 and all of Ephesians 2 explain the magnitude of God's incredible unifying work in Jesus: Gentiles who once had no hope at all are now as eligible for membership in the family of God as Jews. Who would have believed it? That is, what orthodox Jew would have? God's amazing purpose is being realized in "you Gentiles"!

Paul's intercessory prayer begins with thanks for the reports of his readers' *faith* and *love* that have reached him. He has "not stopped giving thanks" for them (Ephesians 1:15), because they exhibit these basics of true Christianity.

They have *faith*. It's a specific faith. (The Bible never applauds faith in faith, the kind so popular in modern folk theology— "Pray to whatever god you believe in.") Their faith is in the Lord Jesus. They do not believe in belief, but in Christ. For them, the church is not just another religious or social organization, but a congregation of persons who have received Jesus as the Christ, the Son of the living God. He is their Lord.

151

But they have not stopped with faith. Jesus has warned that not everyone who says "Lord, Lord" will enter the kingdom of Heaven, "but only he who does the will of my Father who is in heaven" (Matthew 7:21). Another essential is needed—and these Christians exhibit it. They have added to their faith *love*. They do not practice the religion Jonathan Swift decried: "We have just enough religion to make us hate, but not enough to make us love, one another."

When they pray, "Lord, increase our faith" (Luke 17:5), they do so knowing that growth in faith leads as naturally to growth in love as enriching the soil leads to larger harvests.

They love *"all"* the saints" (Ephesians 1:15), commendable and not altogether commonplace behavior. We can all love some of our fellow Christians—we may even love most of them—but it takes real virtue to love all the saints! No wonder Paul gives thanks for them.

Having acknowledged their faith and love, Paul prays that God will give them the "Spirit of wisdom and revelation, so that you may know him better" (Ephesians 1:17). He wishes all Christians to combine faith and love with knowledge and wisdom, especially that knowledge of God that leads to wise action. His prayer is as timely today as it was for first-century believers.

We know why he prays this prayer. Knowledge and wisdom are not possessions everybody enjoys. They are not even attributes everybody desires. Ask people what they want in life, and they will tell you happiness or pleasure or wealth or success. Who, besides some rare latter-day Solomon (see 1 Kings 3:9), desires to be wise above anything else?

True love is often praised, seldom practiced; true faith suffers the same neglect. Even national leaders exhort their fellow citizens to adhere to their faith, without bothering to ask in what or in whom that faith consists. Because of this time-honored praise of love and faith without content, Paul prays that God will reveal himself to us, so that our knowing Him better will lead us to act more wisely. Then we will see that the Bible never praises love in itself; it commends love *for* God and neighbor. Nor does the Bible praise faith alone; it teaches faith *in* God and faith *in* the Lord Jesus Christ.

So Paul prays for knowledge and wisdom to complement faith and love. Even though, as Arnold Toynbee has reminded us, "thinking is as unnatural and arduous an activity for human beings as walking on two legs is for monkeys," a *thoughtful* faith and an *intelligent* love are the marks of a wise, mature Christian.

There is a refreshing candor in Paul's prayer, isn't there, especially for today's reader? Our age has so praised open-mindedness and tolerance and so berated narrow-mindedness and any sign of religious conviction that it is downright inspiring to hear from somebody who believes something. Not somebody who pretends to believe something, or who enjoys posturing as a highly principled individualist, but somebody whose quiet strength and immovable virtue betray an inner iron will born of genuine faith. Too much open-mindedness is something to fear. G. K. Chesterton described H. G. Wells as a man who "reacted too swiftly to everything"; he called Wells a "permanent reactionary."

> I think he thought that the object of opening the mind is simply opening the mind. Whereas I am incurably convinced that the object of opening the mind, as of opening the mouth, is to shut it again on something solid.[34]

It is that "something solid" that Paul prays God to give his readers. He wants "the eyes of your heart . . . enlightened in order that you may *know*" the abundant blessings God has in store for you (Ephesians 1:18). Paul's prayer is not for revealed knowledge alone. He knows with Alfred North Whitehead that "a merely well informed man is the most useless bore on God's earth." He prays for wisdom, which involves both head and heart. He wants us to *see,* so that we will *feel,* so that we will *do.* Add to your knowledge compassion and to your compassion, action! When the eyes of your mind and the eyes of your heart are enlightened, then your love will be intelligent—and busy.

In the Bible, the heart is more than the center of one's understanding. All of one's personality—intelligence, moral judgment, emotions—emerges from the heart. When this vital organ is "enlightened," then, one's entire being sees as it has never seen before. (For additional insight into "enlightenment," see Isaiah 9:2; 35:5; 42:6, 7; 60:1-3, 19; Matthew 4:16; John 1:9; Ephesians 5:8.)

---

[34]G. K. Chesterton, *Autobiography* (London: Hutchinson, 1937), pp. 223, 224.

153

With enlightenment you will surely know three things: your hope, your wealth, and your power. All these are yours in Christ Jesus.

Your Hope

You will know "the hope to which he has called you" (Ephesians 1:18). In the second chapter, Paul will remind us Gentile Christians that we were at one time "separate from Christ, excluded from citizenship in Israel and foreigners to the covenants of the promise, *without hope* and without God in the world" (Ephesians 2:12). And now we do have hope, an eternity of hope, with God. Paul wants every Christian to be hopeful.

Such hope makes all the difference in the way we live. When we are tempted to become discouraged, hope keeps us going. When we are stricken with heartache or bereavement or illness, hope won't let us give up.

This is true for the Christian even though his whole culture may be in mourning. If you would like to become really depressed, spend some time reading the major literary works of the twentieth century. The dominant tone, you will discover, is one of hopelessness. Despair has been the popular mood of modern writers. The brief flirtation with the Death-of-God theology in the 1960s is but one symptom of the general depression of our era. Godless people are hopeless people. They can always find immediate cause for anguish, whether it be threat of nuclear holocaust, rapid devouring of natural resources, rise of crime and violence, poisoned air and water, or whatever the latest popular alarm.

In spite of everything, a God-fearing people has hope. The triumphant ring of hope resounds in the Bible. In the church, it is true, we have our share of heartache. We are not strangers to death or illness or devastating accident. Some of our families suffer beyond the imagination of most persons. But you wouldn't know it to talk to them. They are not defeated personalities. They laugh, they tease, they care, they shine. They know *in* whom they believe and their faith gives them hope that tomorrow will be a better day, and the day after tomorrow will be bright beyond any light on this earth. They *know* the hope to which God has called them.

Vincent Donovan learned about the meaning of hope during his years of pathfinding missionary service among the nomadic Masai people of East Africa. Victims of the worst cruelty that Arab slave traders and their European backers could inflict on the tribe, this proud people gave a name to the last stop on the mainland that captured slaves made before leaving their continent for slavery abroad. They called it *Bagamoyo,* which comes from two words: *bwaga,* which means "to throw or put down," and *moyo,* "heart." The Arab raiders went far inland to capture their human prey, then drove them to the coast toward Zanzibar. From Bagamoyo they sailed. In Bagamoyo, they "put down their hearts," giving up any hope of freedom.

What it must be like to live without hope! Donovan was quick to discover that the Masai language includes no future tense. Masais expect tomorrow to be like today; they will resist anything different, being afraid of any change. People without hope hang tenaciously on to what they already know, preferring the misery they are acquainted with to misery they haven't already experienced. Of one thing they are sure: things will not get better. As a result, Donovan notes, the Masai is practically the only tribe in Tanzania that has been exposed to every kind of change and successfully resisted it. "European clothes, houses, Western education and agriculture have very little value in their eyes."[35]

What a change came into the hearts of the Masai families that let the Lord pick up their burdens! Like the first recipients of the Ephesians letter, they now have *hope.*

Your Wealth

They also know "the *riches* of his glorious inheritance in the saints" (Ephesians 1:18). Christians—even non-Jewish Christians, remember—are going to inherit all God's wealth! As Israel received God's promise of an inheritance on earth, so the new Israel receives an inheritance beyond the confines of this earth.

When you learn you are going to inherit an incredible fortune, you don't act the same. Have you known any young people who knew that when they reached twenty-one or twenty-five they would inherit a large legacy? What a difference that knowledge made in them! Their attitudes toward school, toward people, and toward the future were controlled by that promised inheritance.

---

[35]Vincent J. Donovan, *Christianity Rediscovered* (Maryknoll: Orbis Books, 1978), pp. 4-20.

Their inheritance, however, is nothing compared with ours. The day is coming when we shall inherit everything that is written in the Divine Will for us. Actually, we are already receiving some of it—love, forgiveness, fellowship, the power of the Holy Spirit, a sense of purpose and meaning. But more, much more, is coming. We can count on it, because

> [Our] Father is rich, in houses and lands,
> He holdeth the wealth of the world in his hands. . . .[36]

We are children of a King. What a difference this fact makes!

When Oscar Wilde, not the most democratic of authors, once met an individual with whom he was not overly impressed, he adjusted his monacle, sniffed, and inquired in his most arrogant manner, "Are you anyone in particular?"

No one can get away with that haughtiness toward a Christian. Of course, I'm someone in particular. I'm a child of the King.

French symphony conductor Pierre Monteaux and his wife (and French poodle) were looking for a motel one evening. They drove up to a group of cabins and spoke to a woman standing at the office door. "Sorry," she said curtly, "I have nothing."

A young girl was standing nearby. She whispered to the woman, whose facial expression changed as soon as she learned who these strangers were. Turning back to them, she made a sort of curtsy and said, "Excuse me, sir, I did not know that you were Someone. I think that I can accommodate you."

Monteaux' face became cold and withdrawn. He bowed formally and said, "Madame, everyone is Someone. Au revoir."[37] And with that formal goodbye he drove off.

Paul is writing to Gentile Christians who, up until now have been—at least in the eyes of Paul's race—no one. But in Christ Jesus each has become Someone. A child of a wealthy King.

Your Power

The third item for which Paul prays is that his readers will know God's "incomparably great *power* for us who believe"

---

[36]Harriett E. Buell, "A Child of the King."

[37]*Reader's Digest,* December 1962.

(Ephesians 1:19). It is the same unstoppable power that raised Jesus from the grave and placed Him at the pinnacle of the universe. Paul employs four Greek terms to express the inexpressible magnitude of God's strength in contrast to anything earth can offer. It is *dynamis* (inherent capability), *energeia* (operational or effective power), *kratos* (controlling or resisting strength), and *ischys* (bodily or muscular force). The terms overlap each other, and the definitions should not be pushed. Paul is stressing God's power added to His strength on top of His might multiplied by His energy. All that force, which was able to snatch Christ from the grave and install Him above any other authority in the universe (see Psalm 110:1; Philippians 2:9-11), He makes available to us if we believe.

We, then, who once were spineless nobodies, He makes into powerful somebodies. We who could do nothing to change the course of this world, can now move mountains and do even greater things than Jesus himself did (Matthew 21:21, 22; John 14:12, 13; 15:7).

All this is possible because we are "in Christ." Since we are His body (Ephesians 1:23), what God does in Him, He does in us, the church. "In Christ," we are not subordinate to any, just as no "rule" *(arche),* "authority" *(exousia),* "power" *(dynamis),* or "dominion" *(kyriotes)* can supersede the Lord's anointed (Ephesians 1:21). Note Paul's piling up of nouns again, so that we have no doubt about Christ's exalted position. (He is probably using words that reflect the various degrees of angels in the Jewish heavenly hierarchy, but with Christ's elevation such gradations of power become irrelevant. Only His authority matters now.) In Psalm 8, the "son of man" is recognized as "a little lower than the heavenly beings"; in Ephesians, the perfect Son of Man is acknowledged as above all other claimants to authority. God's complete, perfect, ideal Man now has universal dominion.

He who is head of everything else is of course Head of the church as well. Within the church, thanks to the power of God at work here, we are free from the tyranny of men, of traditions, of heredity, of society, of environment, of principalities and powers—of everything. We have no excuse, then, for our feebleness, our sinfulness, or our failure. God has placed His power at our disposal, if we are in Christ.

When we are in Christ, we share the ruling power.
We triumph in the name of the Conqueror.
We are His body. (See Ephesians 4:4, 12, 16; 5:30.)
Let all Christians know—
  the hope that is yours,
  the riches that are yours, and
  the power that works through you.
You have become Somebody!

CHAPTER EIGHTEEN

From Death to Life

Ephesians 2:1-10

Nine months before he died, the famous English poet Samuel Taylor Coleridge finished writing the epitaph for his gravestone. Probably no other poet in our history had greater genius and yet accomplished less by his own standards than "S. T. C." His disappointment in himself is reflected in this epitaph:

> Stop, Christian Passer-by!—Stop, child of God,
> And read with gentle breast. Beneath this sod
> A poet lies, or that which once seem'd he.—
> Lift one thought in prayer for S. T. C.;
> That he who many a year with toil of breath
> Found death in life, may here find life in death!
> Mercy for praise—to be forgiven for fame,
> He ask'd, and hoped, through Christ. Do thou the same!

For years, Coleridge battled his addiction to opium. He finally became too irresponsible to care for his wife and children and drugged himself into such insensibility that his poetic powers were silenced. He never realized his great potential. If it hadn't been for the kind offices of a gentle physician, Coleridge would have succumbed much earlier, a victim of his drug habit. He had discovered and experienced death in life; fortunately, someone cared enough for him to rescue him from his living death. In the latter years of Coleridge's life, as he fought his way back to sobriety and responsibility, he devoted himself to exploring the meaning of Christian faith. In this century, his theological works command as much respect as his poetry.

When the apostle Paul writes, "For we are God's workmanship" (Ephesians 2:10), he uses the Greek word from which we get our English *poem.* We are God's poetry. The Divine Poet has

159

made of us something beautiful. Coleridge was also a poet, but of less than divine ability. The product of his creativity was a ruined life. His only hope, he realized almost too late, was to throw himself on the mercy of God, whose poetry surpasses his own as far as His grace surpasses the "cravings of our sinful nature" (Ephesians 2:3).

The re-created poet could fully appreciate the praise of the apostle:

> As for you, you were dead in your transgressions and sins, in which you used to live when you followed the ways of this world and of the ruler of the kingdom of the air, the spirit who is now at work in those who are disobedient (Ephesians 2:1, 2).

Paul is writing to people who had been dead and hadn't known it. They lived (*periepatesate*, "walked around") like everybody else in their culture, not realizing they were breathing poisonous fumes exhaled by an evil monarch. Like the opium that at first seemed to solve all Coleridge's problems and gratify the urges of his body, the "spirit who is now at work in those who are disobedient" comes disguised as friend, insinuating his way into control until his helpless victim cannot recover himself. Walking along the wide road that leads to destruction (Matthew 7:13), conforming to and comfortable with the rest of the living dead, the victim still seems quite alive. He would reject Paul's harsh indictment.

Yet transgressions (*paraptomata,* lapses, slips, falls) and sins (*hamartia,* shortcomings) are the inevitable consequences of a life whose activities are dictated by "the flesh" (human nature run amuck—separated from the guiding hand of God, who elevates mere flesh and blood to what He had in mind for humanity when He created us.) Since "flesh" is created, it is temporal, uncertain, and destined to die. Without the life-sustaining support and essential guidance of the divine Spirit, the flesh by itself is subject to decay in body and morality. Human beings, mere flesh without the Spirit, thus "naturally" deserve God's wrath. The surprise to Paul is that instead of reacting to our sins and transgressions in the anticipated manner, God, "who is rich in mercy," chose to make us "alive with Christ even when we were dead in transgressions" (Ephesians 2:4, 5).

Paul pictures both Jews and Gentiles alike, if they are without God, as dead. But they are undoubtedly ignorant of the fact.

They are like a woman who, only recently retired from a brilliant career as a personal secretary, was frightened that her health was deteriorating so quickly. Suffering severe migraine headaches, terrible fits of depression, and fainting spells, she found no relief in anything her series of doctors could prescribe. They concluded there was nothing physically wrong with her. Finally, her doctor, unable to help her, sent her to her minister.

After several appointments with her minister, the truth emerged. Her symptoms had their source in an affair she had thirty-five years earlier. The man was the manager of her company, a husband and father of two children. The liaison went on for six years and was never discovered. They got away with it, they thought. But a third of a century later, in the quiet of her retirement, from out of the depths of her conscience crawled the consequences of her indulgence. For thirty-five years, she had hidden an ulcer of guilt that she would let no one see, even herself. Now her body was feeling the punishment.[38]

What makes her situation intriguing is its commonplace nature. She could easily have said, "Why, all that's in the past. Nobody was hurt. Why do you bring it up now?" Or she could have taken a slightly different tack: "We didn't do anything so terrible. After all, that's the way things are in our modern world." She could have referred to the statistics that frequently appear in popular magazines to prove that most American men and women are unfaithful. Extra-marital affairs are the order of the day.

Or she could have said, "Well, you know, I was very lonely and he was unhappily married. His wife didn't understand him. I could help him. We just brought each other some moments of happiness." You might listen quite sympathetically, but your sympathy would not ease the headaches, dispel the depression, or stop her fainting spells. The fact is, she had followed the course of this world and, like Coleridge, had been almost fatally wounded. "Do not be deceived," the Bible says, "God cannot be mocked. A man reaps what he sows. The one who sows to please his sinful nature, from that nature will reap destruction" (Galatians 6:7, 8).

"The ruler of the kingdom of the air, the spirit who is now at work in those who are disobedient" encourages us (*all* of us—

---

[38]John Sutherland Bonnell, *No Escape from Life* (New York: Harper and Brothers, 1958), pp. 70, 71.

Jews and Gentiles alike) to gratify "the cravings of our sinful nature" and follow "its desires and thoughts." You don't have to subscribe to the doctrine of man's total depravity to feel the gravity of this verse. We are not only *subject* to our own almost overwhelming lusts, but we are also *subjects* of a demonic monarch whose orders we are powerless to resist—without the help of God. It is easier to follow him than to fight him, so we follow. To our everlasting sorrow.

Simply following the course of this world—simply doing what comes naturally—simply doing what everybody else is doing— leads to death. You may already know about Claude Eatherly. He was one of the World War II pilots who dropped the first atomic bombs on Hiroshima and Nagasaki. He came back from war a changed man. He had become sullen, morose, withdrawn. His friends hardly recognized the miserable man. Upon his retirement from service in 1947, he refused to accept a pension from the government. He tried to send his medals back to Washington, but his friends prevented him. He felt so guilty he could not sleep nights. He would wake with a start, crying out for the burning children whose death he had delivered. He apologized to the mayor of Hiroshima for his actions. He sent money to care for the children that he orphaned. He confessed to the council of the city that it was he who had given the go-ahead order. He became a drifter, a drinker, a bum. He abandoned himself to liquor and cards, drifting from job to job, always seeking an escape from his overpowering sense of guilt. The United States government, instead of punishing him for what he did, praised him and tried to make a war hero out of him. But whenever Hiroshima and Nagasaki were mentioned in a conversation, he would blush, his face working with emotion, and walk away. He couldn't stand his guilt.

Since no one wanted to punish him for what he *had* done, he vowed to force someone to punish him for what he *would* do. He began committing crimes, hoping to be caught. He was, only to be convicted, sentenced—and released, either to freedom or an insane asylum. Then he suffered the worst indignity of all: Hollywood offered him $100,000 to make a film of his life.[39]

---

[39]Karl Menninger, *Whatever Became of Sin?* (New York: Hawthorn Books, Inc., 1973), p. 106.

Eatherly could have protested, "But I was only following orders. It is a terrible thing to bomb a city, but it wasn't my fault. I was just following the course of this world." His protest would be correct, of course. But even if we agreed with him, we could not have given him peace of mind; we could not have brought him back from the living dead—because membership in their number is the inevitable result of following the course of this world. And no one but God can wrench us away from the clutches of this world's prince.

Paul understands this. He realizes from personal experience that we are not so much punished for our sins as we are punished by them. The apostle confesses his own guilt: "All of us also lived among them at one time . . ." (Ephesians 2:3). "I know what you were like," he writes, "because I was the same as you."

What's wrong with living like everybody else? Look up—look up as high on the human achievement scale as you want, to the highest realms of government and power. What do you find? You discover corruption and graft and fraud and deceit and lying and treachery, don't you? Then look down, clear to the bottom. There you uncover cheating and stealing and lying and raping and murdering. Where, then, is virtue among mankind? Beware of following the ruler of this world; he presides over the hosts of the living dead.

But you Christians, you are different. "But because of his great love for us, God, who is rich in mercy, made us alive with Christ even when we were dead in transgressions" (Ephesians 2:4, 5). Man may have rejected God for Satan, but God graciously refuses to reject us. Listen to Christians boast. It is never of our pasts, for we were among the human lost. It is never of our personal worth, because we have too keen a sense of our own sinfulness. Yet we are a boastful bunch! We are proud of the fact that God loved us "when we were dead in transgressions." The glory is His, not ours. The difference is not that we were born better than other people. It certainly is not that we have behaved better than others. What distinguishes us is that God has made us alive and given us hope.

It's all a matter of His grace.

Claude Eatherly was not the only pilot who dropped atomic bombs. A few years ago, I heard another of the pilots speak in Portland, Oregon. Addressing a group of Christian men, he told of the horrible feelings he had had to live with. He followed his orders; he dropped the bombs that had wiped out innocent lives. Then he nearly went mad with guilt. He couldn't stand himself any more. The man was speaking in a church building, because when he became fully aware of what he had done, he turned to the only possible source of relief: he asked God for forgiveness and became a part of God's church. He poured out the blackness in his soul and God forgave him and offered him a new beginning.

When I heard him speak, he was a leader in his church. His assigned topic for the evening was the stewardship of his money. He contrasted the life-destroying mission he flew with the chance that God had now given him to spend the rest of his days bringing life to others. He was not defeated; he had not become a drifter. His life was filled with meaning and joy. He was aware of his past, of course, and he hated it. But he was equally aware of what God had given him now and would given him in the future. God had made him fully, completely, joyfully alive. In appreciation, he dedicated the rest of his life to giving others an opportunity to live as well.

It is by God's grace that new life comes to us. "It is by grace you have been saved" (Ephesians 2:5, 8). No one can earn this second chance. No one has the power to persuade the prince of this world to let go. It takes divine intervention to set us free, and in Christ, God has broken Satan's hold on us.

Further, by His grace, we have been incorporated into Christ's body, so that the victory Jesus enjoys at the right hand of God over all other authorities and powers, we enjoy with Him. We are "with Christ" and "in Christ." Even more, we have become God's showpieces, His poems, His workmanship. God intends to show off, using us as exhibits to demonstrate how far His immeasurable grace will extend. Only a God supremely wealthy in grace, only a God whose graciousness exceeds our imagination, would be willing to lavish it (Ephesians 1:7, 8) on the likes of us. Yet that is exactly what He has done.

We have a piece of furniture at our house that has always been the favorite object of conversation with our guests. It's a redwood burl coffee table. My wife's father made it and gave it to us very early in our marriage. Whenever we have moved, we have left behind much of our furniture—but not the coffee table. It will be with us as long as we live. Mr. Whitney found it one day when he and Mrs. Whitney were beachcombing on the northern California coast. As they wound their way among the piles upon piles of driftwood, he spotted the remains of a redwood trunk; on one side there was a large diseased growth, this burl. I'm certain thousands of other beachcombers had also seen it, but it meant nothing to them. But when Mr. Whitney saw the dead, diseased wood, he returned with his chain-saw and sliced off several pieces. One of those slices became our coffee table, an example of beautiful workmanship. A skilled craftsman created an object of beauty and life out of some diseased driftwood. He saw possibilities where others had found only worthless refuse.

So did God. The result is that "we are God's workmanship."

Thus we will do "good works, which God prepared in advance for us to do" (Ephesians 2:9, 10; 4:11, 12). These works are not the means to our salvation, since salvation comes through grace and not works (Romans 3:20, 28; 4:1-5; Galatians 2:16; 2 Timothy 1:9, Titus 3:5; Ephesians 1:7), but an expression of appreciation for His grace and of our faith in Him (James 2:14-18).

CHAPTER NINETEEN

Do Good Fences Make Good Neighbors?

Ephesians 2:11-22

Robert Frost's "Mending Wall" is one of my favorite poems. It's about an annual spring ritual along the stone fences in New England. In the poem, two neighboring farmers meet, as they have for years, to gather the stones that have been knocked off the wall during the winter and put them back where they belong. Every spring, they restore the fence to its function as a barrier between their two properties. It's a meaningless ritual, since one farmer has pine trees on his land and the other grows apples; there has never been any danger that the pine trees would devour the apples. But because a tradition is at stake, the neighbors must be faithful to their annual rite of repairing the useless fence.

Frost emphasizes two sets of attitudes. The poem opens with one of them: "Something there is that doesn't love a wall...."

Later the thought is repeated:

"Something there is that doesn't love a wall,
That wants it down."

Otherwise why would the farmers have to put the fence back in place every year? Something has knocked it down; something wants the stone wall destroyed.

Another attitude opposes the first: "Good fences make good neighbors." One of the farmers likes it so well, this saying of his father, that he repeats it:

"Good fences make good neighbors."

Do they? Not long ago, a friend of mine built a fence. He and his neighbor decided that they would enhance their properties and enjoy more privacy by erecting a wooden fence between them.

They constructed a substantial redwood dividing wall to help them be better neighbors. They purchased the lumber at a discount and worked hard together to put it up. The project went smoothly until my friend decided he wanted to extend the fence fifteen feet beyond what the other neighbor wanted. That created a problem. His neighbor complained, "If you're going to add that much more fence, you can pay for it yourself!"

The problem intensified when my friend painted his side of the fence and a little bit of his color ran onto his neighbor's side. So they aren't speaking. Good fences don't always make good neighbors.

Why have we become so convinced that fences are essential? When we move into a different house, the first thing we do is stake out the boundaries. Then we plant a hedge or build a fence so no one will doubt what belongs to us. Is it some inherent territorial imperative that drives us, or are we really convinced that good fences make good neighbors?

This passage is about fences that have failed. The first words imply an ancient hostility: "Therefore, remember that formerly you who are Gentiles by birth . . ." (Ephesians 2:11). That "you" is the clue that something is wrong. We have already noted that the Jewish people generally separated all persons into two broad categories, "us" and "you." The Jews viewed themselves as the chosen nation of God; they saw everybody else as Gentiles, "the rest." Between these two categories they erected a dividing wall, with everybody who belonged to God on one side, "the rest" on the other. They kept the wall in good repair through their proper observance of rituals like circumcision.

The Gentiles were called "uncircumcised" (*akrobustia,* "foreskin") "by those who call[ed] themselves 'the circumcision' (that done in the body by the hands of men)" (Ephesians 2:11). Cutting off the foreskin of Jewish males was the unmistakable evidence that they were members of the people of God. All others were inferior. Paul recalls the former condition of the Gentile Christians to whom he is writing: "Remember that at that time you were separate from Christ, excluded from citizenship in Israel and foreigners to the covenants of the promise [see Genesis 17:1-14; 26:24; 28:13-15; Exodus 24:1-11], without hope [1 Thessalonians 4:13] without God in the world" (Ephesians 2:12). They had gods, of course, but not God. (See Galatians 4:3; 1 Corinthians 10:20; Isaiah 44:9-20.) They were like Greeks and

Romans, who had many gods but no anticipation of a better future. Their nations looked backward to a Golden Era.

As far as God-fearing Jews were concerned, the fence between Jews and Gentiles was impenetrable. How could the people of God have anything to do with godless Gentiles?

It was customary for Jews to grade all mankind. The two great categories of *Jews* and *Gentiles* could be subdivided into four:

(1) *Jews,* the Chosen Ones.

(2) *Proselytes,* believers in God who had converted to Judaism.

(3) *God-fearers,* non-Jews who had not yet converted to Judaism but who believed in the one true God.

(4) *Gentiles.*

The divisions were obvious to the Jews. Unless you were racially and religiously a Jew, you were forever a second-class citizen. Even if you had converted to Judaism, when you went into the synagogue to pray, your words had to be, "O God of *your* fathers," because God could obviously not be the God of a Gentile's fathers. Even Jews who moved out of the sacred precincts of the holy land were considered second-class citizens, because they were unable to offer their sacrifices in the promised land. And, of course, these considerations were for men only; women and girls were inconsequential, a fact indicated by the role of "male" circumcision.

There were many fences separating those who were really righteous, really of God, from everybody else. They apparently did not make good neighbors.

The other attitude expressed in Frost's poem counters, "Something there is that doesn't love a wall, that wants it down." In Ephesians that something is Somebody, and His name is God. He abolished "the dividing wall of hostility" (Ephesians 2:14). When Christ's blood was shed on Calvary, God was making His supreme effort "to bring all things in heaven and on earth together under one head, even Christ" (Ephesians 1:10).

"Now in Christ Jesus you who once were far away have been brought near . . ." (Ephesians 2:13). *Far away* and *near* are Jewish expressions for the positions of Gentiles and Jews in relation to Jerusalem, hence in relation to God. Only Israel was "near" God. Christ's blood, shed for all mankind, wiped out the distance; even the categories of Jew and Gentile He drained of meaning, since He created "in himself one new man out of the two, thus making peace, and in this one body . . . reconcile[d] both of them to God

169

through the cross, by which he put to death their hostility" (Ephesians 2:15, 16). His message of peace was the same "to you who were far away [Gentiles] and ... to those who were near [Jews]" (Ephesians 2:17).

Paul never lets us forget that only Christ could deliver this peace. By His message, by His sacrifice, by His coming to all of us, He effected an end to the hostilities between man and God and between man and man. All who are in Him are one. For them there can no longer be a "dividing wall of hostility." The allusion here is to the wall that separated the court of the Gentiles from the temple proper in the Jerusalem temple. On that wall was a not very subtle sign warning that no foreigner could enter within the barricade surrounding the sanctuary and its enclosure except on pain of death. Although the temple remained standing until A.D. 70, when Roman forces demolished it, Paul believed it was effectively destroyed by Christ, who "is our peace" (Ephesians 2:14).

Jesus did away with the divisive "law with its commandments and regulations" (Ephesians 2:15). Not obedience to laws but transformation into new being is Christ's goal. The law is too complicated to be perfectly obeyed anyway (Romans 3:19-31; 7:7-12; 8:2-4; Galatians 3:1—4:7). The unity that is God's purpose (Ephesians 1:10) can never be realized legalistically. Only a change in men's hearts will do it, and only Christ can bring it about. And He has done it.

Christ broke down the wall between God and man. The twenty-seventh chapter of Matthew affirms that when Christ died upon the cross, the curtain in the temple was torn in two. Its place in the entry to the Holy of Holies shielded "God" from the presence of unholy humanity. When Christ expired, that curtain was ripped in two; God would no longer be perceived as residing in a particular place. The dwelling place of God would be with men. He would not be separated from any who sought access to Him through Jesus Christ. The wall is gone. (See John 3:16; 12:32; 2 Corinthians 5:19; 1 John 2:2.)

The key word is "access," prosagoges (Ephesians 2:18). In Oriental courts, a functionary served to lead persons into and out of the royal presence. Jesus has become the *prosagoges*. He is the Door and the Way (John 10:7, 9; 14:6). Further, He has revealed how eager the Father is to receive His children. This is the message of the parable of the prodigal son. After the ungrateful young man has squandered his inheritance in the far country, Jesus says he came to himself and decided to return to his home. Now what will he have to do in order to regain access to the father he has spurned? Recite some ritual, perform a sacrifice, obey some legal prescription? None of these. Jesus says he went back to his father who, with open arms, received him. The access was there all along, because of the father's love.

When Jesus broke down the walls of hostility, He gave us access in the Holy Spirit to the Father.

Christ also broke down the wall between Jews and Gentiles. This is the immediate social concern Paul addresses here. To be reconciled to God is also to become one with all of God's children. The One who is our peace with God (Isaiah 9:6f; 53:5; Haggai 2:9; Zechariah 9:10) is also our peace with nations.

Jesus speaks of Jews and Gentiles; we could as easily speak of our enemies. Whenever I visit England, a land I love more with each journey there, I cannot help remembering that at one time we Americans were bitterly shooting at the hated Redcoats. Yet now Americans can travel all over the islands as friends of the English, for our dividing wall of hostility has been leveled. We are at peace.

When our family lived in Tennessee, we visited many of the southern Civil War sites. We recalled that at one time no Yankee would dare venture into southern territory, for there was a dividing wall of hostility that must not be crossed. Yet we traveled without fear.

In Europe, you can visit the famous "Nuts" Museum in Bastoigne, Belgium. You will see memorabilia from the Battle of the Bulge, including handwritten notes on the walls, placed there by grateful Europeans thanking Americans for freeing them from Nazi tyranny. You can leave there and drive on into West Germany, because the dividing wall between Belgians and West Germans is gone. (Tragically, Communists have erected yet another one, as men who resist the peacemaking efforts of Christ have always done.)

Paul's gratitude is that a very specific dividing wall has melted away in the dissolving blood of Jesus. The categories "Jew" and "Gentile" no longer exist in Christ, because "Something there is that doesn't love a wall, that wants it down."

God has also torn down the wall of hostility between Christians and non-Christians. That doesn't mean Christians cannot be distinguished from those who do not follow Christ, but that as the Jews no longer have a right to boast that they alone are the children of God, neither can Christians give way to self-righteousness because we now are His children. For God desires an end to all hostilities; His children cannot brag about their elevated status—they are too busy doing their work as servants. To make the gospel available to everyone, Christians have to go everywhere in love.

In Christ, salvation and access to God are available to all people who believe and obey. God is no respecter of persons, as Peter learned in his encounter with Cornelius (Acts 10 and 11) and the Jerusalem church was forced to conclude through the ministry of the apostle Paul (Acts 15).

Every few years, the United States receives another wave of immigrants—from Cuba, Haiti, Vietnam, Cambodia, Mexico in recent years, and earlier in our history from England, Europe, Ireland, and Asia. In a sense, America is a nation of refugees, many of whom came to escape the tyranny of hostile governments and repressive religions. A refugee nation. Yet within a few generations, the refugees become indistinguishable from those whose lineage traces a longer period of residence here. Give us a little time together, and we are "no longer foreigners and aliens, but fellow citizens" (Ephesians 2:19) in the nation's household. If someone were to pass a law saying that all refugee families would have to return to the land of their ancestors, we would almost all have to leave, for we're either refugees or sons and daughters of refugees. But we are now fellow citizens, and our past is not held against us.

In the church, Christians are likewise refugees who have found safety. We have escaped into the loving fellowship of the body of Christ, thus finding refuge from the tyranny of sin. Having had no hope, we now have a future; having had no peace, we now relax in the strength of the Lord. And what has happened to us, God wants for everybody. We Christians have no right to boast and no permission to withdraw from non-Christians into self-righteousness. God wants all people on the same side of the fence!

He has also abolished the wall between races. Race distinction (as between Jew and Greek, for example) does not exist in the heart of Christ. Of course, differences in pigmentation and other superficial characteristics remain, and certain cultural accoutrements haven't been erased, but in the Lord these are of no significance. Essentially, before God, we are equal.

This equality was graphically demonstrated during the racially tense years of America's mid-century in a sit-in demonstration in Atlanta, Georgia. William Sloan Coffin, Jr., Yale University chaplain, recalls his part in it. Eighty-two black students had been jailed for participating in sit-ins. He went to visit them in the Fulton County Jail in Atlanta. While he was there, they asked their chaplain if they could have Communion. In the waiting room outside, Coffin noted, people drank their water out of fountains marked "White" or "Colored," but on the inside of the bars, people of both races drank the wine from a common cup. He writes,

> The wrongness of the one and the rightness of the other were quite overpowering. "This is my body, broken for you. This is my blood, shed for you." Somehow in that moment in the crowded cell all the sin and suffering of Atlanta, the South, the nation, and even the world seemed reconciled in the sure knowledge of a God who "so loved the world that he gave his only begotten son that whosoever should believe in him should not perish but have eternal life."[40]

God has broken down the wall between races. (See Acts 2:39, "The promise is for you and your children and for *all* who are far off".)

He broke down the walls between all persons, including men and women. Remember the Jew's prayer, "I thank Thee God, that Thou hast not made me a woman." Women were looked upon as property, but Galatians 3:28 asserts that in Christ "there is neither Jew nor Greek, slave nor free, male nor female, for you are all one in Christ Jesus." There is no second-class citizenship in the kingdom of God for male or female.

In a recent transcontinental flight, I learned firsthand about the difference between first and second classes. The first obvious

---

[40]William Sloan Coffin, Jr., "The Word," *Sermons to Intellectuals,* ed. Franklin H. Littell (New York: Macmillan, 1963), p. 8.

distinction is that the seats are bigger in first class. Perhaps that's because "first-class" passengers have always eaten better! I paid for a tourist seat, but a mother and her little children needed my seat, the flight attendant told me, so he asked me if I would mind taking a place in the first-class section. I was the only one there. I had the whole tray of *hors d'oeuvres* to myself as I sat in one of those great wide seats.

It was fun to be temporarily in first class. But it is spiritually dangerous to believe that God makes any such distinctions according to class or caste or race or sex. Christ has made it apparent once and for all that He recognizes no such dividing walls. He has made new creations of us all by the cross (Romans 5:10; 2 Corinthians 5:18-20; John 17:20-23; Colossians 1:22).

We are still "foreigners and aliens," but with a difference. Once God, the Word, the church, and the way of Christ were all distant from us. We were cut off from them. Now, thanks to Christ, we are inside. From our new position, "near to the heart of God," the world we left now seems hostile, confused, strange. As T. S. Eliot discovered, we are no longer at home here, "among an alien people clutching their gods,"[41] even though we used to be just like them. So Christians sing the chorus,

> This world is not my home,
> I'm just a passing through.
> My treasures are laid up,
> Somewhere beyond the blue.[42]

We live in a new dwelling, "God's household," which is "a holy temple in the Lord," "a dwelling in which God lives by His Spirit." (Remember that in the Old Testament, Jews believed that God resided in the tabernacle or temple. Now His home is in the lives of His gathered people.)

The apostles and prophets are the foundation of God's household, the church, because they stand for all time as the indispensable witnesses to who Christ was and what He did on earth.

---

[41]T. S. Eliot, "Journey of the Magi."

[42]Albert E. Brumley, "This World Is Not My Home."

174

Without them, we would not know Him. Thus we speak of the "apostolic church." Christ, of course, is the cornerstone, the One who holds the entire structure together (Psalm 118:22; Mark 12:1-11; 1 Peter 2:4-10).

"Something there is that doesn't love a wall, that wants it down." That something is Somebody, and His name is God, and His church is the means by which He continues to abolish the fences that separate Jews from Gentiles, Christians from non-Christians, race from race, and man from woman.

CHAPTER TWENTY

What God Is Doing Through Me

Ephesians 3:1-13

Because of the awesome work of Jesus in unifying Gentiles and Jews into a single household (Ephesians 2:19) or building ("temple"—Ephesians 2:20, 21) in which God himself dwells (Ephesians 2:22), Paul starts to offer a prayer of thanksgiving and petition—then abruptly digresses and does not return to the prayer until the fourteenth verse. He can't continue his prayer without becoming quite personal. Having stated what God has already done for him (and other Jewish Christians—Ephesians 1:3-14) and what He has done for the formerly alienated Gentile Christians (Ephesians 1:15--2:22), Paul wants to express what this means to him personally—and what God is right now doing through him. He offers his personal testimony.

We pay close attention, because what Paul says God is doing through him differs little from what he does through all Christians.

Note the self-assurance that permeates these verses. Having turned his life over to the Lord to be used as Christ sees fit, Paul experiences nothing of what we like to call our "identity crises." He knows both who he is and what is expected of him. He bears no resemblance to the little chameleon Carl Sandburg used to like to tell about, who got along just fine adjusting to his environment until he happened one day to cross a patch of Scotch plaid. Sandburg says he died at the crossroads, heroically trying to relate to everything at once.

The chameleon exemplifies modern life, doesn't he? Not knowing who we are, we try to adjust ourselves to fit the demands of the job, of the home and family, of the playground, of the church, or of our section of society, each time performing a different role to meet conflicting expectations. In the process, we tear ourselves apart.

Paul does not have this problem. He knows what has happened to him and who he is. It is interesting that the apostle, whose conversion changed his whole life and abruptly set him in pursuit of a new career, does not speak of any of the matters that would concern us in such a vocational change. He doesn't mention job security; there's not a word about benefits or retirement program, nor any hint of opportunities for advancement. Notice further that even though we acclaim him a great religious leader, in his description of what God is doing through him, he does not use the accepted religious titles of his day.

For example, he has no aspirations of being honored as a rabbi, an honored teacher. He is neither a priest like the Levites nor a prophet like Elijah or even John the Baptist. Although before becoming a Christian, he prided himself in being a Pharisee and the son of a Pharisee (Acts 23:6), he does not deign to mention his Jewish religious credentials here because they pale beside the significance of his new position in the Lord. Once in God, a person has little use for man-made or man-honored titles.

The apostle mentions or implies several titles that he now wears with pride. Thanks to the grace of God, he has become a *prisoner of Christ Jesus* (Ephesians 3:1), *an administrator of God's grace* (3:2), *one of the holy apostles* (3:6), *a servant of this gospel* (3:7), *a saint—one of ("the least of") God's people* (3:8), *a preacher to the Gentiles* (3:8), and *a sufferer* (3:13).

Nothing very religious about this list, at least as religion was defined by first-century Jewish believers. Yet through these titles, Paul expresses his joy in being used of God to convey the wonderful "mystery" of His purpose on earth (Ephesians 3:4-6, 10-12; see the following section).

We have already examined the meanings of *apostle* and *saint*. (See comments on Ephesians 1:1, 3-14, above.) Here we shall concentrate on Paul's work as *prisoner, administrator, servant, preacher,* and *sufferer.*

The Prisoner of Christ Jesus

We begin with *prisoner.* "For this reason I, Paul, the prisoner of Christ Jesus for the sake of you Gentiles ..." (Ephesians 3:1). Now here is a religious vocation for you! When Paul became a follower of Jesus, he voluntarily "turned himself in." He gave up his freedom. He made Jesus his Lord, thus becoming a slave.

178

Of course, Paul is literally in prison. He is probably writing this letter during his Roman imprisonment. Although he receives certain privileges in his confinement (for example, the right to live in his own dwelling under house arrest, and the right to receive visitors), he still is bound by chains to his Roman guard and confined to the premises. His incarceration does not matter to him, however, because when he became a Christian, he said, in effect, "I'll serve the Lord regardless; no matter where He wants me to go, no matter what He wants me to do, I'm His. As His prisoner, it does not matter which side of the bars I live on."

He had already learned to be content in any state (Philippians 4:11) and knew that God would bring good out of any circumstance (Romans 8:28), so he did not chafe at his confinement. We thank God for it, of course, since we would not have many of his letters without it. He used his prison terms to catch up on his correspondence. We are the beneficiaries of his suffering, God using this time for the sake of all succeeding generations of Christians.

Every Christian is a "prisoner of Christ Jesus," but that fact should concern us as little as it did Paul. Real freedom is a chimera, anyway. Most people are not aware of it, but they are prisoners of something, chained to habits, to harmful attitudes, to overbearing employers, to overweening ambition, to drives and lusts—and sometimes to literal chains clamped on by political or military enemies. The Christian's imprisonment differs from these, however, in its voluntary nature. We choose to give ourselves up to the Lord, since He alone chains us to himself in order to free us from everything and everyone else. His is the bondage that releases, the burden that lifts (Matthew 11:28-30).

An Administrator of God's Grace

Paul is an *administrator.* "Surely you have heard about the administration of God's grace ..." (Ephesians 3:2). The word is not a religious one. Sometimes translated "stewardship" or "dispensation," *oikonomian* was a common word referring to the administration of a household. The one in charge was called the administrator or steward; he was not the owner, of course, but the one who took care of affairs on behalf of the owner.

Paul's task is to be the manager of what God has given him. He is quite specific: He is in charge of "the mystery" God gave him for the sake of the Gentiles (Ephesians 3:3-6; see Acts 9:15;

Ephesians 1:9, 10; 3:9-12). This mystery is obviously not something he owns, even though he temporarily possesses it; God gave him this knowledge, as God gives us everything, for the sake of others.

As we read the New Testament, we are impressed by the fact that ownership of personal property, whether houses or lands or fishing boats, takes an insignificant place in the apostles' lives. Ownership was obviously unimportant to them. What a contrast between first-and twentieth-century Christians! Nothing means more to us than the houses we live in, unless perhaps it's the cars we park in from of them. We have centered our lives on our possessions, acting as if they were ours!

We do the same with our abilities. We pride ourselves in our athletic skills, our intellectual achievements, our musical talent, as if we alone are responsible for our having them and as if we possess them for our own sake. Yet if a Christian is a prisoner of Christ and an administrator of God's grace, then everything he has belongs to the Lord and is to be used on His behalf. We simply manage what has been temporarily entrusted to us.

Paul frequently returns to this theme in his writings. The most famous passages are these:

Ephesians 4:11-13. God has given gifts to the church in order to assist the members of the body to give themselves in service. God's gifts are people—apostles, prophets, evangelists, pastors and teachers.

1 Corinthians 12:1-31. The Holy Spirit gives different kinds of abilities to members of the body for the sake of the common good. These gifted people are thus gifts to the church, as the church is God's gift to the world. As the church is to be administered for the sake of the world God wants to save, so individual spiritual gifts are to be administered for the sake of the church, with every Christian making his contribution to the total ministry of the body.

Romans 12:4-8. Whatever "grace" God has given us, we should administer our gifts for the sake of our fellow members. Again, our abilities are "gifts" from God, not something we own. So we are administrators.

A Servant of This Gospel

Paul calls himself a *servant:* "I became a servant of this gospel by the gift of God's grace" (Ephesians 3:7). The Revised Standard

Version, following the King James, reads, "Of this gospel I was made a *minister*. ..." The New International Version does us a service in returning to the original meaning of the Greek *diakonos* here, since we have robbed *minister* of its service and turned it into a clerical office. *Diakonos* is variously translated "minister," "deacon," or "servant." We prefer the first two, but we should stick with the last, since the Lord intends to reverse the world's values. In daily life, we do all we can to climb the ladder of success. Each succeeding rung has a higher-sounding title. In the Lord's scale of values, however, the only way up is down (John 13:14-17; Mark 9:33-37). Service, not position, is honored.

How "the ministry" is misunderstood! One mother wrote to encourage her son to become a minister because, she said, "the work is easy, the social status good, and you don't really have to believe in God."[43] Paul would have been scandalized by her letter, not only because of her hypocrisy but also because she fails so completely to understand that ministry is servanthood. The church does not have only a handful of ministers that it ordains to do the work; every Christian is a servant (or a priest—1 Peter 2:5, 9), every servant a "minister." However we earn our living—tentmaking, banking, teaching, farming, truck driving, computer operating—our calling is to be ministers of the gospel.

A Preacher

Paul is a *preacher*. "This grace was given me: to preach to the Gentiles the unsearchable riches of Christ ..." (Ephesians 3:8). Again, the word in our English language, scrubbed holy by well-meaning religious types, has assumed a halo it shouldn't have. In the Greek of Paul and his contemporaries, a preacher was not a frocked man behind an elevated pulpit, handing down pious platitudes to an adoring audience of like-minded listeners. He was not even a religious man. He was an announcer, a herald; he had some news to deliver.

Paul's word here is *euangelisasthai*, which literally means "to announce good news." From it, we get the word *evangelism*, which is the proclaiming of good news to those who have not heard it before. Paul's commission is to take this good news to

---

[43] Quoted in John C. Wynn, *Pastoral Ministry to Families* (Philadelphia: Westminster, 1957), p. 182.

Gentiles, who have hitherto been excluded from the people of God but are now being invited in (Ephesians 2). What God has in store for the Gentiles is so great it cannot be described; the riches are "unsearchable," too vast to be measured. However, God's purpose in uniting Gentiles with Jews in Christ can now be made very plain, so the good news can be communicated to everybody.

Paul will transmit the message through the grace God has given him; we will do the same, using whatever talents and abilities ("gifts") God has made available in us.

A Sufferer

Paul's last title is *sufferer.* "I ask you, therefore, not to be discouraged because of my sufferings for you ..." (Ephesians 3:13). The man knows something about suffering—see 2 Corinthians 11:23-28). His message differs starkly from today's purveyors of easy religion. He has suffered and evidently accepts suffering as one of God's means of revealing himself and a cause for rejoicing in the Lord (2 Corinthians 4:7-12; Colossians 1:24).

Suffering is related to the gifts God gives us, in that God is always concerned about what we do for others. A musical talent or mathematical genius, for example, could either be a simple ability—or a gift of God, depending upon whether it is used by its recipient as a means of self-enhancement or service to the church and through the church to the world God loves. The Christian recognizes that whatever he has received from God is also God's call to service, with His gift as the means of serving.

In this sense, suffering can be a gift, since God can use it to help the church. Paul readily accepts his suffering, since it is a means of blessing those to whom he is writing.

A cartoon some time ago depicted an overstuffed, prosperous businessman stomping out of church, grumbling to his wife about the sermon: "It's easy for him to talk about doing to others as you would have them do to you. He's not in a dog-eat-dog business."[44] But who, more than Christians, are in such a world? Their "dog" is the devil himself. Turn to the book of Acts. There you discover that the one who could write, "Rejoice in the Lord always. I will say it again: Rejoice!" (Philippians 4:4) suffered incredibly for his faith. He was misunderstood, rejected, driven from cities, beaten

---

[44]*Saturday Review,* May 1, 1965.

with rods and whips, stoned, shipwrecked, imprisoned, and frequently at the point of extreme exhaustion. He certainly understood the "dog-eat-dog" business.

All Christian history testifies that Paul's sufferings were not unique. Even our own century has lost count of the number of believers murdered for their faith, not to mention the many more who have been imprisoned, persecuted, or otherwise hounded by their enemies.

Yet Christians do not become finally discouraged, because in everything God works for good (Romans 8:28). Through His power He turns suffering into victory.

CHAPTER TWENTY-ONE

The Mystery of Christ

Ephesians 3:1-13

We did not do justice to this passage in the last chapter. There we concentrated on what God has done for the apostle Paul—and what He wishes to do for us. Here we must study the real focus of the passage, which is not on the writer but on the mystery God revealed to him: "In reading this, then, you will be able to understand my insight into the mystery of Christ" (Ephesians 3:4). When God made this secret known to Saul of Tarsus (beginning with his experience on the road to Damascus, Acts 9), the revelation transformed his life.

The mystery was *made known* to Paul (Ephesians 3:5). The grammar student notes immediately that he employs the passive voice here. Paul nowhere claims credit for discovering God's will. He knows that unaided human intelligence cannot discern the mind of God. What we know of God's plans came to us only because God told us, not because of our research or contemplation or sacrifices or rituals. We like to talk about man's search for God, but the Bible reverses the order, presenting instead a God who searches for man, showing something of himself to men and women who seek but can never find without His help.

When God does reveal himself, He discloses truth we could never have imagined. This is what happened to Paul. Always a God-fearing man, he had given his heart and soul to fight Christians, because he had believed them to be the enemies of God. It was while on the way to Damascus, on one of his anti-Christian crusades, that Christ stopped him in his tracks and turned his life around. Paul (then known as Saul) was convinced that he was serving God by attacking Christians. He had studied to know God's will, and he sought to do it. But by his own efforts, he would have remained forever in darkness. Heaven had to come down to turn Paul around. (See also Acts 22; Acts 26.)

Paul calls his new knowledge from God a *mystery*. The word means "secret." Before Christ spoke to him, no evidence on earth had suggested to Paul that God's plan was that Gentiles *and* Jews should all be in the same family. Remember Ephesians 1:9, 10, the stated purpose of the Ephesians letter?

> And he made known to us the mystery of his will according to his good pleasure, which he purposed in Christ, to be put into effect when the times will have reached their fulfillment—to bring all things in heaven and on earth together under one head, even Christ.

It was indeed a mystery, for until God revealed this insight, who could have guessed that God's overarching desire was for universal unity?

Jews, for instance, worshiped God—but they staunchly withheld themselves from fellowship with Gentiles, whom they considered inferior. No unity there.

Greeks? Take Athens, for example. This "home of democracy," this model for all later democratic countries, this showplace for the enlightened teachings of western civilization's greatest philosophers, still harbored a slave population, a sharply discriminating class system, and contempt for all "barbarians." No unity there.

Romans? The Empire drew a sharp distinction between citizens and non-citizens and had no qualms about enslaving their conquered foes. No unity there.

Does it seem obvious today, as you watch members of the human race killing each other off, that God desires unity? The constitutional fathers of our country spoke glowingly about the rights of life, liberty, and the pursuit of happiness—but the men who signed the documents owned slaves, withheld the vote from women, and did not dream of the universal freedoms of our day. Did even they understand that God wants all people one?

Dare we hope for unity among nations? No, not as long as each government pursues foreign policies designed to further national interests at the expense of international ones.

So it seems that Paul, in his Saul of Tarsus days, was only being human when he breathed fire against Christians. He had never heard, in either political or religious circles, that the goal of God's love is unity among Jews and Gentiles, among all people everywhere. To him, it was the simplest possible truth: to be for God

186

was to be wholeheartedly, even violently for *his* religion and against anyone else's, especially the Christians.

Like the rest of us, Saul felt that to be totally for some*thing* he had to be staunchly against some*body*. Patriotic Americans have trouble being for America without hating Communists, for example. During World War II, United States propagandists persuaded Americans not only to hate Nazism but to hate Germans as well. Patriotic speakers frequently insist that their audiences cannot be genuine, one-hundred percent Americans unless they hate with a passion those people the speakers hate.

In such a world, is God's plan possible?

Paul was a Jew. His people had fought the Moabites, the Ammonites, the Assyrians, the Babylonians, the Egyptians, the Romans. It was only natural to fight the Christians.

This is why Paul required divine revelation to learn that God wanted the hated Gentiles to be fellow heirs with Jews, members of the same body *(sunsoma)* with them, partakers of the same promises in Christ. He does not blame his ancestors for their ignorance of this secret. He says (in Ephesians 3:5) that God had not made this fact known earlier. It is recent news.

And it still seems like news today. A war-weary world yearns to hear such news. It needs to learn that prejudice will not be allowed in the kingdom of God. God wants everybody; He loves everybody. "Red and yellow, black and white, they are precious in His sight."

All this we noted before, in the comments on Ephesians 1:9, 10. But there is a new insight here: The mystery should be made known through the church (Ephesians 3:10). What God has already told Paul, He now expects the church to tell to the world. When God commissioned Paul to a new ministry among the very Christians he had formerly persecuted, and sent him specifically to the Gentiles he had always despised, He expected Paul to be the first of countless ambassadors of unity among men.

Simply stated, when Paul became a disciple of Jesus Christ and experienced a transformed life, he had to tell others about it. So do we.

Many Christians have had real conversion experiences, some rather dramatic, others quieter but just as real. They can't help talking about it. And, like Paul, they talk to everybody, without prejudice. Neighbors, friends, fellow workers on the job, and even strangers, regardless of color or position or anything else.

They are surprised by their own boldness, but they can't help it. Something wonderful has happened and they have to talk about it.

In one of his books, Elton Trueblood says that this kind of turnaround belongs to middle age. Genuine conversion, he believes, doesn't happen so frequently among the young as among more experienced men and women. In their maturity, they discover new possibilities of what their lives can become. Maybe the young can't fully appreciate the alternative Christ gives them. They are not able to say, with one man who gave himself to the Lord with obvious relief, "For fifty-three years, I tried to do it my way, and it didn't work. Now I am going to do it God's way."

Whether young, old, or middle-aged, when something wonderful happens, you can't keep quiet. Tell a new parent that he cannot let anyone know he has a son. See what happens! Here's a better one: tell new grandparents that they cannot tell anyone about their grandchild. You can't keep them quiet! They are like the man in a train lounge car. He approached a fellow passenger and asked, "Do you have any grandchildren?"

"Yes," responded the smiling passenger.

The first man abruptly left him and walked through the car to another, whom he asked the same question. When that person also said "yes," he again hastily moved on to the third one.

"Do you have any grandchildren?" he asked the man.

"No sir, I don't," he said.

"Good," the first man said as he reached for his wallet. "Let me show you pictures of mine."

As I said, when something wonderful happens, you can't keep quiet. So we identify with Paul's enthusiasm in making "plain to everyone the administration of this mystery" (Ephesians 3:9). He preaches—and we preach through the church—"the unsearchable riches of Christ" and "the manifold wisdom of God" (Ephesians 3:8, 10). We talk to everyone, from the lowest to the highest, working with God so that even the loftiest spiritual forces ("the rulers and authorities in the heavenly realms," Ephesians 3:10) will understand what God has accomplished in Christ.

God does not confront every person as He did Paul on his journey to Damascus. Instead, He has established a church to reveal His secret. Through the church, the message is to be proclaimed: "Jesus loves the little children, all the children of the world." "For God so loved the world. . . ." "In Him and through faith in Him we may approach God with freedom and confidence" (Ephesians 3:12). God wants us all to be one in Him. He wants peace.

The church's message was preached dramatically several years ago in Berlin. The Communists had erected their ugly wall of hostility separating East from West Berlin. Shortly thereafter these words appeared on the wall of the Versohnungskirche (Church of the Reconciliation) in Berlin: "Wir sind doch alle Bruder" ("Nevertheless, we are all brothers"). That's the message the church has to proclaim. Nevertheless, in spite of every human design to block God's will, God wants us all to be brothers and sisters in Christ.

Earlier, in 1937, an Ecumenical Conference on Life and Work convened in Oxford, England, just after Japan's invasion of China. Both Japanese and Chinese Christians were in attendance at the conclave. These Christians, whose governments were at war with each other, clasped hands and pledged that no matter what their governments imposed upon them, they would always remember that in the enemy country was a group of their fellow Christians. They promised that after the war, they would seek to work again to establish peaceful and helpful relations between their peoples. They were, you see, brothers! They believed that God wants peace, wants all people—Chinese, Japanese, Russian, American, Cuban, Puerto Rican, African, Latin American—to be united in Christ Jesus.

For in Christ, we are all one; there are neither slaves nor aliens. Epictetus tells about a slaveowner, Epaphroditus, who sold a shoemaker whom he thought was worthless. By some accident, the former slave of Epaphroditus was purchased by one of Caesar's men, and he became a shoemaker to Caesar. All of a sudden, the slave Felicion became quite important in the eyes of his former master, so that Epaphroditus felt compelled to pay him all the deference he could muster. To anyone who could give him information he would ask, "How does the good Felicion? Kindly let me know." And when he needed any help or advice, he would hasten to consult with his former slave. The fact that he had been purchased by Caesar had made all the difference.

That is the difference that being purchased by Christ Jesus has made in our lives. We might have been of little importance before, but now we have achieved status. We have access to the eternal Emperor. We were aliens; now we are fellow citizens. We were slaves; now we are sons. We were Gentiles, now we are Christians.

And as members of the church, we have a tremendous responsibility, for the church must let this message be known throughout the world, that Gentiles—outcasts, aliens, strangers, call them what you will—wherever they are now have access to God through their faith in Jesus Christ.

CHAPTER TWENTY-TWO

Praise to the Father and Prayer for Us All

Ephesians 3:14-21

If we could ask whatever we want from our parents, what would we ask for? Let's talk about one parent, the father. When we were children, we thought—at least until we knew better—that our fathers could give us anything we wanted, if they only would. We early developed the habit of asking Dad for favors, lots of them. We probably never thought to question what it was that we wanted more than anything else.

Our desires change, of course. There are some things we wanted at six that we didn't want at sixteen and certainly had no use for at twenty-six or older. But there is one desire that has remained constant through the years, one that ranks higher than all the others. It is each child's greatest request: "Please help me, Father, to please you."

It's a longing we never entirely outgrow. Whatever our age, we want to be a credit to our parents. Even in old age, when our parents are dead, we still hope that our lives would not be a disappointment to our parents if they were living. When we were youngsters, still dependent upon our parents for food, clothing, and shelter, the help we most wanted from Dad was the necessary money or assistance to do the things that would make him proud.

The apostle Paul writes this letter to Gentile Christians who have now been brought into the family of God. They can call God Father with a new sense of intimacy and belonging. (See Ephesians 2 for the full significance of their acceptance.) They want to please their Father. Paul's prayer is that the Father will give them the help they need in order to make Him proud.

"For this reason" (Ephesians 3:14) refers us back to the first verse of this chapter, where Paul began his prayer before his long parenthesis (verses 2-13). The reason is the wonderful news that Gentiles are now full members of the household of God in Christ along with Jews. So unexpected and overwhelming is this revelation, Paul does not assume the usual Jewish prayer stance—standing with arms raised and outstretched, with palms turned upward toward Heaven—but kneels in adoration and submission to the God who has accomplished this marvel.

He kneels "before the Father, from whom his whole family in heaven and on earth derives its name" (Ephesians 3:14). Paul has exclaimed over the open access all believers now have to God (Ephesians 2:18; 3:12). He makes it possible for all who are in Christ to reach Him without intermediaries other than the Lord himself. This Heavenly Father is the model for all fatherhood, and this Father gives His name to His children just as earthly fathers do. In fact, fatherhood itself takes its name from God, since from Him we earthly fathers learn what our role entails.

To such a Father, Paul offers his prayer on behalf of his readers. He includes three petitions: (1) for the strengthening through the Spirit, (2) for the indwelling of Christ, and (3) for the fullness of God. Paul calls all of God (Father, Son, and Spirit) to the aid of His children.

Strengthening Through the Spirit

"I pray that out of his glorious riches he may strengthen you with power through his Spirit in your inner being" (Ephesians 3:16). Peter promised that when we become Christians, giving ourselves to Christ through faith, repentance, and baptism, we receive the gift of the Holy Spirit (Acts 2:37, 38). The New Testament mentions the Spirit over three hundred times, and almost without exception, it is associated with power. Among the "glorious riches" (Ephesians 2:4, 7) Paul mentions is this indescribable power (*dynamis, kratos, ischys*—Ephesians 1:9), which prevents our giving in to discouragement (*enkakein*—vs. 13) by strengthening (*krataiothenai*—vs.16) us in our struggles.

Some sons ask their fathers for strength and receive only weakness. No one is more the object of our pity than the weak son of a weak father. The son begs for what the father cannot give.

Matthew Arnold, on the other hand, praises his father, the famed headmaster of Rugby School in England, for being a "strong soul" who "upraisest with zeal, the humble good from the ground." The younger Arnold was not blind to the rarity of his father's qualities. He could not resist painting the contrast between his father's character and the weak souls around him:

192

Most men eddy about
Here and there—eat and drink,
Chatter and love and hate,
Gather and squander, are raised
Aloft, are hurled in the dust,
Striving blindly, achieving
Nothing; and then they die—
Perish;—and no one asks
Who or what they have been,
More than he asks what waves,
In the moonlit solitudes mild
Of the midmost Ocean, have swelled,
Formed for a moment, and gone.[45]

Such men have little to give their children.

Our Heavenly Father, however, who has riches unimaginable, can be the source of His children's strength. His power flows through our veins, if we let it. We have but to ask to give it a chance to do its work. The secret of obtaining this divine strength is to remember that it is our Father's: He controls it and directs it. Our task is but to be open channels to allow the Spirit to work through us, like a river rushing between its banks. It is His "power that is at work within us," "able to do immeasurably more than all we ask or imagine" (Ephesians 3:20). To sincerely request His help is to refrain from fighting Him by insisting, "I'd rather do it my way." His power is beyond our direction. This is why we gladly sing the chorus of a favorite gospel song:

His power can make you what you ought to be,
His blood can cleanse your heart and make you free;
His love can fill your soul and you will see
'Twas best for Him to have His way with thee.[46]

The Indwelling of Christ

Paul also requests "that Christ may dwell in your hearts through faith" (Ephesians 3:17). The Spirit gives strength; the

---

[45] Matthew Arnold, "Rugby Chapel."

[46] Cyrus S. Nusbaum, "His Way With Thee."

Son gives direction, purpose, and substance to life. To have Christ dwelling in your heart is to believe in Him, to be taken over by His example, His teachings, His commands, and His love, so that you can say with the apostle Paul, "I have been crucified with Christ and I no longer live, but Christ lives in me" (Galatians 2:20). Paul's prayer is that Jesus' words may come true in our lives:

"If you remain in me and my words remain in you, ask whatever you wish, and it will be given you"; and "I am the vine; you are the branches. If a man remains in me and I in him, he will bear much fruit; apart from me you can do nothing" (John 15:7, 5). Paul petitions that we may be on just such intimate terms with Christ, so that we can ask and receive and so bear fruit worthy of Him.

A young man learned from his employer what it means to have Christ dwelling in him. Ray Hoo had just graduated from Iowa State University and returned to his home in Jamaica to try to find a job. His brother had arranged an interview for him with the chairman of the Jamaican banana industry.

The interview went well. The chairman was willing to make an opening for Hoo, even though there were no vacancies. But then the candidate ruined his chances.

"What do you like to do in your spare time?" the chairman asked.

Hoo, who later became a leader in The Navigators fellowship, volunteered the information that he liked reading and sports, particularly soccer and basketball. Then he added, "I also spend a lot of time in Christian activities because I hope to someday give my life to Christian missions."

That did it! The chairman could not in good conscience spend the money necessary to train a new man only to have him leave for the mission field. So he said, "Young man, your ambitions are noble; but we want men who will give their lives to bananas."[47]

To give your life to bananas. That is the goal of the masses. They dedicate themselves to bananas or oil or corn or automobiles. To "give your life" for your job is to have it dwelling in your heart. It defines your faith: what you believe in, what you work for, what you give yourself to, is your faith.

---

[47]*The Navalog* (Colorado Springs: The Navigators, 1975), p. 3.

The Fullness of God

When you become Christ's disciple, you can no longer give yourself to any kind of "bananas." You have given it to Christ.

Paul Tournier tells of a friend who rose from his knees one day with a new insight into God's will. "I understand now. What I have to do is to put my signature at the foot of a blank page on which I will accept whatever God wishes to write. I cannot predict what he will put on this blank contract as my life proceeds—but I give my signature today."[48] That's it. The Christian gives his life as much to his Lord as others give themselves to bananas. We sign the contract and God fills in the terms. We aren't gambling, though, since we are signing a contract with our Father. He wants nothing less than the best for us and we want nothing less than to please Him. This is the fullness of God in our lives.

When we have the strength of the Holy Spirit, an abiding faith in a Lord who abides in us, and an understanding of God and His word that is "rooted and established in love", we have it all! Paul's prayer is answered.

Then we can make our Father proud of us. And He "who is able to do immeasurably more than all we ask or imagine, according to his power that is at work within us" (Ephesians 3:20) will give us everything we need to accomplish everything He wills for us. His love is greater than our ability to comprehend it on our own, but He does not leave us on our own.

The church glorifies Him by doing His will, just as Jesus Christ obediently fulfilled God's every wish for Him. Even so, Paul prays, you will be able to bring Him glory through your life in the church because of His strength empowering you.

So be it. ("Amen").

---

[48] Paul Tournier, *The Adventure of Living*, Edwin Hudson, tr. (New York: Harper and Row, 1963), pp. 194, 195.

CHAPTER TWENTY-THREE

How to Get Along With One Another—Even in Church

Ephesians 4:1-6

The Church is God's Exhibit A, His demonstration of His desire for peace on earth and unity among men. We recall God's revelation to Paul that there should be no more disunity among men, but that He wanted to "bring all things in heaven and on earth together under one head, even Christ" (Ephesians 1:10). Further, Paul writes, God intends that this purpose should now be made known to everyone through the church (Ephesians 3:10). He wants the church to broadcast this clear message, that He has already begun His great unifying work by bringing Gentiles and Jews together as "one new man" in Christ (Ephesians 2:15). The church can easily tell this story, since its members have already experienced genuine unity with each other in Christ, regardless of the disparities among our backgrounds.

With God's great purposes in mind, Paul now turns from his prayer *for* his readers (Ephesians 3:14-21) to what he expects *of* them. In these six verses (Ephesians 4:1-6), he lays three charges before us, exhorting us to live up to our calling, our character, and our convictions.

Live Up to Your Calling (4:1)

"As a prisoner for the Lord . . ." (Ephesians 4:1). Before urging us to respond to his exhortations, Paul reminds us of his right to talk to us in this way. He is in prison—for the Lord, and for the sake of his readers. He has earned the privilege, even the responsibility, of challenging us to a closer walk with God.

"I urge you to live a life worthy of the calling you have received." We do not use this old-fashioned word *calling* much any more. Its equivalent is *vocation,* which suggests more than *job* or *occupation.* It connotes a divine appointment. All Christians have received God's call to be His people, His saints; that is our

197

vocation. Jesus called tax collectors, fishermen, men and women of all walks of life to be something different in the world. No matter how they earned their living, they were really pursuing a divine calling that lifted them above the masses.

God has called all Christians. He has called us *up* to a higher standard of living, a more rigorous morality. Christians cannot be content with behaving like everybody else. The ways of the world are not our ways. We desire to live a more noble life. (This is easily misunderstood. More than one would-be Christian has hesitated to declare himself for Christ because of this or that imperfection in himself. He wants to improve himself first. His decision is well-meant but misguided, because by delaying, he forfeits the help of the Holy Spirit in walking the higher road. But at least he understands that God calls us *up.)*

A Christian may be called *on,* also. Like a physician who is on twenty-four hour call, Christians are called on to be witnesses to the grace of Christ in their lives, and to be His servants, all the time. Our whole beings are given over to others. We may not like interruptions, but in a sense, a Christian's job is to be interrupted for the sake of people who need us.

And we are called *forth* to battle. We are soldiers on alert. In the Middle Ages, Christians were summoned to holy crusades. Our battles, fortunately, are not martial but spiritual; nonetheless, we crusade for truth and righteousness and justice and goodness. We are prepared to do battle for our Lord.

So Christians are called *out* of the world to be different *from* the world for the sake *of* the world we live *in.*

Live Up to Your Character (4:2, 3)

Building on the improved character Christians have as new creations (John 3:3; 2 Corinthians 5:17; Galatians 6:15), Paul urges his readers to exhibit attitudes that contribute to unity in the body of Christ.

"Be completely humble and gentle" (Ephesians 4:2). "Lowliness and meekness" are the King-James words here. What a strange charge this was to Paul's first readers, whose culture encouraged a more macho stance. Pride, not humility, and force, not gentleness, were the marks of a real man. Neither Greeks nor Romans (nor, for that matter, Jews) found it easy to prefer others to themselves, or to assume the lowest seat or perform the meanest job in the house.

Jesus caught His disciples by surprise when He urged them not to be like Gentiles, whose great men lord it over their subordinates (Matthew 20:25). He baffled them when He stooped to wash their feet (John 13:1-17). He challenged all their previous conditioning when He demanded that they follow His example in humility.

Gentleness or meekness is never to be confused with weakness. It is, instead, the characteristic of a well-trained animal that responds in a disciplined manner to its master's commands. Meekness is power under control, in this case, under God's control. (See 1 Corinthians 4:21; Titus 3:2.)

These Christian virtues are demonstrations of love for our brothers and sisters. We deliberately give them preferential treatment. What other organization besides the church demands such generous character? Most human groups exploit our natural desire to get ahead or prove ourselves better than our peers. But in the church, we are charged to put others first.

"Be patient, bearing with one another in love" (Ephesians 4:2). The King James' *longsuffering* is to be preferred here, since we have milked *patience* of much of its power. Whichever term you use, it is apparent that Paul has found Christians not always easy to get along with!

The fact is, most of us believe in these virtues—for everybody else. Longsuffering, patience, meekness, humility.... Without such, there can be no unity in the church. Each congregation is composed of vastly different personalities, no few of them prickly! How will they ever get along? They won't, unless Christians grow Christian virtues. When Christians will not be patient with one another, they violate the will of God for His holy church and condemn it to confusion.

"Make every effort to keep the unity of the Spirit through the bond of peace" (Ephesians 4:3). Unity mattered so much to Jesus He made it a matter of special prayer:

> I pray also for those who will believe in me through their [the disciples'] message, that all of them may be one, Father, just as you are in me and I am in you. May they also be in us so that the world may believe that you have sent me (John 17:20, 21).

Why did He pray for unity? Because He wants the world to believe in Him. A fighting, scrabbling, bickering church can never prove to a fighting, scrabbling, bickering world that Jesus is

Lord. If He does not make a difference in the way we live and treat one another, why should the world accept Him?

We frequently turn to Abraham Lincoln for examples of the virtues Paul commends. When General Robert E. Lee's surrender was announced in Washington, the city exploded in celebration. On April 10, 1864, delirious crowds stormed the White House, demanding a speech from the President. He told them it was a serious moment and that he had no speech ready for them. But he added,

> I have always thought "Dixie" one of the best tunes I ever heard. I insisted yesterday that we had fairly captured it. I presented the question to the Attorney General and he gave his opinion that it is our lawful prize. I ask the band to give us a good turn upon it.

That was it. He claimed a song. When you think what a more vindictive President Lincoln could have wrung out of the helpless South, you have to praise his generosity. "With malice toward none," he had promised in his second inaugural address; "with charity toward all."

To our great shame, the church of Jesus Christ has not always been so charitable. When a congregation divides over such momentous issues as whether the new building shall or shall not have a belfry, or whether its doorknobs will be brass or glass, or whether the hour of worship shall be eleven o'clock or ten thirty, the real cause for division is seldom discussed. The cause is unworthy character. "Make every effort. . . ."

Live Up to Your Convictions (4:4-6)

The apostle now turns to the unifying faith of his readers. "There is one body and one Spirit—just as you were called to one hope when you were called—one Lord, one faith, one baptism; one God and Father of all, who is over all and through all and in all" (Ephesians 4:4-6).

W. A. Criswell recalls his visit to postwar Germany in 1947, followed by subsequent journeys in 1950 and 1955. On that first visit, the Baptist church building in Munich was destroyed, the people scattered, and the remnant congregation mostly refugees. They met underground by the light of a coal lamp, worshiping one God in their various languages, former strangers finding comfort in midst of devastation. They had so little; they needed so much. Yet when he returned in 1950, the band of believers had built a church building. Criswell took home with him the German believers' practice of joining hands at the Lord's Supper and singing, "Blest Be the Tie That Binds." Criswell recalls especially this stanza:

> We share our mutual woes,
> Our mutual burdens bear;
> And often for each other flows
> The sympathizing tear.[49]

These survivors of history's worst conflagration, who at first did not even know how to talk to each other, at least were certain of this: they belonged to one body and they had the same hope.

This unity means everything to the apostle Paul. Remember that he was born and nurtured as a Jew. He had believed the pathway to acceptability to God was obedience to the hundreds of commandments in the law. He was overwhelmed by God's demands and despaired of satisfying Him.

He also knew that Gentiles had equal reason to despair. They had many gods. They could choose which one to offer their sacrifices before, but they were gambling their lives that the god or goddess they chose was real.

In Christ, Jews who formerly were enslaved by law and Gentiles who bowed before a confusion of gods are now united. They have one faith, faith in the Lord Jesus Christ; one baptism, baptism into the Lord Jesus Christ; one God, the Father of the Lord Jesus Christ, whose body, the church, is one body.

In this short passage, Paul uses the word *one* seven times and *all* four times. He can't emphasize it enough: We are one! Our one Lord reigns (Philippians 2:9, 10; Romans 15:4-13); there is therefore no comparative god, no comparative religion. Our hope (Hebrews 6:11) and faith (Romans 10:9, 10) are in Him alone. With gladness, then, we are baptized into Christ (Romans 6:1-10), thus demonstrating our total submission to the only true Lord.

---

[49] W. A. Criswell, *Ephesians* (Grand Rapids: Zondervan, 1974), p. 179.

CHAPTER TWENTY-FOUR

The Fine Art of Growing Up

Ephesians 4:7-16

With Ephesians 4:7, Paul shifts from thinking of the church as a whole to its individual members. He focuses on what Christ has given "each one of us." Still pursuing the major theme of this letter, the unity God has ordered the church to realize and exhibit for the world, Paul spells out for his readers what Christ has done for us (Ephesians 4:7-10), what He has given us (Ephesians 4:11-13), and what He now wants from us (Ephesians 4:13-16).

What Christ Has Done (4:7-10)

"But to each one of us grace has been given as Christ apportioned it" (Ephesians 4:7). Paul refers here, as elsewhere (Ephesians 3:2, 7, 8), to our opportunity to serve the Lord as a special favor from Him. Grace not only saves us (Ephesians 2:5, 8) but also equips and commissions us for service.

Christ has the authority to give us this grace, because of His descent from Heaven to earth and His victorious ascent from earth to Heaven. When He returned to Heaven, He "led captives in his train and gave gifts to men" (Ephesians 4:8, from Psalm 68:18). Paul's picture here is that of a triumphant Roman general returning to his capital city at the head of a parade (called a "triumph") of his soldiers and the enemies he has captured and the booty he has stolen. In this case, we are the captives ("But thanks be to God, who always leads us in triumphal procession in Christ, . . ." (2 Corinthians 2:14), rescued from sin and liberated in Christ.

We who were formerly His enemies have now been made members of His body. He has taken us to himself and made us His courtiers. More generous than any medieval liege lord, He passes out gifts to members of His court.

Paul's quotation of Psalm 68:18 is altered from the original, which reads:

> When you ascended on high,
> you led captives in your train;
> you received gifts from men . . ."

Here we read,

> When he ascended on high,
> he led captives in his train
> and *gave* gifts to men.

By His grace, then, our conquering Lord deigns to share the riches of His kingdom with us (Ephesians 1:7, 18; 2:7; 3:8); even more, He grants us the privilege of laboring with Him in the church.

His descent was no lazy cruise on quiet waters. He landed in first-century Palestine, as turbulent then as now, the cross-roads of the ancient near east, with a cacophony of languages bouncing off each other (Greek, Latin, and Aramaic being the most common) and a wild assortment of Judaistic religious sects warring with one another (Jesus could have chosen to join the ascetic Essenes, the conservative Pharisees, the liberal Sadducees, or the fiercely patriotic Zealots. Instead, He chose the lonelier course, joining battle with the devil in a single-handed struggle of cosmic consequences). Paul Scherer would have us remember that "the gospel didn't get up out of a feather-bed to yawn its way sleepily through the earth; it got down off of crosses, came stalking up out of fire, with the smell of flames on it."[50]

Jesus' descent was to the depths (Philippians 2:7—"taking the very nature of a servant"). First Peter 3:19, 20 and 4:6 report that Jesus penetrated into the underworld in the interval between His death and resurrection, but Paul does not seem to have this in mind here. Rather, he contrasts Christ's Heavenly dwelling with His earthly sojourn.

---

[50] Paul Scherer, *Love is a Spendthrift* (New York: Abingdon-Cokesbury, 1945), p. 51.

In our century, the Hindu Mohandas Gandhi, inspired by his studies of Leo Tolstoy and Jesus Christ, made a similar though more modest descent. A well-educated, respectably cultured gentleman in his early years, Gandhi determined to do something to make life easier for the miserable people of India's lowest caste. Called "untouchables," "pariahs," "depressed classes" or "outcasts," these downtrodden people were treated as somewhat less than human by their more fortunate compatriots. Gandhi began a systematic campaign to lift them up, giving them the new name of "Harijans," Children of God.

He did more. He gave up his upper caste comforts. He began working with his hands, as the Children of God had to do. His riskiest step, however, was taken when he adopted an outcast girl, insisting that his wife Kasturbai accept her as a daughter. His biographer says that bringing her into his home was "like bringing a Negro daughter-in-law into the pre-Civil War mansion of a Southern lady."

Gandhi said, alluding to the Hindu doctrine of reincarnation, "I do not want to be reborn, but if I have to be reborn I should be reborn an untouchable so that I may share their sorrows, sufferings, and the affronts leveled against them in order that I may endeavor to free myself and them from their miserable condition."[51] He would descend in order to ascend as the leader of captives of the caste system.

This is what Christ did. He has *descended* and *ascended*. He has lifted us out of the prison of sin on earth and, because of His ascent, we who are in Christ look forward to our own resurrection, since "as in Adam all die, so in Christ all will be made alive" (1 Corinthians 15:20-22).

What Christ Has Given (4:11-13)

"It was he who gave some to be apostles . . ." (Ephesians 4:11). Paul now becomes specific about the "grace" mentioned in verse 7. Still concentrating on the oneness we have in Christ, he turns to the diversity within the unity. God in His grace uses all kinds of persons to accomplish the church's task. It is in harmony with the tone of this passage to read, "'It was he who gave some to be

---

[51] Louis Fisher, *The Life of Mahatma Gandhi* (New York: Harper and Row, 1950), p. 144.

apostles, some to be prophets, some to be evangelists, and some to be pastors and teachers,' some to be doctors, some to be lawyers, some to be mechanics, some to be farmers, some to be truck drivers, some to be housewives," and so on. We have many occupations but one calling, various abilities but one supreme responsibility.

Yet Christ has especially blessed the church in the gifts He gave in the beginning. Although some of the gifts (apostles and prophets) are no longer needed, the others (evangelists, pastors and teachers) continue to lead the church. His gifts were some to be sent (apostles), some to speak forth the word of God (prophets), some to travel from place to place proclaiming the good news, and some to stay at home to care for and teach local congregations.

Apostle literally means "one sent forth," an authorized messenger. The twelve apostles of Christ were apparently selected because they would see the risen Lord and be commissioned by Him (1 Corinthians 9:1f) and be able to do signs and mighty works (2 Corinthians 12:12). When Judas was replaced by Matthias, Peter laid down the condition that the new apostle must have been among Jesus' followers during His ministry and have been a witness to the Lord's resurrection (Acts 1:21, 22). The apostle Paul did not qualify according to Peter's statement, of course, but was especially appointed by the risen Lord himself (Acts 2; 22).

Linked with the apostles (Ephesians 2:20, 3:5) in the founding of the church, *prophets* were inspired preachers who "forth-told" God's message. Their work was especially important before the documents of the New Testament were formed into the canon (authorized collection) we now have. The prophets occasionally "foretold", also, as in Acts 11:27, 28 and 21:10, 11.

We can agree with William Barclay in calling the *evangelists* (see Acts 21:8; 8:5-40; 2 Timothy 4:5) the missionaries of the early church.

The *pastors and teachers* were probably leaders of local bodies of believers. If the apostles, prophets, and evangelists planted churches, pastors and teachers built them up in the Word of the Lord. Teachers are linked with prophets in Acts 13:1 and follow them in Paul's list of God's appointments in the church in 1 Corinthians 12:28. Pastors tend the sheep of God's flock, following the example and admonition of Christ: John 10:11, 14; 1 Peter 5:2; John 21:15-17; Acts 20:28.

What sometimes startles the modern church member out of his slumber as he reads this passage is Christ's reason for giving the church these leaders: "to prepare God's people for works of service" (Ephesians 4:12). These leaders do not constitute the church, nor are they to do the work of the church: they are to make it possible for all the church's members to perform their individual services for God as a part of the church.

Several years ago, this writer had an opportunity to be in the grandstands for the famous Indianapolis 500 race. For years, I had known of A. J. Foyt, Gordon Johncock, the Unser brothers, and other superbly skilled race drivers, but never before had I seen them in action. The event was breathtaking and very instructive. Not until that day had I fully realized how dependent the famous drivers are on their pit crews. Without the precision timing and deft abilities of these teammates, whose names never make the newspapers, the drivers are helpless. The whole team works to promote the driver. Their function is to make him look good.

I left the race pondering the church's team. The local church works the same way as the pit crew at the 500—only in reverse. The job of a church's driver (the pastor or teacher or pastor-teacher, by whatever name he is called) is to make the crew (the members of the body) look good. He is doing today what all the leaders Paul names did in the beginning: He is preparing "God's people for works of service."

How far the church has fallen from this Scriptural prescription! A pastor was not too gently reproached by one of his flock because a member was in the hospital and the minister did not call on him. According to this passage, is the minister guilty of negligence? Or is the member who reported? Whose responsibility is it to perform such services? In this case, the pastor reminded his critic that hospital calling was not his job any more than his critic's. He said he would visit, but as a Christian brother, not as a hired employee of the church.

Congregations that hire paid professionals to do the church's "works of service" face three consequences:

(1) They will kill their minister, or at least wear him out. He cannot carry this burden alone in a growing church.

(2) They will guarantee the non-growth of their congregation. It will remain as small as the time and energy and ability of one man. This one fact explains the large number of small churches.

(3) They will stunt the growth of the members of the church. They'll never grow up to assume their Scriptural responsibilities.

But they must become servants in the church "so that the body of Christ may be built up" (Ephesians 4:12). When all the members give themselves to the Lord in ministry, the whole body grows numerically, the members grow spiritually, and the entire kingdom of God is blessed by their service.

Church, then, is no longer a place to go to, but a service agency to work in. Dennis the Menace speaks for too many church members in the cartoon depicting him walking toward the car with his family, scrubbed and polished and calling out to his pal, Joey, that he's going to church but he'll be himself again after lunch. For Dennis, religion is a spectator sport. For Paul, it is a call to ministry. (It was for Jesus, too, who came not to be served but to serve—Matthew 20:28.)

The goal for the church is to "reach unity in the faith and in the knowledge of the Son of God" (Ephesians 4:13). Paul never loses sight of God's overarching concern, "to bring all things in heaven and on earth together under one head, even Christ" (Ephesians 1:10). Every leader in the church—apostle, prophet, evangelist, pastor, teacher—is charged to lead the church's members, all of them, to build up the church of Jesus Christ until the whole world can be united in one faith and a common knowledge of the Son of God. Paul treats the church here as the "one new man" in Christ (Ephesians 2:15). Individualism, then, is out. It is a mark of immaturity. Cooperation, interdependence, mutual assistance, communion of effort—say it however you will—has replaced it. Every member wants the whole body to be built up.

What Christ Wants (4:13-16)

Christ wants us to grow up "and become mature, attaining to the whole measure of the fullness of Christ" (Ephesians 4:13). So that we don't miss his point, Paul says the same thing again: "Then we will no longer be infants." And again: "We will in all things grow up into him who is the Head, that is, Christ" (Ephesians 4:14, 15). We can't escape the implications: To grow up is to become like Christ. To fail to grow toward Christ is to remain infantile.

One day, Paul Hitt and his wife were talking about growing up in Christlikeness. One asked the other, "Who among our friends reminds you most of Jesus Christ?"

They could not answer immediately. They counted many very prominent Christian leaders in their circle of friends, and they thought about all of them, but in the end, they could name only two women who made them think of Jesus. They were not even the leaders, but wives of leaders who had devoted their lives to Christian service. The Hitts knew hundreds of Christian leaders, but could name only two that fit this category.[52] Yet this is what Christ wants, isn't it?

Paul's language requires individual response. Every Christian is to grow up. "Each part does its work" (Ephesians 4:16). No member can excuse himself from maturing.

We tend to minimize our personal importance and divert Scriptural challenges to our fellow members. Since we are unimportant in God's scheme of things, we reason, it is up to others to carry the load. Yet Henry David Thoreau reasons wisely on this point in his *On the Duty of Civil Disobedience.* Appealing for America to abolish slavery, Thoreau correctly saw that the battle was not to be waged in legislatures nor courts so much as in individual human hearts:

> I know this well, that if one thousand, if one hundred, if ten men whom I could name,—if ten *honest* men—ay, if *one* HONEST man, in this State of Massachusetts, *ceasing to hold slaves,* were actually to withdraw from this copartnership, and be locked up in the county jail therefor, it would be the abolition of slavery in America. For it matters not how small the beginning may seem to be: what is once well done is done forever.

To take such courageous stands, however, men and women must "no longer be infants, tossed back and forth by the waves, and blown here and there by every wind of teaching and by the cunning and craftiness of men in their deceitful scheming" (Ephesians 4:14). Children chase after this leader and that, after this fad and that fancy, with little stability and no far-reaching principles. Paul's word for "tossed back and forth" is *kludonizomai,* which is the verb form of the word Luke uses (Luke 8:24) for Jordan's raging waters and James (James 1:6) for a wave blown and tossed

---

[52] Russell Hitt, *How Christians Grow* (Oxford: Oxford University Press, 1979), pp. 27, 28.

by the wind. The second word ("blown here and there"), *periphero,* is like the first yet connotes an even more forceful tossing. The contrary doctrines of heresy were already rushing against Christian believers as Paul was writing; it was frighteningly easy for them to be deceived. They must hold on to each other as they seek to know more of and become more like Christ. Only in fellowship and service and maturity would they be safe.

More than one observer of the modern church has commented regretfully on the infantile state of most members. Looking to their pastor as father, they expect him to feed them, lead them, think for them, pray for them, serve for them, and protect them from all harm. They turn this passage upside down, demanding maturity of their leaders so that they may remain children.

To just such spiritual infants Paul writes: "Instead, speaking the truth in love, we will in all things grow up into him who is the Head, that is, Christ" (Ephesians 4:15). R. A. Knox has noted that a baby's head is unusually large in comparison with the rest of its body. As it develops, however, the body grows into its proportionate size.[53] The Head of the body of Christ is waiting for the rest of the body to grow to its natural size in relation to Him. When people look at the body of Christ, they should be able to recognize that it belongs to the Head!

The body must grow "in all things." Not just intellectually, spiritually, or physically, but totally. James Fowler wisely comments that when he was invited to teach in Harvard Divinity School's department of applied theology, his goal was to make his classes different from those to which he had been exposed. They forgot, he complained, that the students had ever been children, so they did not deal with the "powerful images of God and experiences of the holy" that pre-school children have.

"The other mistake," he added, "was that I was taught theology as though my body began with my neck and went up. But I knew as a Southerner that I thought with my glands."[54]

---

[53] R. A. Knox, *St. Paul's Gospel* (London: Sheed and Ward, 1953), p. 84.

[54] Quoted in Harold Straughn, "Stages of Faith: An Interview with James Fowler," *The Journal of the Minister's Personal Library,* Volume III, No. 1, p. 2.

So must the church and every member of the church grow in all aspects of their being.

Our growth is into Christ. He is the Vine and we are the branches (John 15:1-17). We abide in, even as we grow toward, Him, until we have so identified with Him that we are no longer entirely distinguishable from Him, like Paul who writes, "I no longer live, but Christ lives in me" (Galatians 2:20).

I understand that on a wall near the main entrance of the Alamo in San Antonio, Texas, a man's portrait hangs. The inscription tells why it is there:

> James Butler Bonham—no picture of him exists. This portrait is of his nephew, Major James Bonham, deceased, who greatly resembled his uncle. It is placed here by the family that people may know the appearance of the man who died for freedom.

No portrait of Christ exists, either, but if the church grows up into Him, so that "the whole body, joined and held together by every supporting ligament, grows and builds itself up in love, as each part does its work," then the world will recognize Christ. It will see His likeness reflected in in His body.

CHAPTER TWENTY-FIVE

Off With the Old,
On With the New

Ephesians 4:17-32

Paul continues his challenge to "live a life worthy of the calling you have received" (Ephesians 4:1). The unity in the universe and in the body of Christ, which is Paul's overriding concern, has a two-fold basis: what Christ has already done for us (He called us to be His) and what we do in response (we change our manner of living).

Paul repeatedly calls us to full partnership with the Lord:

(1) He calls; we live a life worthy of the call (Ephesians 4:1).

(2) Christ gives gifts to the church; members of the church do works of service for Him (Ephesians 4:11, 12).

(3) We grow up in Christ, doing our individual work; Christ assists the body to grow (Ephesians 4:15, 16).

(4) We put on a new self, which God created to be like Him (Ephesians 4:23).

(5) God forgave us; we forgive each other (Ephesians 4:32).

(6) God made us His children; we imitate God (5:1).

Paul specifically insists that as God's partners we can no longer live the way we used to, like Gentiles (men and women who do not belong to the people of God). They live in the dark: "For you were once darkness, but now you are light in the Lord" (Ephesians 5:8).

The change Christ effects in a believer's life is like switching on the light in the darkness. It is the difference—and here Paul borrows the old distinction again—between the Jews (God's people) and Gentiles (from the Jewish point of view, all non-Jews, who are thus really nobodies in their eyes). From the Jewish perspective, these nobodies live subhuman lives, since they do not have God in their lives. Spiritual Gentiles are, as Paul describes them here, despairing, lost souls, darkened in mind, separated from God, and hardened of heart (Ephesians 4:18).

Darkened in Mind. Their thinking is futile; it goes nowhere. Their understandings are darkened; seeing, they see not.

They can't see ahead (they live without vision and purpose). They can't see around or over (their troubles thus defeat them). They can't see through (they are easily deceived). They can't see in (they don't even really know themselves). They can't see up (even God is hidden from their blind eyes).

They blithely drift on the tide of their times, boasting of their sophistication, reveling in their "new morality." To call immorality "new morality" doesn't change a thing, though:

> In vain we call old notions fudge
> And bend our conscience to our dealing:
> The Ten Commandments will not budge,
> And stealing will continue stealing.

No matter what name we give it, sin remains sin.

Separated from God. "Separated from the life of God because of the ignorance that is in them . . ." (Ephesians 4:18). They don't know and they don't want to know. They are strangers to God and they do not want to become acquainted.

Hardened of Heart. "Ignorance . . . due to the hardening of their hearts." Christ's way is to stand at the door and knock, not to batter it down. A calloused, unfeeling heart renders a person practically (but for the grace of God) beyond salvaging.

Every pastor can bewail his discouragement after pouring prayers, money, time, attention, affection—everything he has—on a person in distress, only to watch in dismay as the man or woman returns to the same behavior that caused the distress in the first place. Such persons often pray, "Father, forgive me—I don't know what I'm doing—and please don't tell me." Their ways are futile. In time, through continued disregard for what is right, their hearts become unresponsive. There is no feeling for God left. For that matter, there is little genuine feeling at all: they have "lost all sensitivity" (Ephesians 4:19; see Romans 1:24-28).

And "they have given themselves over to sensuality so as to indulge in every kind of impurity, with a continual lust for more" (Ephesians 4:19). That "continual lust" is greed (*pleonexia*); they can't get enough. They are unable to resist, whether the temptation is sexual abandon, gambling, drink, or any other form of self-indulgence.

A young student of mine confessed that she had enrolled in our Christian college in an earnest attempt to escape the stranglehold of the drug culture she had belonged to. She was also seeking relief from the guilt of her two abortions. Her sexually loose life had virtually destroyed her self-respect. She tried for a while to adjust to the straight atmosphere of the campus, but she didn't succeed. She left us, returning to the former life-style that had captured and held her. Even now, when I think of her, I remember her rather beautiful face and her old, old eyes; she had been exposed to too much for her years and her eyes were strained from their too much staring into darkness.

"Having lost all sensitivity," spiritual Gentiles scrounge like dogs among the garbage cans, craving immediate sating of their lusts. Theirs is a subhuman existence. What God created in His image to be pure and holy has rotted away, the cancerous cells of sensuality having done their corrupting work.

This was the condition of Paul's readers before the Lord got ahold of them (and us). The Lord calls us up to Him (Ephesians 4:1). But His calling is not enough: We must also "live a life worthy" of that calling. In Ephesians 4:22 and 23, Paul gets specific: "put off your old self," "be made new," and "put on the new self."

Put Off Your Old Self (4:22)

Having heard of Jesus and having been taught the truth that is in Him, you must now take charge of your life. You must decide. No more old life; your old self must control you no longer, since it "is being corrupted by its deceitful desires" (Ephesians 4:22). The action is continuous—"is being corrupted"—so long as you give in to it.

These powerful urges are hard to control. That is why, on our own strength alone, we find it so hard to live an ethical, upright life. Sportswriter Red Smith spoke for most of us when he delivered the eulogy at the funeral of his longtime friend Fred Corcoran. Facing the mourners in their pews, Smith said, "Dying is no big deal. The least of us will manage that. Living is the trick."[55]

You can't keep living, in fact, if your old self rules. Its ways drive you to death. Therefore, put off these things.

---

[55]Red Smith, *To Absent Friends* (New York: Atheneum, 1982), p. 7.

Put off **falsehood** (Ephesians 4:25). A physical body cannot work unless its various members send out honest signals. A lying nervous system kills the whole body. No personal relationships can work, either, unless they are held together by the truth. There is truth in Jesus (Ephesians 4:21); thus, those who are in Jesus must also be truthful. When one puts on Christ, he abandons deceit.

Put off **anger** (Ephesians 4:26). Paul's words seem a little confusing, at first, to people who have been taught that all anger is sin. This is not what Paul says. Admitting that anger is a normal emotion, Paul's quotation of Psalm 4:4 implies that the emotion can be expressed in non-damaging ways. You must, however, refuse to grant your emotions control. When they rule, the devil can manipulate us for his own purposes. You dare not allow the immediate anger to degenerate into harbored bitterness. Take care of the problem today and then forget it. Do not take it to bed with you. (Even the Mosaic law insisted that wages were to be paid and transactions settled before nightfall—Deuteronomy 24:13-15.)

Put off **stealing** (Ephesians 4:28). There must have been thieves in the early church—just as there are today. William Barclay says that theft was rampant in the ancient world, especially at docks and in public bathhouses. Of today, Barclay would have had to add that theft is rampant on income tax forms, in government offices, in business deals, and everywhere else. Notice that Paul does not appeal for a stop to stealing in order that Christians might boast of their purity. His appeal is on behalf of the needy, as always. Let the Christians work with their own hands, not with a purpose of making themselves wealthy, but so they may have money to give away (see also 1 Corinthians 4:12; 1 Thessalonians 4:11, 12). Those "on the take" will not be "on the give."

Put off **unwholesome talk** (Ephesians 4:29). As the thief stops stealing and starts giving for the sake of others, so all Christians stop gossiping and slandering and cursing and start controlling their speech for the sake of others. The old person cared only for pleasing himself; the new self never stops thinking—and talking—for the benefit of others.

Put off **grieving the Holy Spirit** (Ephesians 4:30). When the Lord saved us, He gave us the Holy Spirit as a guarantee of our inheritance (Ephesians 1:14). The Spirit is not an unfeeling, impersonal object, but caring and personal. His heart can be broken and His wishes thwarted by insensitive persons.

Finally, put off **"all bitterness, rage and anger, brawling and slander, along with every form of malice"** (Ephesians 4:31). These characterized the person you used to be, but are foreign to the person you are becoming in Christ. Instead, be made new!

Be Made New in the Attitude of Your Minds (4:23)

You see, you can't expect the Lord to do everything. He'll renew you, but you must do something about your attitude. You must become "kind and compassionate to one another, forgiving each other, just as in Christ God forgave you" (Ephesians 4:32). Kindness, compassion, forgiveness—these are in *your* control. God has forgiven you, given you another chance. Now you must do the same to any who has offended you (Matthew 6:14, 15).

This is Paul's familiar coupling of God's work with our work, as in Philippians 2:12, 13—"Continue to work out your salvation with fear and trembling [our part], for it is God who works in you to will and to act according to his good purpose [God's part]." Romans 12:1, 2 urges us to offer ourselves as living sacrifices to God, but Paul can so challenge us because of God's mercies toward us.

Paul's position is consistent: It is "by grace" we are saved (Ephesians 2:5, 8), but we are not passive recipients; we are active partners with God. When Jesus spoke to Nicodemus about the necessity of being born again, He taught that new birth involves spirit and water, indicating God's initiative and man's response (John 3).

Preaching seems to have difficulty finding the balance between these two. If in past centuries preachers were guilty of teaching salvation by works and overlooking the grace of God, more modern preaching often says so much about the grace of God that it appears there is nothing at all that we have to do. God does everything. Just believe. That's it. Such preaching is an insult to intelligence and a violation of Scriptural teaching.

Peter Gillquist translates the story of the rich young ruler (Luke 18:18-27) into discussion between a "modern Christian witness" and "the ambitious young mayor of a midsized American city." After the Christian finishes speaking for a fellowship breakfast in a hotel dining room (on the theme "A Purpose for Living"), the mayor approaches the speaker, compliments him on his message, and then asks specifically what a fellow has to do to receive Jesus Christ and gain that purpose for living.

The speaker tells him he doesn't have to do anything, really. It's all free.

The mayor is astonished. He can't believe he won't have to change.

The speaker insists that he won't have to do a thing. Just ask Jesus into your heart, he assures him, and Jesus takes it from there.

The mayor presses him. He wonders about some decisions he makes in his position. He wonders whether he can be a true Christian and continue doing as he has been doing.

Still the Christian insists. No strings attached to the Good News.

Then they step over to the side of the room, and the speaker asks him to repeat a simple prayer asking Jesus into his heart, and that's it.[56]

Gillquist contrasts this modern, painless preaching with Jesus' demand that the rich young ruler give up his materialistic comfort for the strictures of discipleship. There is no "cheap grace" in Christ. He demands, according to Paul, a changed attitude, a transformed mind. It is imperative, then, to "put on the new self, created to be like God in true righteousness and holiness" (Ephesians 4:24).

Put on the New Self (4:24-32)

This is the third requirement: First, "put off your old self"; second, "be made new in the attitude of your minds"; and finally, "put on the new self." Again, Paul alludes to our partnership with God. It is He who *created* us to be like Him, He who treats us as if we were righteous and holy (Romans 5:1-5; 1 Peter 2:5, 9). He has removed every barrier to fellowship with Him; all we have to do is put on the new self He has created for us. It's a decision.

We put on **new words** (Ephesians 4:29). Even our speech is affected when we become Christians. We do not "let any unwholesome talk come out of [our] mouths."

We put on **new actions** (Ephesians 4:26-28). We do not let our emotions control us, we don't steal any more, and we do not lust after another person's body. We take seriously such advice as this

---

[56] Peter Gillquist, *Why We Haven't Changed the World* (Old Tappan: Revell, 1979), pp. 24, 25.

from the Roman philosopher Marcus Aurelius, "No longer talk about the kind of man a good man ought to be, but be one."

We put on **holiness** (Ephesians 4:24). Having been called by God to be His special people, we want to live a life worthy of the call. Being a part of God's people implies living for others on behalf of God. Holiness lives with hands open to give and help. It weeps for the suffering in this world and works to lighten their burden. It thanks God for His blessings beyond numbering, and becomes a channel for God's blessings to flow through to the people He so loves in this world that He wants His Son to save them, too. Holiness rejoices in the victory of the good, in the harmony between God and His people everywhere. Holiness appears eccentric in a world gone amock; to act holy will seem quite insane in a mad world. Holiness involves a reckless giving of yourself away—and discovering there's more of you left over than there was before.

Holiness means taking your place as a member of the body of Christ and doing everything to help the body to grow up into Christ.

Holiness does not come naturally. You decide.

In verse after verse, Paul stresses the Christian's responsibility for his life in Christ. An infant (Ephesians 4:14) simply reacts to stimuli; a mature person is goal-directed, decisive, self-motivated, and in harmonious relationship with other members of his group. A child blames others; an adult assumes responsibility.

Susan Ackerman of Phoenix was the subject of an August, 1983, feature article on the disease anorexia. Her follow-up letter to the editor was more instructive than the article itself, especially for its evidence of Ms. Ackerman's maturity:

Editor:
I am the 32-year-old woman who is recovering from anorexia, written about in an article on Aug. 7.
While the article was on the most part factual about my physical condition and what my family went through, there are a few things I would like to correct and other points I would like to clarify.
I am not a "victim" of a disease. A victim is a person injured by others or by a lack of self-control. I was injured by no one but myself, and by no way was it by a lack of self-control. I injured myself with a great deal of self-control.

A victim has no choice. I did. I chose this behavior to avoid dealing with feelings I had over events in my life that I would not accept and could not face. I chose this way to escape. No one forced this on me. How much I weigh, or how much I eat or do not eat, is not important and should not have been concentrated on in the article. Food is not the issue. Weight is not the issue.

Even if I were to die, it still would have been my choice. I would not have died a victim of a disease, but rather by my own hand from a disorder that I chose.[57]

So long as Ms. Ackerman was under the sway of her old self with her poisonous attitudes, she was catapulting herself toward certain death. No one else could save her. Not until she decided to "put off" her old self, "be made new in the attitude" of her mind, and "put on" a new self, a mature, responsible, goal-oriented self, could she cast off her anorexia.

In *Love Is Letting Go of Fear,* Dr. Gerald Jampolsky encourages his readers to take control of their lives by casting off their former robot-like existence and recognizing that they can decide their responses for themselves. He challenges them to say, "I claim my freedom by exercising the power of my decision to see people and events with Love instead of fear."

As an illustration of what he means, he recounts an incident from his days in medical school. While there, he noticed that a surprising number of his classmates came down with whatever disease they were studying at the time. In his case, he was deathly afraid he would contract tuberculosis. He was assigned a month on the TB service as an intern in Boston. At the end of the first day, he was a wreck, so great was his fear. Then at 11:30 he received an emergency call. A 50-year-old woman, tubercular and an alcoholic with cirrhosis of the liver, had vomited blood. He checked her pulse and couldn't find any. He massaged her heart and removed the blood from her throat with a suction machine. The oxygen machine wouldn't work at first, so he administered mouth-to-mouth resuscitation. Her pulse came back and she began to breathe again. She made it.

---

[57] Susan Ackerman, "Letter to the Editor," *Arizona Republic* (August, 1983).

Back in the interns' quarters, Jampolsky looked at himself in a mirror. He was a bloody mess. He then realized he had given himself totally to saving the woman's life and was never afraid. He had acted in love.

He thought about what he had learned. When he was totally absorbed in worry over what he could catch, his fear nearly paralyzed him. But when he forgot himself in service, he felt no fear at all. "By letting go of the past, by putting my full attention into giving in the now, I forgot about fear and could see things differently."[58]

He put on love.

---

[58] Gerald Jampolsky, M.D., *Love Is Letting Go of Fear* (Celestial Arts, California, 1979), pp. 78, 79.

CHAPTER TWENTY-SIX

In the Likeness of God

Ephesians 5:1-7

What an audacious thought! That you and I could become imitators of God! Yet nothing less than this lofty standard is acceptable to the apostle Paul. "Put on the new self, created to be like God in true righteousness and holiness," he has already written in Ephesians 4:24. Then, becoming more specific, he urges us to be "kind and compassionate to one another, forgiving each other, just as in Christ God forgave you" (Ephesians 4:32).

From holiness to forgiveness—and then on to every other expression of love: "Live a *life* of love, just as Christ loved us and gave himself up for us" (Ephesians 5:2). In mind and heart and deed, we imitate God by imitating Christ. ("To this you were called, because Christ suffered for you, leaving you an example, that you should follow in his steps"; 1 Peter 2:21.)

In its call to pattern ourselves after God, Ephesians 5:1, 2 takes it place beside Jesus' equally demanding appeals: "Be perfect, therefore, as your heavenly Father is perfect" (Matthew 5:48), and "Be merciful, just as your Father is merciful" (Luke 6:36). In Ephesians, as in the New Testament generally, the writer urges the highest standard of living for the sake of others. Christ sacrificed himself because He loved people; the Christian's conduct is likewise governed by his concern for others. The great missionary to Africa, Albert Schweitzer, explains why this conduct is so critical in our service to God: "We have constantly to remember the inexorable law, that we can only bring so much of the Kingdom of God into the world as we possess within us."[59]

It is a truth even a child can understand. A few years ago, the Christian Missionary Fellowship published a little missionary

---

[59] Joy, ed., *Albert Schweitzer: An Anthology,* p. 112.

223

recruitment pamphlet inspired by seven-year-old Christopher Corts. On the title page, he printed in his uncertain hand, "STEPS OF Becoming a Missionarie." On succeeding pages he listed the ten steps as he saw them:

1. Think—Do I want to become a missionary?
2. If so where at?
3. After this go to a counsler.
4. Memorize scripture.
5. Be sure you know the languge!
6. Decide what group you want to work with.
7. Be married!
8. Let the people study you!
9. Be sure they understand gods word!
10. Baptize!

It's that eighth step that stops us. Christopher has been well taught. The primary subject studied by people wherever missionaries are sent is the life of the missionary himself. If he does not imitate God, how can the people come to know God? If they don't see holiness and righteousness and kindness and compassion and forgiveness and love acted out before them by the missionary, how will they ever come to know the God in whom these qualities find their perfection?

Implicit in these verses (Ephesians 5:1-7) are three contrasts that bear examination: (1) the children of God versus the sons of disobedience; (2) the life of love versus a life of lust; and (3) worship of idols versus worship of the true God (2, 4, 5).

The Children of God
vs. the Sons of Disobedience (5:1, 6, 7)

As always in the New Testament, the challenge to righteous living emerges from our relationship with God. "As dearly loved children," we imitate God, not as fearful servants of a fearsome deity. "This is love: not that we loved God, but that he loved us and sent his Son as an atoning sacrifice for our sins. Dear friends, since God so loved us, we also ought to love one another" (1 John 4:10, 11). He not only loved us, but He adopted us to be His very own children (Galatians 3:26, 27), even though we were far from deserving this kindness (Romans 5:6-11). Thus, we don't struggle to live a righteous life in order to earn God's approbation. We have been accepted by God already, even when we were unacceptable, so we imitate God's holiness because we are so thankful to be members of His family (Ephesians 5:4).

The choice is mutual. He has chosen us; we in turn have chosen Him. We would rather be His obedient children than be partners with the sons of disobedience (Ephesians 5:6, RSV) who deliberately rebel against Him.

For Paul, the choice is obvious: you will align yourself with God or with those who are disobedient. You will be a "fellow citizen with God's people" (Ephesians 2:19) or a partner with the disobedient (Ephesians 5:7). Mere lip service in the cause of Christ is not sufficient; the struggle against Satan is too fierce for casual allegiance (Ephesians 6:10-18). Complete dedication to—and imitation of—the Lord is required of God's children.

The final chapter of the life-long struggle of Mahatma Gandhi to free India from British imperialism helps us grasp what Paul is calling for in Ephesians. Gandhi was crushed by the defection of his disciples. He had worked sacrificially, and non-violently, to bring freedom to India and unity to India's divided Muslims and Hindus. But he labored in vain. On August 15, 1947, Islamic Pakistan was partitioned away from Hindu India in a bloody and violent separation. With the division, Gandhi believed that his thirty-two years of hard labor were coming to an inglorious conclusion. He had preached unity and non-violence; his disciples tore at each other with violent animosity. He had failed.

Gandhi's biographer poignantly describes his failure:

> Millions adored the Mahatma, multitudes tried to kiss his feet or the dust of his footsteps. They paid him homage and rejected his teachings. They held his person holy and desecrated his personality. They glorified the shell and trampled the essence. They believed in him but not in his principles.[60]

His experience parallels that of Jesus centuries earlier. That's why He warned His disciples, "Not everyone who says to me, 'Lord, Lord,' will enter the kingdom of heaven, but only he who does the will of my Father who is in heaven" (Matthew 7:21).

---

[60] Louis Fischer, *The Life of Mahatma Gandhi* (New York: Harper and Row, 1950), p. 473.

Cheap lip service can't fool the Lord of Truth. Only true obedience, only deliberate imitation of God, is worthy of a child of God.

The Life of Love vs. a Life of Lust (5:2, 3, 5)

If love is perfected in Christ, it is most surely perverted in lust. To think of love is to picture Christ on the cross, voluntarily giving His all for the sake of the ones He loved. What a gross profaning of this selfless expression of love it is to describe sexual immorality as "making love"! Anton Chekhov captures this perversion by observing that in nature, a repulsive caterpillar turns into a lovely butterfly, but with human beings, it is the other way round: a lovely butterfly turns into a repulsive caterpillar.

The language of love asks, "What can I do or give for you?" The Christ of the crucifixion answers the question once and for all.

The language of lust asks, "What can I get for myself?" An impassioned crowd yelling, "Crucify Him," is the answer we must hear, though we would rather not.

Love gives for the sake of another, even if it must die to express its love. Lust takes for the sake of self, even if it must kill to get what it wants.

Sometimes lust covers itself with a cloak of theological respectability. In the early days of Christianity, there was a hint of the full-scale gnosticism that would rock the church in the second century. Some of these heretics were masters of this kind of deceit. Professing to believe in a kind of philosophical dualism that proclaims mind good and body evil, they could then insist that what their bodies do is irrelevant to their religious condition. What matters is what their minds think about God and goodness, not what their bodies practice. In the name of their self-proclaimed philosophical sophistication, then, they could indulge themselves in the grossest forms of sexual immorality while professing to be quite religious.

To combat this heresy, Paul writes, "But among you there must not be even a hint of sexual immorality, or of any kind of impurity, or of greed [which, in this context, suggests the coveting of another person's body]" (Ephesians 5:3). The Christian, like the Jew before him, must view a person as an integrated whole. In a real sense, the Bible does not teach that a person has a soul, but that he is a soul, and that his body and spirit unite to form the soul, which means "life." What the body does, then, cannot be separated from what the mind thinks.

That's why "obscenity, foolish talk or coarse joking [ribaldry]" are prohibited (Ephesians 5:4). Jesus had said, "What comes out of a man is what makes him 'unclean'" (Mark 7:16). James warns that "the tongue also is a fire, a world of evil among the parts of the body" (James 3:6). The Bible never takes our modern view that words are "just words." Words have power to heal, to change, to damage, to kill. Persons, then, who persist in foolish or obscene joking are profaning what is holy and propagating what is evil. As the body can't be separated from the mind, neither can words be unharnessed from their effects. So—some things must not even be mentioned, lest the power of lust overwhelm the effect of love.

Worshipers of God vs. Worshipers of Idols (5:2, 4, 5)

To imitate God is to offer Him our highest form of worship; to disobey is to chose another, less worthy god in His place. As Canon E. C. Raven of England has written, "To rest content with less than the best, to set up as our ideal a loyalty that is deliberately selfish, second-rate, is to be guilty of idolatry."[61] Undoubtedly, an immoral, impure, or greedy person seldom thinks of himself as a worshiper of any kind, yet that is what Paul labels him: "Such a man is an idolater" (Ephesians 5:5). In spurning God he has set up another god in His stead.

These gods make their own demands. A favorite cartoon appeared in the *Saturday Review* some years ago (March 30, 1963, to be exact). It depicted two scientists examining the tape of a gigantic computer (they were much, much larger in those days). The scientist holding the tape, a worried expression on his face, tells the other, "It's very, very angry and it's demanding a sacrifice." The Bible frequently calls us to offer ourselves as sacrifices to God (Romans 12:1, 2, for example), using Christ as the supreme example to be followed, but our sacrifice is offered in love for God and others, not in lust for selfish satisfaction. As a result, our offering "smells good" to God (note this language in Genesis 8:21 and Exodus 29:18, 25, 41). In fact, *we* become a fragrant offering, like Christ (2 Corinthians 2:15, 16).

---

[61] Quoted by Luccock, *Halford Luccock Treasury,* p. 423.

In the Old Testament, God was pleased to receive animal or cereal sacrifices; in the New, Christ offers himself on behalf of all, so nothing else is required. Our own offerings are purely voluntary, motivated only by thanksgiving. "Obscenity, foolish talk or coarse joking" may be appropriate in the worship of idols, but never in the worship of God; what He wants from us is an expression of gratitude.

Paul warns us that it is possible to offend God, even though some preachers are guilty of preaching otherwise. "God's wrath comes on those who are disobedient" (Ephesians 5:6). He cannot countenance idolatry.

Imitation of God requires total commitment. There must be no cheating, no holding back from complete allegiance. Dale Hays has published an excellent illustration of the meaning of such commitment. He writes that he heard a Haitian pastor tell his people a parable about a man who offered his house for sale for $2,000. His prospective buyer couldn't afford to pay the full price, so after the usual haggling, the seller came to terms: he would let his house go for $1,000 with only one stipulation. He would retain ownership of a small nail that protruded from just over the door.

That seemed reasonable enough, so the buyer took possession on these terms. Several years went by and the original owner decided he wanted his house back, but the new owner refused to sell. So the first man went out, found the carcass of a dead dog, and hung it from the single nail that he still owned. The stench soon rendered the house uninhabitable, and the residents were forced to sell the house back to the owner of the nail.

The pastor concluded, "If we leave the Devil with even one small peg in our life, he will return to hang his rotting garbage on it, making it unfit for Christ's habitation."[62]

It doesn't take much to make a bad stench. Such foul-smelling things are not even to be mentioned, let alone done. They are the stuff of idolatry.

True worship of God, which is living a life that imitates Him, is the genuinely fragrant offering He seeks from us. Christ has shown us how to offer such worship.

---

[62] Dale Hays, "Total Commitment," *Leadership,* Spring 1983.

CHAPTER TWENTY-SEVEN

Light in the Lord

Ephesians 5:8-14

The movement toward Christ is from darkness to light, from the black night on a Judean plain to the brilliant aura of angels announcing the Messiah's birth, from the bleak darkness of Good Friday to the blazing brightness of Easter.

> The people walking in darkness
> have seen a great light;
> on those living in the land of the shadow of death
> a light has dawned (Isaiah 9:2; cf. Matthew 4:16).

Ever since Jesus arose from the dead, His disciples have believed that in Him God sent His light and truth into the world. "In him was life, and that life was the light of men. The light shines in the darkness, but the darkness has not understood it. . . . The true light that gives light to every man was coming into the world" (John 1:4, 5, 9).

The light of Jesus casts out spiritual blindness, mental darkness, and moral blackness. Those He enlightens in turn become lights in a dark world. In Christ, they are people of the light.

People of the Light (5:8)

Of himself, Jesus said, "I am the light of the world." Of His disciples, He added, "Whoever follows me will never walk in darkness, but will have the light of life" (John 8:12). Even more, they will become the light of the world themselves (Matthew 5:14). The New Testament repeatedly stresses the Christian's transformation from living in darkness (and thus being darkened) to living in the light of the Lord (thus actually becoming light, the source of enlightenment, for others—see John 3:19; 12:36; Acts 13:47; 26:18; Romans 13:12; 2 Corinthians 4:6; Colossians 1:13; 1 Thessalonians 5:5; 1 Timothy 6:16; 1 Peter 2:9; 1 John 1:5-7).

229

As we used to sing in Sunday school, God expects Christians to "brighten the corner where you are." We understand the difference between *belonging* to a church and *being* the church. If asked by some street-corner surveyor, "Where is your church?," many Christians would give precise directions to and the exact address of their church building. They might throw in the worship hours and some information about the church program as well. But they would not have given Paul's answer.

He would answer, "Why, our church is over there at the grocery store, it's at a nearby service station, over at the beauty shop, down at the doctor's office, and out there on the playfield. Wherever our members are, there is where our church is. We are the church, and our members are shining as people of the light."

In 1973, a Cambodian school teacher and his wife accepted Christ as their Lord and Savior in an evangelistic campaign in their country. Sin Soum and his wife then felt called of God to leave their home and move into a large refugee settlement outside Phnom Penh where they had learned there was not a single Christian. It was a decision involving many personal hardships for them. Shopping, for example, meant a half-day journey, and the nearest water was a fifteen-minute walk. They had to construct their own shelter, which was only a tiny thatch hut.

Within six months, however, this light-filled couple had led thirty refugees to the Lord. After two years, without any formal training in evangelism, they were taking care of a congregation of over one thousand members, almost all of whom were their spiritual children or grandchildren.[63]

They were passing on the light. T. R. Glover of Cambridge once remarked that if the church had accomplished nothing else during its history but keep alive the memory of Jesus Christ, the church would have justified all it has cost to maintain. When you think of the difference the knowledge of Jesus meant to the thousand refugees, you quickly agree with Glover. You can also comprehend why Jesus, the light of the world, did not waste His time on earth forming an army, fomenting a political revolution, or writing treatises. Instead, He left behind an enlightened community, the

---

[63] Reported by Stanley W. Mooneyham, *Christianity Today,* September 18, 1981.

church, to carry on His life-giving, light-bearing work. So the work goes on, even in refugee camps, because people who once were darkness (Ephesians 2:1-3; 3:17-24, 1 Peter 2:9) "are now light in the Lord" (Ephesians 5:8).

You can identify them because people of the light bear the fruit of the light.

The Fruit of the Light (5:9, 10)

"The fruit of the light consists in all goodness, righteousness and truth" (Ephesians 5:9). Paul is still thinking in contrasts. Go back to Ephesians 5:3-7, where he describes the darkness. It involves sexual immorality, any kind of impurity, greed, obscenity, foolish talk, and coarse joking; a person who gives himself to these pursuits has no "inheritance in the kingdom of Christ and of God" (Ephesians 5:5). Children of the light dare not "be partners with" such a person (Ephesians 5:7).

That humorous but dissipated British cartoon character, Andy Capp, unwittingly illustrates Paul's emphasis here. He was having another of his famous evenings at the pub and, as usual, had consumed several pints too many when the bartender of the Star and Garter yanked him from the bar, dragged him out of the pub, and dropped him unceremoniously on the steps of another pub across the street, the Dog and Duck. A rather disheveled Capp then peers at the reader to complain, "This is the only trade where a gaffer is ashamed of 'is best customer."

Unfortunately, it isn't the only trade that hurts most its most faithful customers. The roadside inns along the broad way that leads to destruction are many. And in the darkness, one's companions do not appear dangerous and their pastimes do seem so attractive! So, for the sake of our staying in the light, the apostle warns us not to become partners with these "best customers."

The darkness that confuses a lost pilgrim is black indeed. Elsewhere Paul says, "Formerly, when you did not know God, you were slaves to those who by nature are not gods" (Galatians 4:8). In Romans he speaks with equal vividness:

> Therefore God gave them over in the sinful desires of their hearts to sexual impurity for the degrading of their bodies with one another. They exchanged the truth of God for a lie, and worshiped and served created things rather than the Creator—who is forever praised. Amen (Romans 1:24, 25).

Evidence of the darkness is everywhere. On June 3, 1973, Henry Brisbon, Jr., stopped two different cars within an hour, robbed the woman in the first and the couple in the second. His total take from the three was $54, two watches, and two rings. For the sake of this pittance, he cold-bloodedly killed all three.

Five years later, Brisbon was finally brought to trial and sentenced to a term of 1000 to 3000 years—the judge didn't want him ever to set foot in freedom again. Just a year later, he was back in court, however, this time for stabbing a fellow inmate to death with the sharpened handle of a soup ladle. At this trial, the state's attorney described Brisbon as such a terrible human being that he was a walking testimonial for the death penalty.

Brisbon disagreed. Of himself he said, "I'm no bad dude, just an antisocial individual."

Brisbon's self-characterization is the perfect description of darkness. From a Biblical perspective, you can't be antisocial and "not bad." Christian virtues are social virtues. Darkness is by definition antisocial (compare Ephesians 5:3-7 with Galatians 5:19-21). Light is what pleases God and so is good for everybody.

> Is not this the kind of fasting I have chosen:
> to loose the chains of injustice
>   and untie the cords of the yoke,
> to set the oppressed free
>   and break every yoke?
> Is it not to share your food with the hungry
>   and to provide the poor wanderer with shelter—
> when you see the naked, to clothe him,
>   and not to turn away from your own flesh and blood?
> Then your *light* will break forth like the dawn,
>   and your healing will quickly appear;
> then your righteousness will go before you,
>   and the glory of the Lord will be your rear guard.
> Then you will call, and the Lord will answer;
>   you will cry for help, and he will say: Here am I.
> If you do away with the yoke of oppression,
>   with the pointing finger and malicious talk,
> and if you spend yourselves in behalf of the hungry
>   and satisfy the needs of the oppressed,
> then your *light* will rise in the darkness,
>   and your night will become like the noonday (Isaiah 58:6-10).

Darkness took over the city of New York for a brief but frightening time in 1977. It was the second of two electrical power failures to afflict the metropolitan area. The first was the subject of many good-natured jokes and no one worried much. But the second left all observers anxious about the city and about humanity. For what seemed an unbearably long time, the city sweltered in darkness that summer night when lightning chanced to set off a chain reaction of power failures that left New Yorkers in utter darkness. The blackness was not merely physical; it was also moral. Out of the gutters of human depravity crawled every conceivable sin against men and property. While policemen stood by helpless, rampaging mobs looted stores, burned buildings, and ravaged people. So-called "normal, law-abiding citizens" joined hardened criminals in indulging every sinful desire.

There were some, journalists duly reported, who blazed like fires of goodness against the blackness. Their honesty, their kindness, their genuine decency offered hope that human civilization may still have some reason to exist. New York in the dark helps us understand Jesus as never before: "My disciples *must* be the light of the world."

A few years earlier, in St. Louis, the manager of a 700-family housing project lost his job for being too helpful! Burt Steingruby, a forty-three-year-old father of five, had done nothing dishonest; to the contrary, he was dismissed by the local housing authority because it was discovered that he had been stealthily helping people. Under questioning, Mr. Steingruby confessed that he was guilty of helping about 1000 project families out of his own pocket during the years he was manager.

He assisted them, he said, because nobody else would. He wasn't trying to be a hero; he just didn't want to see anyone evacuated when a little temporary financial help would make the difference. Most repaid him; many did not, but he simply wrote off his losses as charity.

So he was fired, even though he used only his own money. He eventually found a factory job at half his former salary. He didn't have any regrets, he said, and he would do the same thing over again.

Journalists picked up the story because Mr. Steingruby's kindness was, in their opinion, such an unusual departure from normal behavior. It was, you could say, like a ray of sunlight shining in the darkness.

This, then, is the fruit of the light: in place of malice, goodness; in place of injustice, righteousness; in place of falsehood, truth; in place of sin, "what pleases the Lord" (Ephesians 5:10). Wherever it shines, men will see the effect of the light.

The Effect of the Light (5:11-14)

The light exposes the deeds of darkness. Their shamefulness will become fully evident.

The light will effect a change in the believer:

What a wonderful change in my life has been wrought,
Since Jesus came into my heart,
I have light in my soul for which long I had sought,
Since Jesus came into my heart.[64]

This is the change described by Malcolm Muggeridge, the former editor of Britain's *Punch* magazine. When this literary rascal accepted Christ as the Lord of his life, he did so with a full understanding that a revolution in his behavior was called for, especially with respect to wine and women. It was a change he wanted to make. Having looked "far and wide, inside and outside" his own head and heart, he found no one but Jesus to offer "any answer to the dilemmas of this tragic, troubled time." He described Christianity as

a very bright light; particularly bright now because the surrounding darkness is so deep and dense; a brightness that holds my gaze inexorably, so that even if I want to—and I do sometimes want to—I can't detach it.

Muggeridge took seriously Christ's injunction to become "the light of the world," letting "our light shine before men." He identified partaking of the light, keeping it in one's eye as John Bunyan's Christian (in *Pilgrim's Progress)* was told to do, as Heaven itself, while being cut off from it is hell.

---

[64]"Since Jesus Came Into My Heart," Copyright 1914 by Charles H. Gabriel. © Renewed 1942 by The Rodeheaver Co. (A Div. of WORD, INC.) All rights reserved. International copyright secured. Used by permission.

Away from the light, one is imprisoned in the tiny, desolate dungeon of one's ego; when the light breaks in, suddenly one is liberated, reborn.[65]

Muggeridge experienced what Paul is calling for. Note Paul's verbs: They are imperatives. He does not think of walking in the light as some kind of supernatural religious experience, but as a deliberate moral decision. Although Christ called him by a blinding light on the road to Damascus (Acts 9), Paul does not use his experience as the standard for all Christians. Instead he appeals to his readers' wills. Every sentence assumes our ability to decide for ourselves: put off your old self, be renewed in the attitude of your minds, put on a new self, imitate God, let no one deceive you, do not be partners with them, find out what pleases God. Let the light of God shine in you.

Through all these verbs, Paul pleads for us to draw near to God. "Following after God," the great Christian leader Augustine has written,

> is the desire of happiness;
> to reach God is happiness itself.
> We follow after God by loving Him;
> We reach Him, not by becoming entirely what He is,
> but in nearness to Him,
> and in wonderful and immaterial contact with Him,
> and *in being inwardly illuminated and occupied by His truth and holiness.*

The newly enlightened believer becomes, in turn, the light that exposes the unmentionable secrets of the night. By refusing to participate, by speaking against, and by demonstrating better alternatives to the "fruitless deeds of darkness," the Christian, like his Lord before him, "makes everything visible" for what it is.

Paul's quotation (Ephesians 5:14—not an Old Testament quotation, although its words can be traced to Isaiah 9:2; 26:19; 51:17; 52:1; 60:1) abruptly turns our attention from moral questions to the dynamic center of the Christian message. What is so

---

[65] Malcolm Muggeridge, *Jesus Rediscovered* (London: William Collins Sons and Co., 1969), pp. 109, 110.

revolutionary about the faith is that it is *not* primarily concerned with ethical behavior. Even in the midst of this discussion of Christian conduct, Paul subtly asserts that we're dealing with God's offer to move us out of darkness into His marvelous light. It's an offer for more than just an improved quality of life, although it is certainly that. It is Christ's offer of himself to us. The Light of the world, the Light that gives life, has himself arisen from the dead and now awakens us from our death in sin (Ephesians 2:1-6) and shines *on* us and, to the extent that we let Him, *through* us.

The darkness of the crucifixion hours could not conquer the Light. Death could not destroy Life. Thus, "I am the resurrection and the life. He who believes in me will live, even though he dies; and whoever lives and believes in me will never die" (John 11:25, 26).

CHAPTER TWENTY-EIGHT

Walk in Wisdom

Ephesians 5:15-20

This is WISDOM, maids and men:
Knowing what to say and when.
Artists with the master touch
Never use one word too much.
Jesus preaching on the Mount
Made His every sentence count.
Lincoln's Gettysburg address
Needs not one word more or less.
This is WISDOM, maids and men:
Knowing what to say and when.
—Anonymous

This isn't all there is to living "not as unwise but as wise," but it is a good beginning. To be able to think and speak precisely *is* a mark of wisdom.

It is also, in an era "when the days are evil," a refusal to be locked into prevailing prejudices, an attitude that makes good sense in every field of human endeavor. Henry Bessemer, who invented the famous Bessemer process in steel production, for instance, attributed his breakthrough in modern refining methods to the fact that he had no fixed ideas, traditions, or prejudices to control his mind. He did not suffer from the general belief that, in the metal refining industry and in everything else, whatever is, is right.

The world does not always honor nonconformity like Bessemer's, of course. Worldly wisdom is more often defined as "getting along by going along." What is expected is not that we should be reasonable or independent, but that we should adapt to the mood of the day: if there is peace, we should be for peace; if there is war, we should fight. If the prevailing moral code is

Victorian, we should be prim and proper; if the new morality has taken over, we should die rather than be prudish. We are to be, as a popular book title labeled us a few years ago, *A Nation of Sheep*.

Going along may ease your way through life, but this so-called common sense sets you adrift on a current away from the wisdom of God (1 Corinthians 1:18-31). What is missing is any sense of purpose, any connection with eternity. As William Beebe once explained the scientist's attitude, "The isness of things is well worth studying; but it is their whyness that makes life worth living."[66] That whyness is life's purpose, without which life loses meaning.

"If I had to die now, I would say: 'Was that all?' And: 'That is not really how I understood it.' And: 'It was rather noisy." These are the words of the Berlin Jewish writer Kurt Tucholsky, who committed suicide in 1935, in despair over the growing power of the Nazis.[67] In his confusion, if not in his honesty, Tucholsky represents the majority of mankind who don't know how to live and, even more anxiously, don't know why.

"Be very careful, then, how you live," counsels the apostle Paul (Ephesians 5:15). You Christians are not to be unthinking children, "tossed back and forth by the waves, and blown here and there by every wind of teaching" (Ephesians 4:14). You are to be mature sons and daughters of God, imitating Him (Ephesians 5:1) and not your corrupt contemporaries.

You must walk in wisdom. As people of the light you are to "see to it" *[blepo]* that you live [*peripateo* — "walk about"] carefully. During World War II, some experiments at Ohio State University proved that Air Force applicants were normally using their eyes to only about twenty per cent of their real capacity. This visual "laziness" could cost the life of a pilot who has to see clearly, discriminate quickly, and identify accurately the whizzing sights in the skies. His optical sense must be heightened beyond the norm. He must "be very careful."

---

[66]William Beebe, quoted by Konrad Lorenz, *On Aggression*, Marjorie Kerr Wilson, tr. (New York, Harcourt, Brace and World, 1963), p. 21.

[67]Quoted by Hans Kung, *Does God Exist?* (New York: Doubleday, 1978), p. 479.

The Christian lives with heightened sensibilities. He sees more clearly, feels more deeply, hears more discerningly, and walks more carefully. Henry James, the father of novelist Henry James Jr. and philosopher William James, once congratulated the senior Oliver Wendell Holmes (physician and poet and father of a future Supreme Court Justice): "Holmes, you are intellectually the most alive man I ever knew."

"I am, I am," the doctor agreed. "From the crown of my head to the sole of my foot, I'm alive, I'm alive!"[68]

To be in Christ is to be so alive! Even though Mumford Jones is undoubtedly right in complaining that "ours is an age which is proud of machines that think and suspicious of men that do," Christians think. They want *to know,* not just to feel, "what the Lord's will is" (Ephesians 5:17). They want to walk carefully. They heed the counsel of C. S. Lewis:

> God is no fonder of intellectual slackers than of any other slackers. If you are thinking of becoming a Christian, I warn you you are embarking on something which is going to take the whole of you, brains and all. But, fortunately, it works the other way round. Anyone who is honestly trying to be a Christian will soon find his intelligence being sharpened: one of the reasons why it needs no special education to be a Christian is that Christianity is an education in itself.[69]

In Ephesians 5:15-20, Paul suggests three characteristics of the person made wise in Christ. In the first place, the wise person makes the most of every opportunity (Ephesians 5:16). Second, he discerns the Lord's will (Ephesians 5:17). Finally, he is filled with the Spirit (Ephesians 5:18-20).

"Making the Most of Every Opportunity" (5:16)

He knows he does not have much time, so he does not waste what time he has. He "buys back the time" (*exagorazomenoi ton kairon*), or redeems it. A good, long lifetime of eighty years is a brief moment when measured against the history of mankind, and

---

[68]Donald Hall, ed., *Literary Anecdotes* (Oxford: Oxford University Press, 1981), p. 67.

[69]C. S. Lewis, *Mere Christianity* (New York: Macmillan, 1952), p. 61.

compared with the promise of eternity, it is a fleeting instant. Since our time is so short, we ought to make the best of it. One of Charles Schulz's delightful greeting cards depicts Charlie Brown pondering some of the philosophical greats: "Cervantes said, 'To do is to be.' Descartes said, 'To be is to do.'" On the inside of the card is a laid-back Snoopy, wearing sunglasses and musing on the words of a more recent thinker: "Sinatra said, 'Dooby Dooby Doo.'"

Snoopy's style is not the Christian's. There is an intensity about a disciple's life. He knows the "days are evil" (*poneros* refers to moral evil), his days are few, and his responsibilities in Christ are pressing.

His days on earth are few. The time is coming when he will work no more. Wisdom faces this fact. It is a theme Jesus repeatedly discussed. His parable of the five foolish and five wise bridesmaids (Matthew 25:1-13) concludes with the warning, "Therefore keep watch, because you do not know the day or the hour."

No one does. Wisdom makes provisions, therefore, and is ready, even though it is more common for people to fumble through life making excuses for their tardiness. One day, it will be too late for excuses.

If eternity is a reality, how then can we "Dooby Dooby Do" our time away? And how can we expect to spend eternity with our Lord if we don't make time for Him now?

Another of Jesus' famous parables is of the prosperous farmer who decided to tear down his barns and build bigger ones to store up his hoard for himself (Luke 12:16-21). Then he'd say to himself, "You have plenty of good things laid up for many years. Take life easy; eat, drink and be merry."

But God said to him, "You fool!" Strong language, but precise. "This very night your life will be demanded from you. Then who will get what you have prepared for yourself?" Such, Jesus alerts us, will be the divine judgment on "anyone who stores up things for himself but is not rich toward God." When held against the night of death, how trivial seems the building of bigger barns.

At a funeral, there is little praising of barns and warehouses and harvests. Talk turns instead to souls and values and the race of time toward eternity.

"Understand What the Lord's Will Is" (5:17)

"But," someone inevitably protests, "how can we know the inscrutable will of God?" It is not as hard as we like to pretend. Scripture is undisturbingly clear on many specific matters. While they do not spell out whether you should be a butcher or baker or candlestick maker, they teach that whatever your occupation, you should live up to your calling as a Christian and pattern your behavior after that of God (Ephesians 5:1).

Ephesians gives excellent instruction in the will of God. Return to 5:3-6. The Lord obviously wants us to be highly moral persons, pure in action, having no other god before God. We cannot hide from these sentences: they are the will of God. Further, the consequences of disobedience are drastic: "No immoral, impure or greedy person—such a man is an idolater—has any inheritance in the kingdom of Christ and of God" (Ephesians 5:5). The word of the Lord cannot be communicated any more clearly than this!

Matthew Arnold, one of Britain's leading literary figures in the nineteenth century, quotes a favorite bishop's advice for upright living: "First, never go against the best light that you have; secondly, take care that your light be not darkness." Good counsel, for although the fool may say, "There is no God" (Psalm 14:1), the wise man believes in God and obeys Him. He follows the best light available to man.

"Folly," the late Dietrich Bonhoeffer wrote,

> is a more dangerous enemy to the good than evil. One can protest against evil; it can be unmasked and, if need be, prevented by force. Evil always carries the seeds of its own destruction, as it makes people, at the least, uncomfortable. Against folly we have no defense. Neither protests nor force can touch it; reasoning is no use.... So the fool, as distinct from the scoundrel, is completely self-satisfied.[70]

There is no way to help someone who insists on his right to be foolish. The door to his mind is closed; he has shut himself against the will of God. He has been deceived with empty words, his understanding darkened by long agreement with the perverted practices of his world. He may protest that he seeks God's will,

---

[70]Bonhoeffer, *Letters and Papers from Prison,* p. 10.

yet he is unwilling to worship Him and live a morally pure life. He is not convinced that

> The law of the Lord is perfect,
>   reviving the soul.
> The statutes of the Lord are trustworthy,
>   making wise the simple.
> The precepts of the Lord are right,
>   giving joy to the heart.
> The commands of the Lord are radiant,
>   giving light to the eyes.
> The fear of the Lord is pure,
>   enduring forever.
> The ordinances of the Lord are sure
>   and altogether righteous.
> They are more precious than gold,
>   than much pure gold;
> they are sweeter than honey,
>   than honey from the comb.
> By them is your servant warned;
>   in keeping them there is great reward (Psalm 19:7-11).

Be Filled With the Spirit (5:18-20)

The pagan world, on the other hand, fills up on alcohol. In America, for example, a 1983 Gallup poll found that drinking problems afflicted one third of our nation's families. (That figure, by the way, was up from 22 percent in 1982.)

Drunkenness is no new sin. In Paul's day, drunkenness was rampant; its effect was "debauchery" (*asotia*), a condition vividly described in Proverbs 23:29-35.

> Who has woe? Who has sorrow?
>   Who has strife? Who has complaints?
>   Who has needless bruises? Who has bloodshot eyes?
> Those who linger over wine,
>   who go to sample bowls of mixed wine.
> Do not gaze at wine when it is red,
>   when it sparkles in the cup,
>   when it goes down smoothly!
> In the end it bites like a snake
>   and poisons like a viper.

Your eyes will see strange sights
   and your mind imagine confusing things.
You will be like one sleeping on the high seas,
   lying on top of the rigging.
"They hit me," you will say, "but I'm not hurt!
   They beat me, but I don't feel it!
When will I wake up
   so I can find another drink?

The drunkard's condition is pitiful. The Scripture's prescribed antidote is straightforward: "Do not get drunk on wine" (Ephesians 5:18). Period.

If you really want some kicks in life, seek them in the Spirit, not in spirits. "Be filled with the Spirit."

It is a surprising contrast, isn't it? Paul does not advocate temperance, but another form of intoxication. The disciples demonstrated it on the Day of Pentecost. Peter had to dispel the impression that they were drunk before he could preach (Acts 2:15).

The contrast is accurate. People drink primarily to relieve their tensions, to assuage their guilt, to feel more at ease socially, to gain a greater sense of strength or security, or to experience a warmth and glow that is not normally theirs. These are precisely the results of being filled with the Holy Spirit. Watch some really joyful Christians at a church party. They, too, could be accused of being drunk, they act with such merriment and abandon. Outwardly, they have several of the marks of those who have been filled with wine; they are enjoying a quite different Spirit, however, and this intoxication does not pass away the next morning.

Paul uses the imperative mood of the verb here: "Be filled." It is within the power of the individual to allow himself to be taken over by the Holy Spirit. There isn't anything mystical going on here. Just as the drinker submits to the power of his drink, the Christian submits to the power of God in his life. One surrenders to alcohol, the other to the Spirit.

The Holy Spirit has been promised to every Christian, of course (Acts 2:38), but unfortunately, not every believer has really opened himself to the control of the Spirit. Paul is not suggesting that we need to somehow get more of the Holy Spirit in our lives—we already have Him. What Paul urges, however, is that we let the Holy Spirit have more of us! That we actually surrender to

243

the will and power of God. That we be truly "in Christ" and that Christ be just as truly "in us."

The effect of this filling is, to say the very least, singing and praising and giving thanks (Ephesians 5:19, 20).

We sing "psalms" (originally, singing accompanied by the harp) and "hymns" (in classical Greek, festive lyrics sung in praise of gods or heroes)—in other words, we sing whatever will praise and glorify God. The music comes from the heart, testimonies in song to accompany our testimonies of word and life. Peter explains it best: "Though you have not seen him, you love him; and even though you do not see him now, you believe in him and are filled with an inexpressible and glorious joy" (1 Peter 1:8).

In everything, we give thanks. According to William Law, this is the essence of wisdom. This eighteenth-century man of prayer declared emphatically, "If anyone would tell you the shortest, surest way to all happiness and perfection, he must tell you to make a rule to yourself to thank and praise God for everything that happens to you." By doing so, Law insisted you can turn even an apparent calamity into a blessing. The Spirit, after all, is in charge, and the ways of the Spirit of God are wise beyond our knowing. (See also Romans 8:28; 2 Corinthians 4:16-18; 1 Thessalonians 5:18.)

CHAPTER TWENTY-NINE

The Marriage Ideal

Ephesians 5:21-33

Paul never loses sight of the theme of his letter, although from time to time it might seem so. Even in these verses, however, when he speaks of such domestic matters as relations between a husband and a wife, he is still concerned about the unity of everything in Christ (Ephesians 1:10). God's purpose is to bring all things into harmony, even husbands and wives.

Scholars often give the discussions introduced here the technical name *Haustafel,* "Table of Household Duties," a treatment of practical advice found in Jewish, pagan, and now Christian documents. (See Colossians 3:18—4:1 for another example.) Paul includes advice for spouses (Ephesians 5:21-33), for parents and children (6:1-4), and for slaves and masters (6:5-9). It is noteworthy in our litigious age that Paul stresses duties, not rights. To demands one's rights is to guarantee one's misery and to shatter the unity that God wants.

In Ephesians 5:21-33, Paul concerns himself with the power struggle that threatens the most intimate of human relationships. While our era holds seminars in assertiveness training, Paul counsels submission of selfish interests for the good of the relationship. Whenever husband or wife insists on rights instead of duties, on dominating instead of serving, the unity of the home is shattered.

Hardheaded pragmatists will object that Paul presents an idealized view of matrimony here. Granted. His description of the sacrificing husband and the submissive wife looks too good to be true—unless you have been fortunate enough to see a real husband and a real wife take his words seriously. Then you know he speaks the truth. To make his ideal the goal of our marriages instead of the self-serving struggle for our "rights" that leads to such fictions as "marriage contracts" (permitting cohabitation without benefit of genuine love) is to adopt the only sensible road to the goal of harmony in the home.

The honest alternative would be to rewrite the wedding vows to sound something like this: "I, Roy, take thee, Joy, to be my lawfully wedded wife and hereby lay claim to all the rights, privileges, and perquisites appertaining thereto." To promise undying loyalty, "for better or for worse," while at the same time expecting "to get my rights" is to do violence to marriage before ever leaving the altar.

In his novel *Reuben, Reuben,* Peter de Vries' first paragraph describes the course of contemporary matrimony:

> Given a little money, education and social standing, plus of course the necessary leisure, any man with any style at all can make a mess of his love life. And given these, plus a little of the right to self-realization that goes with modern life, a little of the old self-analysis, any woman with any gumption at all can make a shambles of her marriage.

Once upon a time romantic confusion was "the privilege of a few," but now, deVries concludes, everybody can get in on it.[71] How can a modern couple escape the confusion? By heeding Paul's counsel. It is admittedly tough medicine, since sacrifice and submission do not come to us easily, but it is undeniably the best prescription available.

"Submit to one another out of reverence for Christ" (Ephesians 5:21). This principle governs *all* relationships in the Lord. Unless we honor one another above ourselves (Romans 12:10), God's desired unity is stifled by self-serving. Peace in the world—like peace in the home—is achievable only through mutual submission. Paul's word (*hupotasso*) is found twenty-three times in his writings, always denoting subordination to a person of excellent character or elevated position.

Following the general principle, Paul becomes very specific: "Wives, submit to your husbands as to the Lord" (Ephesians 5:22). It is impossible to misunderstand Paul here. We may ignore his advice, or deliberately counteract it, but we cannot claim that we do not understand. Many Christian ministers include these

---

[71]Peter de Vries, *Reuben, Reuben* (Little, Brown, 1964).

verses to the wife and husband in wedding ceremonies, sometimes to the consternation of the modern participants who can scarcely believe that something so old-fashioned would be demanded of today's bride and groom. They would much prefer the words of a cartoon, in which the presiding minister asks the couple, "Do you promise to love, honor, and relate to one another?" "Relating to one another" somehow seems easier than submitting, because we can "relate" in a variety of ways. To promise "to relate" is to promise nothing at all.

Paul's starting point is not with the bride or the groom, but with the Lord. Submission begins with respect for the Lord, who desires that His disciples respect one another, even at home, and even between sexes (Galatians 3:28). Paul's instructions for Christian behavior in the church and world (Ephesians 4:1—5:21) apply to the family as well. Although Greek and Roman (and, for that matter, Jewish) cultures treated men as superior to women, Christ elevated women to the level of men. But this must be understood in the context of Ephesians 5:21 to be one of mutual submission, not mutual dominance. Male and female kneel together before Christ; male and female serve each other in humility. The woman "submits," the man "loves" with *agape* love, a love that sacrifices for the sake of the loved one.

Paul's counsel is quite in harmony with other Bible verses regarding the role of women in marriage. She was created to be a companion and helper suitable for man (Genesis 2:20). The Lord told her that her desire would be for her husband, who would rule over her (Genesis 3:16). Colossians 3:18 echoes Ephesians: "Wives, submit to your husbands, as is fitting in the Lord." First Corinthians 11:3 reads, "Now I want you to realize that the head of every man is Christ, and the head of the woman is man, and the head of Christ is God." We cannot escape the implications of the words. They do not imply the inferiority of woman, of course. Terribly cruel and distorted applications of these verses have made more than one woman's life miserable. These Scriptures have to be read in harmony with Galatians 3:28 ("neither male nor female") and with an appreciation for the way Jesus treated women and the large role they played in the early church. Paul intends no put-down for women here.

He certainly does not intend that a woman becomes her husband's slave. A few years ago, a *Dennis the Menace* comic strip illustrated how easy it is for a husband to take advantage of his submissive wife. Dennis is at the Wilsons, having cake and milk. Mr. Wilson is trying to read his paper as Mrs. Wilson washes the dishes. Dennis wonders why Mr. Wilson never goes to work.

Mr. Wilson explains that he is retired.

"Retired! Is that why you loaf all the time?" Dennis asks him.

Mr. Wilson tells him he has earned the right to loaf, since he worked hard for many years so that he could take it easy some day.

That makes Dennis wonder why Mrs. Wilson doesn't retire. He has never seen her loaf.

"She can't retire because she never worked" is Mr. Wilson's unfortunately tactless response.

Dennis can't accept this answer, since Mrs. Wilson is always cooking or washing or sewing.

"That's different," Mr. Wilson exclaims. "She's a housewife! If she retired who'd do the housework?"

"Couldn't *you* help?" Dennis wonders.

"Dennis! Are you trying to make trouble?" an exasperated Mr. Wilson shouts.

At this point Mrs. Wilson intervenes, telling her husband not to yell at the boy. "He's right and you *know* it!"

In the next frame, Dennis is walking up to his mother in her garden. When she asks him what the Wilsons are arguing about over there, he says, "I dunno. I came home 'cause I didn't want to get involved!"[72]

Mr. Wilson probably thinks his is the Biblical understanding of the wife's role, but Dennis is closer to the truth, since he intuitively grasps what it means for a husband and wife to be in mutual submission. The wife is a person in her own right, full of dignity and possibilities, who respects her husband and assists him to fulfill his potential. She is his helper and friend, but never his lackey.

To be in submission, then, is not to be weak, unduly dependent or servile; it is certainly not to become a non-person. What Paul asks is that whatever the wife possesses she places in the service of her husband. She does not demand her way, she is not belligerent or assertive in a self-serving manner, she is not a "nag," if you please, but she cares about what is best for her husband.

---

[72]*Dennis the Menace,* Hall Syndicate, 1973.

Christ is the head of the church as the husband is the head of the wife. The church submits to Christ because Christ has saved the church through His sacrifice. The church has every reason to trust such a "husband."

To husbands, Paul's words seem even more exacting. "Husbands, love your wives, just as Christ loved the church and gave himself up for her" (Ephesians 5:25). There is no hint here that the wife exists for the sake of the husband, or that he depends on her. Many husbands mistakenly hope to prove their love by such "romantic" words as, "I need her so much," or, "I can't get along without her." That is not love, of course, but childishness. Paul calls for greater maturity.

To love as Christ loved the church, for her sake, to perfect her—now that's an order! To love your wife so that your primary concern is for her—her beauty, her holiness, her completion; to love her even if you must die for her as Christ died for the church, this is the husband's role.

The Bible teaches that Christ laid down His life for us (Romans 4:25; 8:32; Galatians 1:4), which is the same as saying that He died for the church. He did so in order "to make her holy"*(hagiazo* — "to set apart"; Ephesians 5:26). There is an old Jewish wedding custom in which the groom, after the ring is given, says, "Behold, thou art sanctified ['made holy,' 'set apart'] to me." This illustrates the marriage between Christ and His bride, the church, for the church has become a "set apart" people, holy to the Lord.

Members of the church have been "washed" (Ephesians 5:26). Paul ties together the *washing,* implying a physical cleansing (an undoubted reference to Christian baptism, although Paul could also have in mind the purification of the bride before the wedding), and the *word,* which may refer to the words spoken at baptism. Titus 3:5 speaks of "the washing of rebirth and renewal by the Holy Spirit" by which God saves us. What Paul is concentrating on here is the effort Christ expends in order to assist the church, His bride, become "radiant, ... without stain or wrinkle or any other blemish, but holy and blameless" (Ephesians 5:27). A Christ-loving husband will expend the same effort to assist his wife, whom he loves as he loves his own body because in loving his wife, he loves himself, since the two are one flesh.

Is it for this that we men marry? Do we actually think about sacrificing ourselves? No. We marry for companionship, for sex, for comfort and security, but few of us marry for love, at least as the Bible defines it. The Biblical ideal is marriage for the sake of our wives, assisting them to realize the potential God gave them. It is no wonder, then, that so many marriages fail. If a man asks a woman to be his wife to serve his selfish desires, his selfishness traps both of them in a prison of bitterness and even hatred. His lusts master them both, and she either becomes his slave or finds a way to get away from him physically or emotionally. But if the man's goal is his wife's good, and the wife's goal is her husband's good, a mutually enjoyable harmony rules in that home.

Christian marriage obviously demands a high view of women. Demosthanes, in the fourth century before Christ, expressed the prevailing view of his day: "We have courtesans for our pleasure, prostitutes for our daily physical use, and wives to bring up legitimate children and to be faithful stewards in household matters." Jewish rabbis in the second century after Christ taught a Jewish man to thank God that He did not make him a Gentile, a woman, or a bore. In Shakespeare's England, it was the custom for a man of means to keep a wife to run his house and a mistress to satisfy his physical needs. Throughout history, men have viewed women as a means to satisfy their desires.

Against them all stands Paul with his Lord. The apostle's ideal of marriage is the highest to be found anywhere. He treats women as worthy of God's love and, hence, worthy of men's love—and sacrifice.

In Christian marriage, therefore, the power struggle is over. Husband and wife do not spar to determine who is the superior or stronger one, or who will serve whom. The two have become one (verse 31).

In Plato's *Symposium,* one of the speakers explains love. The god Zeus, he says, was jealous of the power of men, but he had an idea that would keep them humble. "They shall continue to exist and I shall cut them in two." The theory is that since we are born only half a person, we seek until we find our other half, then the two become one.

That is one explanation of marital unity, but not a very good one. It suggests that each of us has a special other half, and no other person can satisfy us. It is the old "marriages are made in Heaven" theme, only without Heaven. There is no Biblical support for this romantic concept of love and marriage. In this view, marital success is in the hands of fate; we are helpless until fate properly matches us with the one we were destined to marry.

When Paul wrote Ephesians, marriages were arranged by parents. A man and woman did not fall in love and then get married; they got married and learned to love. Only in recent generations have we defined marital love as something we "fall into." Until then, marital love was something we had to grow into.

We must not go to the other extreme, however. If we say on the one hand that marriages are not necessarily made in Heaven (meaning by that that only one person is suited for me and that my marital success is up to Heaven), we must not react by thinking that we are nothing but animals and that what is really important is that we satisfy our physical urges. In the turbulent '60s, an Ohio State University professor was advocating extra-marital affairs as the way to revitalize marriages. At about the same time, another professor asked us to consider the human male in the same category as a normal buck, bull, or stallion that "collects, dominates, protects, and impregnates as many females as he possibly can."

The professor's advice is quite reasonable, if we think of ourselves as just another species of the animal kingdom. But if, in fact, we were created in the image of God, then the comparison should not be with the bull in the pasture but with the Lord of life. So to Christ's view of marriage the apostle Paul turns our attention.

This is why it is imperative that we talk about the marriage ideal. We have had enough talk of bulls and stallions. The marriage ideal, as presented here, is that we adopted sons and daughters of God live up to the standard of Christ's calling in our homes. The fact is that we *can* have ideal marriages if husbands and wives really love and submit to one another. It is quite possible for a woman in love to be in submission to her husband and find in that subjection total fulfillment. It is equally possible for even a selfish, egocentric man to so learn to love a woman that he can give himself up for her, so that she might become beautiful and perfect and holy.

What we have been calling an ideal, Paul calls a "mystery," meaning something that was a secret until God revealed it. In Christ's relationship with the church, God has taught us the proper way for a husband and a wife to relate to one another. Now it is no longer a secret. It has become an ideal, but an attainable ideal.

251

CHAPTER THIRTY

Of Children and Fathers

Ephesians 6:1-4

God wants unity in the home. Wives and husbands are expected to submit to one another in the Lord. With each partner working for the good of the other, harmony is possible and the fullest development of each spouse is the beautiful result.

God wants the same happy relationship between parents and children. Unfortunately, there is no guarantee that great persons are necessarily good parents. Mahatma Gandhi, who modeled his high ethical standards after Jesus Christ, has often been held before us as the model man of our century. Yet Gandhi's son Harilal departed in every way from his father's example. When Harilal's wife died in 1918, he remarried, but the new marriage did not stop his disintegration. He buried himself in alcohol and women; he disgraced his Hindu father by attacking him in print, then signed his name "Abdulla," a Moslem name. Through his conversion to Islam, his drunkenness, and his womanizing, Harilal seemed to be doing everything he could to hurt his father.

When Oral Roberts' oldest son Ronald committed suicide in 1982, fellow Christians all over America were shaking their heads in pity for the family. Ronald was helplessly addicted to drugs, the condition that led to his suicide. Oral Roberts' oldest child, daughter Rebecca Roberts Nash, was killed in an airplane crash in 1977. Richard, the third child, was divorced in 1980. Even as optimistic a person as the famous faith healer must have had some long, long thoughts about the agonies of parenting and the delicate relationships between parents and their children.

Comedienne Phyllis Diller has had such thoughts. She said, "The reason I'm not an alcoholic is because I don't like to drink in front of the kids, and when I'm away from them, who needs it?"

But parenting is no joking matter. The disharmony between generations is a perennial problem, with all adult ages worrying about what's happening to the race as they watch their obviously inferior offspring get ready to take their places. It is reported that in the fifth century B. C. a philosopher grumbled,

> Our youth today love luxury. They have bad manners, contempt for authority, disrespect for older people. Children nowadays are tyrants. They contradict their parents, gobble their food and tyrannize their teachers.

Whether the report is accurate or not is debated, but the sentiment probably accurately reflects adult worries of every century.

Paul discusses parent-child affairs in three brief sentences here. He is still tracing the implication of his theme of unity in Christ (Ephesians 1:10). His point is that as self-assertiveness can destroy the unity between husband and wife, so can it separate parents from their children. His words are correctives. If you follow his advice, there can be peace in your home.

The Words to the Children (6:1-3)

"Obey your parents in the Lord" (Ephesians 6:1). To a generation fed on permissive theories of child-rearing, this counsel sounds terribly old-fashioned. With some schools offering classes on "How to get what you want from your parents" and some lawyers encouraging children to sue their parents for their rights, this verse seems to fight against the trends of the times. It sounds especially simplistic when Paul adds his reason for telling children to obey: "for this is right." That's it. No further argument.

The apostle would have been astonished if he were to observe the disobedience of some children—and the fear of their parents. When I was teaching high school, I happened to walk into the principal's office one morning just as he came out of his inner office, shaking his head. He said he had just received a telephone call from a father who complained that he couldn't get his son, a high school junior, out of bed on school mornings. He wanted advice from the principal.

I had never heard of such a thing. I certainly could not imagine my own father complaining to someone else that he couldn't make me get out of bed in the morning! (I did recall a ritual of earlier years, however, when in the mornings my mother would call me ... and my mother would call me ... and my mother would call me ... then my father would call me and I'd get up!) My father had no fear of his son, I assure you.

In her youth, Alice Roosevelt, Teddy's daughter, was what the newspapers of her day called a "madcap." She broke all the rules, including smoking cigarettes, drinking champagne until all hours, and publicly ridiculing national leaders. Her father despaired of controlling her. "I can either run the country or control Alice," he explained. "Not both."

He is not the only parent ever to have lost control. Yet, the Bible says, children are to obey their parents. Their obedience is essential for an orderly society and for personal spiritual ("in the Lord") growth. As we obey God our Father, so He expects us to obey our parents in the Lord. We never outgrow the need to be obedient to higher authorities.

How, then, do children learn to obey? There is no secret. They learn obedience from parents who obey God and expect obedience from their children.

It's unfortunately very easy for parents to teach their children to disobey them. They do so by not meaning what they say. They fall into the trap of repeating themselves three, four, or five times before they really mean business. Their kids can count, so they know they don't have to pay any attention until the fifth time.

When I was in college administration, the president of the college's student council and I brought the student government to the edge of extinction. Three times, he had requested a fundamental change in the council's stated operating authority; three times, acting on behalf of the administration, I had refused the requested permission. He then proceeded to make the changes himself in direct violation of college policy. I stopped him and, in the process, threatened to eliminate the council entirely unless it could operate within the college's guidelines.

Later I asked him why he had gone ahead when I had clearly told him no three times.

"I wanted to see if you really meant it," he told me. In that short answer, I learned a great deal about him. He had apparently been conditioned to believe that the first three refusals don't count. (Of course, this young man, if he were telling the story, would have some things to say about a stubborn administrator who was unaware of the changing times. And he'd probably be right!)

The Old Testament word to children is even stronger than *obey.* "*Honor* your father and mother" (Exodus 20:12; Ephesians 6:2). Treat them with respect, give them the deference due to those worthy of tribute. As you outwardly obey their desires, inwardly nurture the attitude that keeps you at peace with them. Your society may encourage you to assert your independence at the expense of your elders, but the Bible doesn't. The unity of your home will be shattered unless this time-honored system is honored. Ogden Nash may have sung somewhere, "Children's aren't happy with nothing to ignore, / And that's what parents were created for," but his song must never be anything but a joke.

Paul underscores the God-given source of the home's unity when he adds, "in the Lord". Husbands and wives must submit to each other "as to the Lord" (Ephesians 5:22). Slaves are to be obedient to their masters "as [they] would obey Christ" (Ephesians 6:5). All Christians are to be strong "in the Lord" (Ephesians 6:10). The Christian life is the God-filled life, according to Paul. "In him [God] we live and move and have our being" (Acts 17:28), Paul assured the Athenians. In all actions, then, even in everyday matters like satisfying your employer or obeying your parents, you are serving the Lord. "So whether you eat or drink or whatever you do, do it all for the glory of God" (1 Corinthians 10:31).

According to the Old Testament, children are to respect their parents because their elders know some things they haven't learned yet. Further, as Deuteronomy 5:16 records it, this commandment includes a promise:

> "Honor your father and your mother, as the Lord your God has commanded you, so that you may live long and that it may go well with you in the land the Lord your God is giving you."

(Some scholars debate whether this is actually the first commandment with a promise, since the second one [Deuteronomy 5:8-10] seems to include one as well. Perhaps that is not so much a promise, however, as a description.) This promise of long life and well-being goes a step beyond Paul's simple assertion "for this is right." A parent's wisdom can help the child prepare for life.

With the advent of psychoanalysis in the twentieth century, we now read this passage with deeper understanding. Rebellious and disobedient children fight all their adult lives against the guilt they incur when they reject their parents' authority. If they were reared in a home fraught with disharmony, they carry a psychic burden that can shorten and certainly sadden their mature years. You must honor your father and mother if for no other reason than to protect your own mental health!

The words to children are *obey* and *honor.*

The Words to Fathers (6:4)

The words to fathers are *instruct* and *train.*

The first readers of this letter would have had no problem understanding why Paul said *"fathers"* rather than *"mothers and fathers."* The preceding verses (Ephesians 5:21-33) demonstrate that the husband is the head of the wife, thus the head of the children. Although the father may delegate most of the immediate responsibility for child care to the mother, he sets the tone in the household and is the source of security and discipline.

A parallel text (Colossians 3:21) urges fathers not to *embitter* their children, lest they become *discouraged.* Fathers are to *encourage,* that is "give heart" to their offspring and not cause them to "lose heart." His teaching ("instruction") and disciplining ("training"), in both word and modeling, come from his own loving heart. He never becomes abusive or tyrannical, but on the other hand, neither does he ever abdicate his responsibility by leaving the nurturing of the children solely up to his wife. As he loves his wife with his whole heart (Ephesians 5:25f), so he loves his children and brings them up "in the training and instruction of the Lord."

Modern fathers are often confused about the best way to apply this verse. A few suggestions are in order.

1. Begin by being a real father figure to your children. To borrow a term that has many uses and return it to the home, may I suggest that all children need someone to fill the traditional role of "father" in their lives. He is their source of psychological support, their counselor, their model. He is a steady disciplinarian, never capricious or petty, but always concerned with what is best for the children. From him, they can learn what it means to be an adult. (His children ought to be able to say more of him than my son said of me a few years ago. During an open house for our church members, one of our visitors was having some fun with Lane, tempting him to betray family secrets. "What does your father do around the house?" he asked him. Lane thought for a while, then honestly answered, "Well, he sleeps a lot.")

Not the best father figure! I must work on my example, so that my son can have as good a model as I had in my father. He taught me more by example than by precept. He gave me the richest legacy a father can bestow—proud memories of a worthy man.

2. *Let your love show.* Every child needs affection and acceptance. Some fathers who love their children deeply nonetheless find it hard to communicate their love. They are afraid to touch, afraid to embrace. Their children grow up starved for affection. They become discouraged.

Some time ago, I read of a nationwide survey that had been conducted among young women who became strip teasers and "go-go" dancers. The surveyors were searching for the reason that they would take up this socially questionable work. The one common element among the women was that none of them enjoyed a good relationship with her father. The attention their fathers had denied them they were now seeking by displaying their bodies before other men. They were, in a word, discouraged women.

3. *Don't be afraid to discipline.* Here is a double danger. On the one hand, you can indulge a child too leniently. "Spoiling the child," we call it. On the other, you can regiment so harshly that you rob the child of any opportunity to make decisions and gradually become self-disciplined.

Several fine books have been written in recent years to help parents find the happy medium between too much and too little discipline. We don't have space here to reproduce their arguments, but we can state the assumption that all of them begin with this premise: the teaching of discipline begins with yourself. You can't expect to foster maturity and self-discipline in your children if you are self-indulgent, lazy, and undisciplined. That is a sure way to "exasperate" your children. Start with yourself; then you have earned the right through example to "bring up" your children "in the training and instruction of the Lord."

4. *Devote yourself to your child's development.* Your child's *total* development, that is. Along with providing adequate shelter, clothing, and food, remember that every child needs help in achieving social, physical, educational, and spiritual goals as well. All of these, including the last, are the father's responsibility. As one smart mother put it, "There are two lasting things I would

like to give my kids. One of these is roots, the other is wings. The first is easier than the second."[73]

5. *Set the emotional and spiritual tone in your house.* If the father is, in fact, head of the house, his attitudes and moods will govern there. Henry Ward Beecher boasted of his father, "I never heard from him a word of uncharitableness, nor saw a symptom of envy or jealousy." He set the spiritual tone for the family.

Howard Hendricks sets down six things "NEVER NEVER (well, hardly ever!) to do" which I'd like to repeat here to help us fathers establish a tone that fosters healthy growth in our children:

Don't threaten—you decimate your own authority.
Don't bribe—bargaining usually makes you the loser.
Don't lose your temper—a clear demonstration of lack of control.
Don't refuse to explain—they'll go elsewhere and you're on the outside.
Don't use sarcasm or embarrassment—the fastest way to demolish a relationship.
Don't dash their dreams—your ticket into the generation gap.[74]

All these words of advice can be summed up in two sentences:
Let your children know you're their father.
Let your children know your Father.

[73]Alan Loy McGinnis, *The Friendship Factor* (Minneapolis: Augsburg, 1979), p. 78.

[74]Howard Hendricks, *Heaven Help the Home* (Wheaton: Victor Books, 1973), p. 39.

CHAPTER THIRTY-ONE

How to Be a Christian on the Job

Ephesians 6:5-9

At first glance, this passage seems to have little to do with us. The age of slavery, at least in our country, has passed. We don't have masters and slaves.

But we do have employers and employees, and with just a little imagination, we can apply the good advice Paul writes concerning masters and slaves to the equally touchy relations between bosses and workers.

Paul is not thinking of industrial plants, of course. He is still thinking in family terms. Having addressed relationships of husbands and wives and of parents and children, he turns now to the other members of a typical Roman-empire family, the slaves. It has been estimated that one third of the Roman population were slaves, so Paul's instructions here were read earnestly by early Christians trying to obey the Lord in their complex culture.

Some of today's readers find the passage not only irrelevant, but offensive. They can't forgive Paul for not blazing away against slavery instead of seeming to accept it meekly as part of the *status quo*. Theirs is a legitimate complaint, but it betrays more a twentieth-century bias than a first-century understanding. The critics fail to note that the Scriptures do not sanction slavery as they do the divine institutions of marriage and family. Instead, they treat it as a prevailing evil for which there is no simple solution.

There are at least three reasons for the Bible's light treatment of slavery. First, when these words were written, Christians had no political or social influence whatever. They could have preached most enthusiastically against this social illness, but they would not have made any impact on the Roman slave system. Secondly, even if they managed to set some slaves free, the freedmen couldn't have found work. When an entire economy is based on endentured labor, who will pay wages to hire a newly freed slave? Thirdly and fundamentally, Christians had a greater challenge before them than transforming the economic system. Their goal was to convert pagans into God-fearers who could then eventually revolutionize the economic system. First things first. God wants both masters *and* slaves re-born as new beings in Christ.

In Galatians 3:28, Paul has written that in Christ, our usual categories no longer apply, since "there is neither Jew nor Greek, slave nor free, male nor female, for you are all one in Christ Jesus." Christians thus are forbidden to think of anyone as "just a woman" or "just a slave." Women and slaves and Greeks are persons and, in Christ, these persons are all brothers and sisters, no matter what distinctions the world acknowledges.

In these few verses, then, Paul the prisoner bids slaves not to think of themselves as fettered prisoners of man but as his fellow prisoners of Christ. He is also their fellow slave, like them a servant of Christ. So to his fellow prisoners and slaves, he says in effect, "When you put on Christ, you became His slaves; whether you work for Christ as a servant of an earthly master or in some other capacity doesn't matter, since as His slave you can serve Him under any circumstances."

Here, then, Paul speaks directly to our modern problems in labor-management relations. His words seem impractical at first, but they aren't. In fact, contemporary studies of the management styles of Japan's and America's best corporations prove that the Bible is unbeaten as a handbook for excellence in business leadership. William Ouchi, in his *Theory Z,* for example, surprises the reader in his preface by claiming that his book, the result of his examination of the best in Japanese management, is about *trust, intimacy,* and *subtlety,* qualities quite removed from the usual stereotype of aggressive, impersonal, goal-oriented industrial leadership. One reads of family feeling, of "clans," of lifetime employment, of "father-son" relationships within corporations. A Christian student of modern management theory feels right at home with "Theory Z" and other person-oriented doctrines. They seem to come right out of Ephesians 6:5-9!

Let's read this passage with employers and employees in today's business places in mind.

A Word to Employees (6:5-8)

Slaves, obey your earthly masters with respect and fear, and with sincerity of heart, just as you would obey Christ. . . . like slaves of Christ, doing the will of God from your heart (Ephesians 6:5, 6).

Work hard in obedience to your superior, even though you don't stand to gain anything materially for your effort (slaves eat the same, whether they really produce or not). Work hard because your real Master is Christ, who became a slave like you in order to serve God (Philippians 2:1-11; John 13:1-17). Work sincerely, obeying your supervisor just as readily as you obey Christ (the advice is the same as it is for wives and children).

Strange-sounding words to today's laborers. Not many Labor Day speeches urge workers to give the best they can, to be loyal, obedient, and productive. Instead, labor leaders urge their fellows to demand more and more, no matter what.

That do-the-least-you-can-get-away-with-for-the-highest-pay attitude was pushed to its extreme in Bristol, England. A United Press International story (August, 1983) exposed some workers at an electronics factory there who had been sleeping through the night shift for more than sixteen years. They had fabricated secret bedrooms in the plant's walls and ceilings. They were only found out when outside contractors found some "spare" electrical cables and traced them through the ceiling and behind sliding hatches to reading lamps beside the beds in these hidden rooms. They also found in the secret compartments mattresses, blankets, pillows, sheets, lamps, and even an alarm clock.

At least three foremen knew about their workers' sleep-in shifts, but they were afraid to report them for fear of losing their jobs.

These workers could profit from Paul's injunction. No Christian could shirk on the job like this, since Christians serve their employers not just "when their eye is on you, but like slaves of Christ" (Ephesians 6:6).

Somebody recently gave me a mathematical explanation of why nobody works around here:

WE'VE FINALLY FIGURED IT OUT
HERE'S WHY NOBODY WORKS

Every year has 365 days	365 days
If you sleep 8 hours a day	-122 days
This leaves	243 days
If you rest 8 hours a day	-122 days
This leaves	121 days
If you don't work Sundays	-52 days
This leaves	69 days
Most take Saturdays off	-52 days
This leaves	17 days
You take 1/2 hour for lunch	-9 days
This leaves	8 days
You get one week of vacation	-7 days
This leaves	1 day
No one works Labor Day	-1 day
This leaves	0 days

NO WONDER NOTHING EVER GETS DONE AROUND HERE!!!

There are some sincere workers, however. They pattern their work lives after Paul's exhortation. One such man, for example, turned down a lucrative job offer. "Well, I can wait awhile—I can wait two or three years for you, if I have to," his prospective employer countered. The man still refused the new job and wouldn't give any promise that he would accept an offer in the future. "I can't give my whole heart to the job I'm doing here," he said, "if I have my eye on your offer." The man believed he couldn't serve two masters. He wanted to be able to work "sincerely," giving his best to his employer.

Remember, Paul is speaking of the same loyalty he has already urged husbands and wives, and fathers and children, to show to one another. His principle is simplicity itself, yet it offers more promise of reforming our corrupted economic system than any of the more elaborate theories we have ever tried. For a laborer to be a productive worker does turn out in the long run to bolster the Gross National Product. Every manager praises the value of a loyal, obedient, honest worker; he not only lauds him, but he also becomes dependent on him.

That dependence, more than any seniority or tenure system, is a worker's best job security guarantee. I once supervised a man who, in his fifty years as a worker, had only had two employers. He was just a year or two short of achieving his goal of retiring when his service to the two had added up to fifty years. When the day came, however, he didn't retire. He had become so valuable that his superiors asked him to remain. He worked ten more years, a desired and trusted laborer.

And he never was one to work just "when their eye is on you." In fact, he worked without direct supervision, "as if . . . serving the Lord." The Living Bible translates these words, "Don't work hard only when your master is watching and then shirk when he isn't looking." A retired business executive was asked once what was the secret of his success. He replied that it could be summed up in three words: "And then some." He said, "I discovered at an early age that most of the difference between average people and top people could be explained in three words, *and then some.*" Top people do what is expected of them—and then some. They are thoughtful of others—and then some. They meet their obligations and their responsibilities fairly and squarely—and then some. They are good friends and helpful neighbors—and then some. They can be counted on in an emergency—and then some.

In Christian terms, what distinguishes them is that they have a higher set of standards, because they have a different Boss. They don't work to impress their employer but their God; they want Him who sees everything to approve. They have an eight-hour job but a twenty-four-hour Lord. They don't need other supervision.

Their devotion to God makes every job, even the most menial, significant to them. You undoubtedly know the old story about Sir Christopher Wren, England's greatest architect. When he was building the famous St. Paul's Cathedral approximately three centuries ago, he went for a walk among the workers, most of whom did not know him. He asked one of them, "What are you doing?"

"Anyone can see I'm cutting stone," the man snapped.

He asked another and was told, "I'm earning five shilling two-pence a day."

But the third man he asked replied, "I'm helping Sir Christopher Wren build a great cathedral."

Dr. Robert Schuller writes that someone sent him a copy of the last will and testament of a poor German worker. In his final bequest, he wrote, "I leave my eldest son my most prized possession, the tool that I used to cut the stone for the Cologne Cathedral."[75] He, too, recognized that his work was for a great purpose. He was doing more than cutting stone.

In a Christian's work, there is a reward: "because you know that the Lord will reward everyone for whatever good he does, whether he is slave or free" (Ephesians 6:8). As Dr. Schuller has noted, among the greatest of these bonuses God pays is self-esteem. Nothing upbuilds like knowing we are working for the Lord and doing it His way. The Christian worker will not stoop to dishonesty or carelessness in his labor. To do so would be to insult the Lord, something a Christian cannot do.

The best reward, of course, will be hearing one day from the Divine Master, "Well done, good and faithful servant! You have been faithful with a few things; I will put you in charge of many things. Come and share your master's happiness" (Matthew 25:21).

A Word to Employers (6:9)

Paul does not have as much counsel for masters as for slaves, for two reasons: first, there were not many masters in the early church (it consisted mostly of the uninfluential poor); second, most of what he has already said applies to masters as well as slaves. "Masters, do the same for the slaves as I have told the slaves to do for you. Treat them with respect. Be as concerned about their personal welfare as you are about your own. Masters, take care of your slaves; employers, take care of your employees."

Somebody will object that Paul's advice won't work now, but remember those words "intimacy, subtlety, and trust" from Ouchi's *Theory Z?* The corporate boss who worries that he'll

---

[75]Robert Schuller, *Self Esteem, The New Reformation* (Waco: Word, 1982), p. 73.

destroy his profits if he puts the welfare of his employees first is out of step with the best thinking in management today. Wise is the employer who genuinely looks out for his employee. God is God of boss *and* worker, rich *and* poor. To such a God, Archie Hargraves prayed at a large gathering of churchmen:

> O God, who lives in tenements, goes to segregated schools, is beaten in precincts, is unemployed, help us to know you. . . . O God, who is cold in slums in winter, whose playmates are rats, from four-legged ones who live with you to two-legged ones who imprison you, help us to touch you.[76]

The God who identifies with the humble will certainly bless those who bless them.

Many Christian businessmen have found, to the surprise of some, that Scriptural principles make good management sense. It is not, they have discovered, necessary to pay any form of bribery in order to land a contract; they are not forced to lie, to advertize falsely, or to defraud in order to get ahead. Attention to quality work has paid handsome dividends, and a reputation for integrity has been like gold in their pockets. (Of course, some Christian businessmen fail, but the fault is not in their Christian convictions but in other poor management techniques or in circumstances beyond their control.)

If in labor-management relations and contract negotiations, somebody from labor could say, "I don't think we should do that because it would hurt the company," or a member of the management team would propose doing something "because it will help the employees," an era of goodwill could begin. It is happening. Many of today's leading corporations base their decisions on the welfare of their employees—and they are prospering. And there are labor organizations that make sacrificial decisions in order to keep the company operating. (Remember Chrysler and the United Auto Workers?) Paul's is most practical advice.

The employer (master) is not to threaten. In New Testament times, since a slave was his master's property, the master had the right of life and death over him. A Christian master voluntarily

---

[76]Ronald J. Sider, *The Chicago Declaration* (Carol Stream, Illinois: Creation House, 1974), p. 82.

gave up that right, however. "Don't rule by threats and ultimatums" would be another way of reading this verse. Today, the employer often holds the right of firing the employee. It is a power that can be too easily abused. Extreme measures lead to rule by intimidation, a leadership style expressly forbidden here. A Christian boss and his Christian employee are brothers in Christ, and as brothers, neither is superior to the other. The glory of the church is that superiors and subordinates on the job are equals on the pew. In the church, they are one; they worship together, partake of Communion together, pray and work as equals. This is the difference Christ makes.

Paul once had to write a letter to Philemon, a slave owner, on behalf of his runaway slave Onesimus. Paul worked to heal the breach between the two by sending the slave back to his owner, instructing him as a Christian that it was his duty to be an obedient worker, but Paul also admonished his Christian master to welcome his repentant slave back as a brother! Employer and employee—brothers. What a difference Christ makes.

Paul's efforts on behalf of Philemon and Onesimus are evidence of a fact every home knows: there is often tension in the family. A famous minister once told a convention of his colleagues that he would never hire a secretary who was a member of his church. Too many problems, he insisted. More than one minister protested. One said, "I have never had a secretary who was not a member of my church, and I never will!" He admitted that there were occasional tensions, but he believed that Christian men and women should be able to work out any problem in the spirit of Christ, but if Christ can't govern in the workplace, where can He govern?

We reach to Colossians 3:17 for the principle that rules in all relationships: "And whatever you do, whether in word or deed, do it all in the name of the Lord Jesus, giving thanks to God the Father through him." And 1 Corinthians 10:31, "So whether you eat or drink or whatever you do, do it all for the glory of God."

CHAPTER THIRTY-TWO

Be Strong in the Lord

Ephesians 6:10-18

This is not my favorite Scripture. The apostle Paul employs one of his most famous, but one of the least comforting, metaphors for Christian life: warfare. Christians are soldiers fighting in a war they are sure to win, but they don't know when. In the meantime, the struggle is fierce.

We have grown weary of war. Our spirits rejoice when Jesus invites all "who are weary and burdened" to find rest in Him (Matthew 11:28), and our anxious hearts relax to His soothing words, "Peace I leave with you; my peace I give you.... Do not let your hearts be troubled and do not be afraid" (John 14:27). We gladly retreat into the haven of rest we call the church, seeking safety from the raging battles outside.

Perhaps our yearning for tranquility deafens us to some of Jesus' other words: "Do not suppose that I have come to bring peace to the earth. I did not come to bring peace, but a sword" (Matthew 10:34). Jesus seems to contradict himself, but He doesn't. His followers have always found a strange and unworldly calm within their souls, the peace He promises, but their inner well-being has seldom been paired with even a brief truce without. Whether we like it or not, Paul's "be strong in the Lord" (Ephesians 6:10) is timely advice.

Earlier, Paul has prayed that we Christians will know "his incomparably great power for us who believe" (Ephesians 1:19). Piling synonym on top of synonym ("power," "working," "mighty strength," "exerted," "rule," "authority," "dominion"; Ephesians 1:19-21), the apostle promises that what God did in raising Christ from the grave to the throne demonstrates what God wants to do for us. He snatched Jesus from the clutches of the prince of death; He will rescue us from that enemy's schemes (*methodeia,* "wiles," "crafty plots"). [The devil's "schemes" are spoken of with the same word used of the "craftiness of men in their *deceitful scheming* "—Ephesians 4:14.]

We need God's strength, His armor (*panoplia*—the whole protective suit), because the struggle against the devil is fierce. Even though we know that victory will be ours if we faint not, we cannot fight alone. We must heed Paul's first word, which is quite specific:

Get Ready for Battle

You won't escape, unless you give in to "the devil's schemes." If you choose to live for God, loving Him and loving other people, prepare to do battle against "rulers," "authorities," and "powers of this dark world" (Ephesians 6:12).

So get ready. "Be empowered," or "let yourselves be strengthened." The verb here in verse 10 is in the passive voice; in verses 11 and 13, the voice switches to active: "Put on the full armor." Paul often uses both voices to indicate the partnership between the believer and God: We do, and God does through us. (See Philippians 2:12, 13—"Continue to *work out your salvation* with fear and trembling, for *it is God who works in you* to will and to act according to his good purpose.")

Make no mistake about it, in a sin-drenched world, God's people will have to take up arms to defend themselves and to protect loved ones. Get ready for battle.

The battle will be against unseen forces. It is first and always spiritual. Look at our own society. We have not solved our racial problems; our crime rates speed wildly out of control, our social injustices threaten to defy correction. Our fellow citizens are paralyzed by anxiety, afraid of the dark, afraid to venture out at night, afraid of living and scared of dying. We have mastered many physical problems and can justly boast of advanced technology, yet the "powers of this dark world" have nearly cornered us.

Charles Malik, former Lebanese President of the United Nations General Assembly, once chastised his friends in the West for placing all our emphasis in the East-West political struggle on arms and technological inventions. "The greatest weakness of Western strategy is its relative neglect of the intellectual and spiritual dimension," he warned. It is in things of the mind and spirit that the West's advantage really lies.

It all depends then whether there are still strong enough forces in the West who passionately believe in and vigorously and constantly work for and boldly and single-mindedly proclaim the original primacy of the mind and spirit.[77]

This is the realm in which the wars that determine destinies are fought. Every schoolchild knows that Roman arms conquered Greece, but Greek culture eventually overtook and long outlived Rome's physical victory.

In our century, Britain provides the best illustration. When Hitler dispatched an average of 200 planes to bombard London for 57 consecutive nights (September 7 to November 3, 1940) as a horrified world watched on the sidelines, even Prime Minister Churchill (he later confessed) expected the city to be reduced to a rubble heap. It seemed impossible for Britain, with so many of its cities crippled by the bombings, to last another week, let alone to emerge victorious. Yet even in the darkest days of the war, British morale did not collapse as Hitler expected, and production, instead of falling off, actually increased through the worst of the blitz. The astonishing fact is that it was Germany, not England, that never recovered from its attack on the island.[78]

What made the difference? The mind and heart of the British. Although they dallied dangerously for a while, when the attack began, they rallied under Churchill's leadership and refused to succumb to Hitler's bullying tactics. They prepared to do battle.

Don't Fight the Wrong Enemy (6:12)

"For our struggle is not against flesh and blood, but against the rulers ..." (Ephesians 6:12). In Ephesians 5:21—6:9, Paul has discussed the most intimate human relationships, stressing the necessity of mutual submission and love in order to achieve peace. Before that, he has spoken at length of peace within the church. His exhortation in 6:10 ("Be strong in the Lord") is his logical conclusion to these discussions. It takes strength of patience not to fight the ones who are closest to us; it takes strength of character to refrain from doing battle with the wrong enemy. The real

---

[77]*Christ and Crisis* (Grand Rapids: Eerdmans, 1962), p. 9.

[78]William L. Shirer, *The Rise and Fall of the Third Reich* (New York: Simon and Schuster, 1960), p. 781.

reason Paul does not want us wasting our energies by turning against one another is that we have a far more strategic battle to fight. Our war is against the evil one and his allies. If we spend our resources demanding our rights in the church or in the home, fighting petty skirmishes with our loved ones or our fellow workers, we won't have them when we really need them to fend off the wiles of the devil. We are scoring touchdowns for the wrong side.

My high school principal taught me an unforgettable lesson on this issue. During my junior year, I paid an involuntary visit to his office. My history teacher had complained to him about me. I had been talking—and talking—when I should have been listening. The teacher felt I was being more than a little disrespectful, and told the principal so. After I had given my version of the exchange, I was surprised to hear the principal side with the teacher. Of course, I now realize how impudent I had been, but then I felt that the righteousness of my cause justified my behavior. After he gently chided me for my pugnacious ways, he wisely added, "Be careful, Roy, that you don't fight so hard to win a battle that you lose the whole war."

It was a good lesson. I have remembered it and applied it sadly to fellow Christians who become so caught up in this or that little issue that they endanger the whole Christian enterprise. It is so easy to win small battles while losing large causes. We turn against "flesh and blood" instead of the more pernicious rulers and "spiritual forces of evil in the heavenly realms" (Ephesians 6:12). We must remember that Christians are not to be spectators in spiritual warfare but more like paratroopers convening on Sunday for a briefing before being dropped behind enemy lines on Monday.

The real enemy is Satan. In the Bible, the world is frequently spoken of as being under his rule (1 John 5:19) and, consequently, in darkness (Luke 22:53, Colossians 1:13). The devil "prowls around like a roaring lion looking for someone to devour" (1 Peter 5:8, 9); he must be resisted (James 4:7). His domain is that unseen but very real world of ideas and influences and forces that impinge upon us. Paul may have in mind either the gods of the many religions popular in his day, or the sometimes weird and usually misleading philosophical speculations that the learned loved to play with, thinking them harmless, or both. In addition, he certainly means the demons and evil spirits that served the hellish desires of the prince of darkness. Believers in the middle ages were still so convinced of their power over people's daily lives that they built ugly gargoyles into their gothic cathedrals to frighten them away.

Modern believers are not so convinced of the reality of these forces. Our battle takes a little different form, but it is just as vital. Our malign influences come into our homes over television and radio waves; they teach through newspapers and magazines; they program us through the pitches and nuances of advertizing. They are made up of the thousands of nuances that form a culture. We are often unaware that they are un-Christian, even anti-Christian. They are, simply stated, "the ways of this world and of the ruler of the kingdom of the air" (Ephesians 2:2). Unless we are on guard, we inhale their noxious fumes without knowing it.

Then we are lulled into ignoring the real issues Christians should be addressing. The battle of the church is to save lives, a fact that is often forgotten in the multiplicity of entertainments that congregations tend to take too seriously. A recruiting letter sent out by the Knights of Columbus, for instance, exhibits the ease with which organizations lapse into spiritual laziness. It is printed here not because it is so unusual, but because it isn't.

> The Knights of Columbus was formed some 87 years ago to meet the challenges of those times and ever since has adapted to meet every new challenge confronting it. If you'd like to see how we're meeting today's challenges, we'd be most happy to show you. We are pleased to invite all men in the parish to an open house to be held at Faith Edwards Parish Center. The highlight of the evening will be the showing of the movies of the 1969 Notre Dame football season, including the Cottonbowl game against Texas. If at this time you would like to participate in the tasks of meeting these challenges we would welcome the opportunity of accepting your application for membership in our council.[79]

Review Paul's exhortation, then reread this letter. It sounds something like this:

> "Finally, be strong in the Lord and in his mighty power. Put on the full armor of God" to watch Notre Dame play football.

---

[79]Urban T. Holmes III, *The Future Shape of Ministry* (New York: Seabury Press, 1971), p. 120.

The right armor, the wrong battle. We have a far, far more important war to win. Our battle is against the spiritual hosts of wickedness that control the thoughts and attitudes of humanity. We must gear up for the fight to unify all mankind under the lordship of Jesus Christ.

When we submit to the generalship of Christ in this battle, perhaps for the first time, we will begin to understand Jesus' Beatitudes (Matthew 5:3-12). What does He mean, "Blessed are the meek"? Or "Blessed are the poor in spirit"? Or "Blessed are the peacemakers"? He is offering blessing to His disciples who are saving their ammunition for the big battles. They are meek and poor in spirit and peacemaking in those multitudinous skirmishes that people fight over things that don't really matter. Jesus' disciples know that nothing at all can separate them from the love of God in Christ Jesus (Romans 8:38, 39), so they march into battle without fear. They aren't afraid of other soldiers, or their weapons, or even of the "flaming arrows of the evil one" (Ephesians 6:16). Their spiritual values are secure, their lives are safe in the Lord, they are at peace with God, they hate what Christ hates and love whom Christ loves. Meekly, humbly, peacefully, they obey their Lord's will. They have put on the whole armor of God.

Put On the Whole Armor of God (6:13-18)

What Paul calls armor, most men would call nakedness. The Defense Department would waste no time on his advice for military preparedness. His armor is for the real battle, not one of our merely political international wars. Modern weapons are designed for destruction anyway, and Paul is more concerned about survival.

When John Steinbeck first viewed the notorious Berlin Wall in 1963, after a two-month tour behind the Iron Curtain, he said of it, "One of the laws of paleontology is that an animal which must protect itself with thick armor is degenerate. It is usually a sign that the species is on the road to extinction."[80] The modern arms race is ample proof that Steinbeck is right. If we continue to stockpile weapons as we have been, extinction of the human race is virtually assured.

---

[80]Quoted in *Time,* December 20, 1963.

274

Russia's Premier Nikita Khrushchev's autobiography includes his reminiscence of a conversation he had with President Dwight Eisenhower at Camp David about the way their respective defense departments were conducting the arms race. Ike said his military leaders would request such and such a program, which he would deny because of lack of funds. Then they would solemnly assure him that the Russians had already appropriated money for their own program and were moving ahead of the Americans. "So I give in," Eisenhower said. "They keep grabbing for more and I keep giving it to them."

Khrushchev said it was just the same in Russia. His military leaders would bring evidence that the Americans were developing such and such a system, and ask to develop their own. He would hesitate, they would persuade him that in a war, the Russians would be ill-equipped if they did not have this program, so "I end up by giving them the money they ask for."[81]

Thus the two countries put on their full armor for their battle against flesh and blood. They think they can solve something that way. History proves them wrong, but they don't believe history. And they don't believe God.

We do, so we put on His armor. We believe that if you "come near to God . . . he will come near to you," helping you to "resist the devil" (James 4:7, 8). Genesis 3:9-13 shows that the first consequence of separation from God is fear. When God sought the disobedient Adam, our ancestor hid, then finally confessed, "I was afraid." He had not resisted the evil one. Yet the devil *can* be resisted (1 Peter 5:9). Paul tells us how.

His advice is primarily defensive. His concern is that we **"stand"** (Ephesians 6:11, 13, 14). Ralph Waldo Emerson wrote that "the hero is no braver than an ordinary man, but he is brave five minutes longer." He "stands" there. The Christian also stands there.

He has put on **"the belt of truth"** (Ephesians 6:14). Without personal integrity, a desire for "truth in the inner parts" (Psalm 51:6), there is nothing to hold the other parts in place.

He wears **"the breastplate of righteousness"** (Ephesians 6:14). God himself wears this mark of character (Isaiah 59:17). It refers

---

[81]*Khrushchev Remembers,* tr. and ed. Strobe Talbott (Boston: Little, Brown and Company, 1970), pp. 519, 520.

to a just, good, upright life. On a visit to India during the "emergency" declared by Prime Minister Gandhi, many Indians shared their worry with me, "How can a government survive when people are not honest?" It was the same question heard in the United States during the Watergate scandal. It's a good question. No government can long endure without righteous leadership.

He has his **"feet fitted with the readiness that comes from the gospel of peace"** (Ephesians 6:15). Ready to advance when called upon by the Prince of Peace, we are not really fighters, as such, but members of a peacekeeping mission. Strengthened by inner peace, we can refuse to do battle with "flesh and blood" but boldly resist the advances of the wicked ones.

He carries **"the shield of faith"** (Ephesians 6:16). We don't defend our faith; our faith defends us from the burning darts of the enemy. The Roman historian Herodotus says it was the custom for soldiers to fashion arrows with points of tow dipped in pitch; they were then ignited and shot at the foe, the fires doing more damage than conventional arrows could do. The faith that shields us here refers to the content (what we believe) and the trust (in Whom we believe) that Biblical faith implies.

He wears **"the helmet of salvation"** (Ephesians 6:17). There is no wavering or doubting for the Christian. He can say, "I know whom I have believed, and am convinced that he is able to guard what I have entrusted to him for that day" (2 Timothy 1:12). The Christian knows God has saved him, is saving him, and will save him. His grace is sufficient.

He carries **"the sword of the Spirit, which is the word of God"** (Ephesians 6:17). Elsewhere, the Bible speaks of the Word of God as a sword (Hebrews 4:12) given by the Spirit (Ephesians 3:5; 2 Timothy 3:16). This Word is a constant source of strength and the weapon by which you can pierce the false arguments of the enemy. Like Jesus, we know that man lives by every word that comes from the mouth of God (Matthew 4:4).

The prayer that is added is not really part of the armor, but it expresses the inner sense of resolve and dependency upon the source of strength. The preparation is incomplete without it.

Now, then, the Christian is prepared. He can withstand anything. Defended by truth, righteousness, peace, salvation, and the Word of God, he is secure indeed. He is certainly no longer a child tossed about by "every wind of teaching and by the cunning and craftiness of men in their deceitful scheming" (Ephesians 4:14).

A Christian leader in India was undergoing a particularly difficult period of harassment from enemies on every side. He was forced to spend countless wasted days in court defending himself against fraudulent charges. Every day, he expected to be tossed into jail. He toyed with the idea of fleeing the country. When he confessed his discouragement to the chief of police in his village, however, the chief, a Hindu, quietly asked the Christian, "Will you explain to me the cross of Christ?"

The pastor answered, "You are right. I cannot run away."

Neither can we. Because of the cross.

We must stand. But we stand in full armor.

CHAPTER THIRTY-THREE

A Final Word of Encouragement

Ephesians 6:19-24

With these words, Paul concludes his great formal treatise on the church, having traced the implications of God's general purpose ("to bring all things in heaven and on earth together under one head, even Christ"; Ephesians 1:10) and His purpose for the church ("through the church, the manifold wisdom of God should be made known to the rulers and authorities in the heavenly realms"; Ephesians 3:10). As we have noted before, the church is Exhibit A in God's case for unity on earth.

Although Ephesians is more formal than Paul's other letters, even here he cannot remain impersonal. The church consists of persons in relationship with each other. They are bound together in one body, with each part caring about the others. This is more than a theoretical dogma; it is a living fact. So here, Paul expresses how much he cares for the readers of his letter. He knows they have been upset by reports they have heard of Paul's imprisonment and suffering, so he adds a final word of encouragement to dispel their anxiety.

These lines closely parallel Colossians 4:7, 8. Paul had written Colossians earlier, then hastened to complete Ephesians so that Tychicus could deliver both letters on the same journey. Tychicus will thus act as Paul's personal ambassador to the churches in Colossae and Ephesus (and the other churches among whom the Ephesians letter is to be circulated). Tychicus appears several times in the New Testament: here; in Titus 3:12, where he is named with Artemus as a potential successor to Titus in Crete; in 2 Timothy 4:12 in connection with a later trip to Ephesus; in Acts 20:4 (where he is mentioned as being from Asia); and in the parallel passage already mentioned (Colossians 4:7-9), where Paul commends him again as "a dear brother, a faithful minister and fellow servant."

In these final verses, Paul states his personal purpose in sending this letter along with Tychicus: "that you may know how we are, and that he may encourage you" (Ephesians 6:22). The New English Bible, making explicit the root meaning of *encourage,* says the purpose is to "put fresh heart" into them. Since they have heard of his sufferings, they need to be aware that his trials have not defeated him.

Prayer (6:19, 20)

He has just charged them to pray constantly "in the Spirit on all occasions" (Ephesians 6:18), including "all the saints." Now he asks for prayer for himself, a request he is never hesitant to make (Colossians 4:3, 4; 1 Thessalonians 5:25; 2 Thessalonians 3:1).

He makes two specific appeals: (1) for words to tell the truth of the gospel, "whenever I open my mouth" (Ephesians 6:19) and (2) for courage. He may be a prisoner, but he wants to be a bold prisoner, fearlessly preaching the "mystery" (Ephesians 6:20; see 1:9, 3:3) of the good news about Jesus. He may be in chains, but he is nonetheless an ambassador in chains, never forgetting for a moment that he is under orders from his Master.

Paul is in Rome, the capital city. Ambassadors from all over the known world are there. He is no less important than they, he implies; to the contrary, he represents the King of the universe. He must not be intimidated by emperors or chains. His is a grave responsibility; he needs their prayers.

Paul's words stop us. We like to think of the great apostle Paul, whose influence on Christianity has been second only to that of Christ himself, as being above human frailty, immune from our weaknesses, exempt from our prayer needs. But he never makes such claims for himself. When he boasts, he doesn't brag about his own strength, but the Lord's (2 Corinthians 12:7-10). In fact, he calls himself the worst of sinners (1 Timothy 1:15) and the least of the apostles (1 Corinthians 15:9). He makes no apologies for his dependence on prayers, his own and those of his partners in the gospel.

In other words, he is one of us. We, too, are sinners. We know what we ought to do, yet we fail to do it. We know what we are supposed to avoid, yet we blunder into it. We'd like to be Christian, we try to be moral, we want to be good, but still we succumb to our lusts and stumble over our sins. As Paul needed the prayers of his friends, so do we.

He doesn't ask for the obvious, however. His petition is not for freedom from his chains, nor for an end to his suffering, nor even for success in his righteous cause. He simply asks for courage to be a bold preacher in hostile surroundings.

Even in friendly territory, such prayers are needed. Most preachers can identify with the young man who preached his first sermon to his first congregation. It was a terrible experience for everybody, including him. In the following weeks, he preached several more sermons, all as bad as the first, if not worse. The church's leaders met in emergency session. People were beginning to complain. What should they do?

Their decision was to talk the problem over with the young minister. Here is what they told him: "You will not see us in worship for the next several weeks. We will be in an adjacent room praying during your sermon." Week after week, they kept their promise, and the effect was dramatic. They prayed him into a great preacher.

You can almost call this the mark of a true fellowship of Christians. They don't judge but instead they pray for one another. Their purpose is to pray each other into strength for their service to God. It is for such power that Paul asks, so that he won't flinch before his opponents. As an ambassador in chains, he has a commission to complete.

Peace to the Brothers (6:23)

Here Paul combines an encouraging word with an implied request. The cheering word: you already have peace from God, who has broken down the walls of hostility among men through the cross of Jesus (Ephesians 2). The request: now live peacefully with each other in the fellowship of the church so that, even if there are battles going on all around you, you Christians may be able to relax in the presence of one another. (Remember: Your real enemy is Satan, never other Christians; 6:10-18.)

My wife and I were in India in 1975 during Prime Minister Indira Gandhi's so-called "emergency." Most of that nation had been turned into a nervous police state. We experienced firsthand (but not for the first time) the restrictions, suspicions, and recriminations that torment people when their government turns against them. Our Christian friends whispered their fears to us: they did not dare to speak aloud lest unseen spies overhear and betray them. Many of their acquaintances had already disappeared suddenly; others were haunted by the suspicion that they were on the government's hit list.

We have since been in several totalitarian countries, and the feeling is always the same. Yet, in spite of the ability that hostile governments have of controlling the people's movements, they can't overcome the Christians' peace with God nor the harmony among fellow believers. Peace is possible under all circumstances among disciples of the Prince of Peace.

Love (6:23)

This peace is the product of Christian love. Just as nothing can separate us from the love of God in Christ Jesus (Romans 8:38, 39), neither can anything nor anyone foster division between Christians who genuinely love each other. (See Ephesians 1:15; 3:17; and Galatians 5:6—"The only thing that counts is faith expressing itself through love.")

Ephesians points to the supreme example of love: "Be imitators of God, therefore, as dearly loved children and live a life of love, just as Christ loved us and gave himself up for us as a fragrant offering and sacrifice to God" (Ephesians 5:1, 2). To love as Christ loved is to accept without prejudice and to work for the good of every person whom God loves (John 3:16).

The extent of this love is described by Bruce Larson, who discovered an enlightening bit of graffiti on a subway wall in New York City. An advertising poster showed a most austere, proper older man recommending a certain product. The poster had been defaced, probably by a small boy writing "the dirtiest thing he could think of." He sketched a balloon coming out of the man's mouth, with these words in it: "I like grils."

Underneath some uptight person had written with a felt-tipped pen, "It's girls, stupid, not grils."

Below that, a third person, with a broader sympathy than the felt-tipped penman, added, "But what about us grils?"[82]

Paul has made as strong a case as possible for the full acceptance into the church of every kind of "gril". Even men and women who "were dead in your transgressions and sins" and who "followed the ways of this world and of the ruler of the kingdom

---

[82]Bruce Larson, *No Longer Strangers* (Waco: Word, 1971), pp. 89, 90.

of the air" (Ephesians 2:1, 2) belonged. Circumcised and un-circumcised were equal members of the household of God (Ephesians 2:11-22); people accustomed to fighting their way through life by lying, stealing, whoring, slandering, and deceiving, with hearts filled with envy, greed, malice, and every other kind of darkness now belonged to the church with all the rights and privileges of every other member. Only love could hold such a disparate crowd together. Paul wishes them such love, so they can be at peace with one another.

Faith from God the Father and the Lord Jesus Christ (6:23)

As peace is rooted in love, so is love grounded in faith. Remember Galatians 5:6? "The only thing that counts is faith expressing itself through love." According to Paul, we find the source of faith in Heaven. God has taken the initiative; He gave us Someone to believe in, the Lord Jesus Christ, who in turn gave us every spiritual blessing we enjoy (Ephesians 1:3). Paul subtly reminds us that our relationship with God is not so much the result of our frantic search for Him as of His determined efforts to reach us to draw us to himself.

In *Christianity Discovered,* Vincent Donovan tells of his discovery of the meaning of faith through his evangelistic work among the Masai people in East Africa. He was talking with a Masai elder about the struggle of belief with unbelief. There was one word for faith, the elder taught him, that meant something like "to agree to," and the example he used was of a white hunter shooting an animal with his gun. Only his eyes and his fingers were involved in the act. This isn't really an adequate word, he said.

For a man really to believe, he said, is more like "a lion going after its prey." The whole beast is involved. His senses of smelling and seeing and hearing detect the prey. The speed of his legs, the power of his leaping body, the deathblow delivered by his front paw, and finally the enveloping embrace of his front legs (his arms, the Masai says) all do their part. Finally, the lion makes the prey part of himself. This, the elder insists, is what faith is.

Then he adds an unexpected twist to his analogy. He reminds the missionary that the Masai did not seek him out. They did not even want him to come. Yet the missionary searched them out, following them into the bush, the plains, the steppes, the hills, their villages, their homes.

You told us of the High God, how we must search for him, even leave our land and our people to find him. But we have not done this. We have not left our land. We have not searched for him. He has searched for us. He has searched *us* out and found us. All the time we think we are the lion. In the end, the lion is God."[83]

The old Masai tribesman and the experienced apostle Paul agree that our God is a searching, seeking, saving God. Without what He accomplished through the death, burial, and resurrection of Jesus Christ, there could be no Christian faith. The *content* of our faith is Jesus, through whom God has done everything He could do to seek for and save us. The *conduct* of our faith is trust in and commitment to Him. "The only thing that counts is faith expressing itself through love."

That love never dies.

Grace to All Who Love Our Lord Jesus Christ With an Undying Love (6:24)

Paul has used this word *grace* several times already: Ephesians 1:2, 7; 2:5, 7, 8; 3:2, 8; 4:7. It always implies the unmerited favor of God upon us, sometimes expressed as a special task to accomplish for Him, sometimes as an opportunity for giving or sharing. It is capable of several shades of meaning. Here, in light of the Christian's spiritual battle (Ephesians 6:10-18) and Paul's own request for prayers for fearlessness, it implies that special strengthening that comes from our relationship with the Lord.

At an annual dinner of the American Law Institute several years ago, Judge Learned Hand concluded his speech with this challenge: "Courage, my friends! Take heart of grace. The devil is not yet dead." Undoubtedly without any awareness of the parallel, the judge used *grace* in precisely the same sense that Paul does. In a dangerous, hostile world ("The devil is not yet dead"), Hand's auditors need to muster up enough courage to do battle with the evil one. They have to "take heart of grace."

They must, because they face powers greater than their own. As Arthur Koestler approached his final days, he must have felt overwhelmed by those same forces, for he chose as his epitaph, "He did his best—and it wasn't good enough."

---

[83]Donovan, *Christianity Rediscovered,* pp. 62, 63.

Neither is ours. Without grace—God's unearned favor to us—we perish. We can identify with the words of Mabel's song in the first act of Gilbert and Sullivan's *The Pirates of Penzance:*

> Poor wand'ring one!
> Tho' thou hast surely strayed,
> Take heart of grace,
> Thy steps retrace,
> Poor wand'ring one!

We Christians have retraced our steps; we have walked back to the Creator, back to the Savior. We believe in God; we believe in His Son Jesus. We have taken heart. We have received grace.

We believe in Christ. More than believe, we love Him with undying love. Undying—that means with a love that won't quit. It won't quit because we will never let go of the Lord and we know He will never let go of us.

LEGALIST....!

JUDIAZERS..... Matt 9:16,17. 1 Tel 2:16 GAl. 1:7
beside your faith you must adhere to the Law. ardem
dietary regulation Observance of religious order
Holy day

PEACE ^{MEANS} — SHALom!

PHARISES--- '
decided that spirituality consists in the abundance of
good Works.

SCribes - who became the lovers of the LAWS.

SANHEdRin... the supreme Court

Jesus who had everything to loose, became a Nobody
in the world in order that (we) might become
somebody. Phil. 2:5—11. Tel 5:1
Jews & Gentiles to Have this freedom (Eph 2:14 — B)